JOHN BARLEYCORN

JACK LONDON was born in San Francisco in 1876. Reared by a family without fixed occupation or residence, he lived along the Oakland waterfront described in *Martin Eden* (1909) and *John Barleycorn* (1913). As a boy he bought a sloop and set up as an oyster pirate in San Francisco bay, as later told in the *Cruise of the Dazzler* (1902) and *Tales of the Fish Patrol* (1905). After work on a sealing schooner, a tramping trip through the US and Canada, and a period of education including a semester at the University of California, he returned to the Oakland waterfront with an interest in sociology and the Socialist party. In 1897 he joined the gold rush to the Klondike, but his attempt at mining was unsuccessful, and stricken with scurvy he returned to Oakland the following year and began to write of his experiences. In 1900 his first collection of short stories, *The Son of the Wolf*, was issued, bringing him national fame for his portrayal of the vigorous, brutal life of the Far North. Continuing to write in this vein, he produced a prolific output of stories and novels, including *The Call of the Wild* (1903), *The Sea-Wolf* (1904), and *White Fang* (1906). In 1902 he went to London, where he made a study of slum conditions for his descriptive work *The People of the Abyss* (1903). The remainder of his short but full life was spent under the heady influence of popularity and success. He travelled as a war correspondent, made lecture tours, went on sailing voyages to the Caribbean and the South Seas, and lived on his great patriarchal estate, Beauty Ranch, in California. He died in 1916, having suffered chronic ill health for a number of years.

JOHN SUTHERLAND is Lord Northcliffe Professor of Modern English Literature at University College London. He is the author of a number of books, among them *Is Heathcliff a Murderer?*, *Can Jane Eyre Be Happy?*, *Who Betrays Elizabeth Bennet?*, and *Henry V, War Criminal? and other Shakespeare Puzzles* (with Cedric Watts). He has also edited Jack London's *The Sea-Wolf* for Oxford World's Classics, as well as *Vanity Fair* and *Pendennis* by William Makepeace Thackeray, *The Moonstone* by Wilkie Collins, and *The Way We Live Now* and other novels by Anthony Trollope.

T0058835

OXFORD WORLD'S CLASSICS

*For over 100 years Oxford World's Classics have brought
readers closer to the world's great literature. Now with over 700
titles—from the 4,000-year-old myths of Mesopotamia to the
twentieth century's greatest novels—the series makes available
lesser-known as well as celebrated writing.*

*The pocket-sized hardbacks of the early years contained
introductions by Virginia Woolf, T. S. Eliot, Graham Greene,
and other literary figures which enriched the experience of reading.
Today the series is recognized for its fine scholarship and
reliability in texts that span world literature, drama and poetry,
religion, philosophy and politics. Each edition includes perceptive
commentary and essential background information to meet the
changing needs of readers.*

OXFORD WORLD'S CLASSICS

JACK LONDON

John Barleycorn
'*Alcoholic Memoirs*'

Edited with an Introduction and Notes by
JOHN SUTHERLAND

OXFORD
UNIVERSITY PRESS

OXFORD
UNIVERSITY PRESS

Great Clarendon Street, Oxford OX2 6DP

Oxford University Press is a department of the University of Oxford.
It furthers the University's objective of excellence in research, scholarship,
and education by publishing worldwide in

Oxford New York

Athens Auckland Bangkok Bogotá Buenos Aires Calcutta
Cape Town Chennai Dar es Salaam Delhi Florence Hong Kong Istanbul
Karachi Kuala Lumpur Madrid Melbourne Mexico City Mumbai
Nairobi Paris São Paulo Singapore Taipei Tokyo Toronto Warsaw

with associated companies in Berlin Ibadan

Oxford is a registered trade mark of Oxford University Press
in the UK and in certain other countries

Published in the United States
by Oxford University Press Inc., New York

John Barleycorn first published 1913
First published as a World's Classics paperback 1989
Reissued as an Oxford World's Classics paperback 1998
Reissued 2009

British Library Cataloguing in Publication Data

Data available

Library of Congress Cataloging in Publication Data
London, Jack, 1876–1916.
John Barleycorn: Alcoholic memoirs/Jack London; edited with an
introduction by John Sutherland.
p. cm.—(Oxford world's classics)
First published 1913; first published as a World's classics
paperback 1989.
1.London, Jack, 1876–1916—Biography. 2. Authors. American—
20th century—Biography.
3. Alcoholics—United States—Biography.
I. Sutherland, John, 1938– . II. Title. III. Series. 89–31677
PS3523.046Z467 1989 818'.5209—dc20

ISBN 978–0–19–955557–4

11

Printed in Great Britain by
Clays Ltd, Elcograf S.p.A

CONTENTS

CONTENTS

INTRODUCTION

I

IN 1912 Jack London was America's best-known under 40-year-old. Hollywood had not yet become our Hollywood, but 'Jack' was recognizably a star and a living legend. His rugged good looks and cocked Irish chin were as well known as Theodore Roosevelt's belligerent squint. (Like Roosevelt, London had a love affair with the camera. Among his literary remains at the Huntington Library are hundreds of photographs, many of himself). For his admiring contemporaries Jack London embodied the irresistible power of American youth. He was Herbert Spencer's social Darwinism incarnate, an overman, a Carlylean hero, a Horatio Alger success story, a champ.

Born into an irregular marriage, the son of a vagabond astrologer and a failed boarding-house keeper in Oakland, California, Jack was a main support of his family at 10 years old, getting up at three in the morning to deliver newspapers. He left school at 14. By 15, he was the 'Prince of the oyster Pirates', poaching in the shallow waters off San Mateo. Before he was 18, Jack had sailed the Siberian waters as a seal hunter; he later plodded over the Klondike snows as a goldminer. In the interim he was one of the enlisted unemployed in Jacob S. Coxey's army as it marched on Washington demanding a new deal. He deserted from Coxey's ranks (inevitably, given his freebooting nature) to ride the rods, hop freight cars and generally hobo all over the northern American continent. He served time in Erie County Penitentiary (he had been to see the Niagara Falls by moonlight—the true London touch). He then returned to enroll in high school. Two years later he entered Berkeley from where, anticipating his hippy successors, he dropped out after one semester. Before he was 30, London had made a reputation as the most intrepid of international correspondents, reporting to the American people from the 'abyss' of London's East End slums and the Russo-Japanese War. Lesser men would have stopped in their careers at any one of these points; but for London it was ever forward on what he called the 'Adventure Path' of life.

Nor was it all grimness and Darwinian struggle. 'Fitness' meant more than survival to Jack; it was part of his joy of being. In his writing prime London gave expression to America's new obsession with manly sports. He was the country's first celebrity sportswriter, covering heavyweight boxing fights, anticipating Norman Mailer (in many ways Jack's literary reincarnation) by seventy years. But—unlike Mailer, the ringside fan—Jack was as much a participant as a literary onlooker. Between writing stints it was, as he tells us in *John Barleycorn*, his habit to take exercise breaks: 'I boxed and fenced, walked on my hands, jumped high and broad, put the shot, tossed the caber, and went swimming.' Again, the bit about tossing the caber catches the sheer fun of Jack's determination to be a great writer with biceps to match. His fiction and non-fiction writing popularized dinghy sailing, equestrianism (the democratic Western, not the patrician 'English' style), bicycling, kite-flying, and target shooting. He loved solo sports and boosted them with the same flair with which Teddy Roosevelt promoted America's team sports (notably college football—in its modern form virtually a Roosevelt invention).

Arguably Jack London's most enduring memorial was his successful transplanting of the sport of surfing from Waikiki to the West Coast of America. This he did by writing what was effectively a user's manual for the sport and by himself practising it. And what London bequeathed to the Beach, as reverent southern Califor-

nians call their seaboard, was not merely the techniques
of riding breakers—in itself as banal as roller skating—but
the mystic *cultus* of surfing which elevates the sport to a
religious celebration of man's domination of the elements.
His description in 1911 of the Hawaian ('Kanaka') surfing
hero articulates beautifully the cool mastery of the ocean's
violence that lies at the heart of the sport:

From out of the sea he has leaped upon the back of the sea, and
he is riding the sea that roars and bellows and cannot shake
him from its back. But no frantic outreaching and balancing is
his. He is impassive, motionless as a statue carved suddenly by
some miracle out of the sea's depth from which he rose. And
straight on toward shore he flies on his winged heels and the
white crest of the breaker. There is a wild burst of foam, a long
tumultuous rushing sound as the breaker falls futile and spent
on the beach at your feet; and there, at your feet steps calmly
ashore a Kanaka, burnt golden and brown by the tropic sun
. . . He is a Kanaka—and more, he is a man, a member of the
kingly species that has mastered matter and the brutes and
lorded it over creation.

While packing in action and joy enough for three
ordinary men's lives, London had educated himself. Life,
of course, was too short for the years and decades that
others might spend training their minds. Not for Jack
the lugubriously slow tempi of high school and college.
Books were his university. As a boy he borrowed them by
the armful from Oakland Public Library, devouring the
printed page as ravenously as he devoured near-raw duck
(his favourite food, lightly seared on a high flame for a few
minutes). At a pinch, books were, in fact, more important
than food to him. During his travels in the Yukon he
packed Darwin's *Origin of Species* into his rucksack where
other men would have stowed pemmican. London told
some tall stories in the course of his career, but never
exaggerated his passionate love of print. In his prosperous
later years he assembled a huge library of around 15,000
volumes—the tools of his trade, he called them. And to

the end of his short life, London read voraciously on every
conceivable topic. As with everything he did, London was
an autodidact of heroic proportions.

Since selling his first story ('To the Man on Trail') in
January 1899, London had written for his living. And—
Midas that he was—he had succeeded fabulously. In his
last years, he was earning around $75,000 annually by
his pen; in modern currency values about a million and
tax free. No author had ever made it so big, even in
new-frontier America. London had taken to himself a
handsome new wife (or 'mate-woman') in 1905. In early
1912 as he planned out the writing of *John Barleycorn*
Charmian was with child and Jack had high hopes of a
'Jack London Jr'. (He had two daughters by his previous
wife, Bessie, from whom he separated in 1903.) In August
1912 London made a new five-year contract with *Cosmopolitan* which was, even by his standards, munificent.
The publisher undertook to pay the author $2,200 a month
for the exclusive right to serialize all his fiction. London
had bought a property in California's Sonoma County
in June 1905—the beginnings of his 'Beauty Ranch'—
which he began seriously to develop in 1911. By 1912
it comprised some 1,000 acres. At its centre he began
erecting a mansion to be called the Wolf House. The
Spanish tile roof alone cost $3,500 and when finished it
would be a fit habitation for one who had shown himself
so indisputably a leader of the human pack.

The American continent was Jack London's to ride
over, the bordering oceans were his to sail as he pleased.
From June to September 1911 he and Charmian took
a four-horse driving trip through the wilds of Northern
California and Oregon. From March to August 1912 they
booked passages on a clipper, the *Dirigo*, and undertook
a bracing voyage around Cape Horn, the most dangerous
sailing waters in the world. (It was on this trip that he began making his first notes for *John Barleycorn*.) London,

it would seem, had it all. Fame, money, physique, good looks, the love of beautiful women and—most important—youth. Everything that he had achieved in his life was his while he was still young enough to enjoy it, with a full head of dark hair. In 1912 he was still only 36 years old.

Such was the public image of Jack London in 1912. And it was an image which he could easily have kept intact, had he so wanted. As is invariably the case with their heroes, the American public wanted desperately to believe in the simple myth of Jack London. More, as it turned out, than London himself wanted to believe in it. All his books were strikingly unlike each other, he told his publisher William Ellsworth in January 1913, but '*John Barleycorn* is unlike any other book ever published anywhere in this world'. It was also a book which would forever complicate the simple image of Jack London, American hero.

After some dickering, London subtitled *John Barleycorn* 'Alcoholic Memoirs'. It is, in fact, more confessional than reminiscential in tone. In these memoirs London proclaims himself to have been—in the past—a chronic boozer. He does not make the admission that he was an alcoholic—indeed, he goes to some lengths to deny any present addiction. But, as he makes clear, he has had in years gone by some major bouts with drink. The effect of *John Barleycorn*'s revelation was, not to exaggerate, similar to that when the world learned in 1985 that the archetypally beefcake Rock Hudson was both gay and dying of AIDS.

One's first reaction to *John Barleycorn* is that London has written an astonishingly honest book, particularly in the historical context of 1913. When a contemporary star or public figure books into the Betty Ford clinic at the aptly named Rancho Mirage, few eyebrows are raised. There may be a little sniggering at the press-released white lies about 'prescription drugs' or whatever, but the general response is one of charitable good will.

'Get well soon' or 'there but for the grace of God' are the commonest reactions. Dependence on, or abuse of, chemical substances have been largely de-stigmatized, thanks—it should be said—to pioneeringly courageous recovered alcoholics like Betty Ford.

The drunk's stigma was, however, indelible in 1913. No-one of London's public standing had ever come clean on the question of problem drinking before—at least not while at the zenith of their power and fame. There were, of course, the decadents: those degenerates such as Swinburne in England or Verlaine in France who were notorious *absinthistes* and inebriates and who actually experimented with the degradations of alcoholic excess. And everyone knew about Coleridge and opium, De Quincey and laudanum. But London was no decadent; he was an advertisement for the white race whose supremacy he trumpeted, a eugenicist's dream, every clean-living American teenaged boy's role model. For him to be at the same time a drunk—albeit a wholly reformed drunk—was very confusing to his public.

It is a major part of *John Barleycorn*'s honesty that it does not glamorize drinking. 'I didn't like the damned stuff', London tells us: 'this physical loathing for alcohol I have never got over. But I have conquered it. To this day I re-conquer it every time I take a drink. The palate never ceases to rebel, and the palate can be trusted to know what is good for the body.' The surgeon general could not have put it better. Among the most powerful descriptive scenes in *John Barleycorn* are those which capture the banality of drunkenness, or as London put it to his publisher, 'the bare, bald, absolute fact . . . of my own personal experiences in the realm of alcohol'. Take, for instance, the cameo of drunkenness in Chapter 6. The 14-year-old Jack, having drunk two grown seamen under the table on the *Idler*, returns to shore in his skiff but topples drunkenly into the low-tide mud of Oakland Estuary:

It was then that my correlations began to break down. I lost my balance and pitched headforemost into the ooze. Then, and for the first time, as I floundered to my feet covered with slime, the blood running down my arms from a scrape against a barnacled stake, I knew that I was drunk. But what of it? Across the channel two strong sailormen lay unconscious in their bunks where I had drunk them. I *was* a man. I was still on my legs, if they *were* knee-deep in mud. I disdained to get back into the skiff. I waded through the mud, shoving the skiff before me and yammering the chant of my manhood to the world.

It is a complex scene. *Inter urinas et faeces*, the child London is being reborn—as a man and a drunkard. Degradation and baptismal rite of initiation mix in this scene of the beslimed lad, emerging bellowing from the foreshore. (It makes a strikingly contrastive parallel to the image cited above of the sun-bronzed Kanaka striding god-like from the waves.)

   John Barleycorn contains many such corrections to the pervasive myths of male drinking—the heroic myths which are nowadays promulgated by beer advertisements. The infantine Jack is bewildered by the first 'man fight' he witnesses between Black Matt ('who, everybody said, had killed two men in his time') and 'strapping' Tom Morrisey. 'Maybe I would see that wonderful thing, a man killed', little Jack gleefully thinks. But so sloshed are the contestants, that all they can do is waltz with each other: 'Black Matt and Tom Morrisey merely held on to each other and lifted their clumsy-booted feet in what seemed a grotesque, elephantine dance. They were too drunk to fight.'

   Throughout *John Barleycorn*, London sustains this tone of ironic wonderment at the sheer idiocy of drinking and not least his own early exploits with the bottle. The grotesque incompetence of alcoholic performance, its heroic aspirations and clownish fulfilments, provide some of the author's finest comic writing (sometimes thought rather a rare commodity with London). Take, for example, *John Barleycorn*'s chapter on Jack's Bonin Islands orgy in Chapter 16. Having been given shore leave in Japan after an arduous voyage, London and his two shipboard companions—'the three sports'—plan various expeditions inland. One is keen to go fishing in a Japanese sampan; another points out a pathway in the volcanic mountains among the palms and flowers that they might explore. Instead—without ever intending it—they follow the example of countless other sailors on shore leave; that is, they get themselves paralytically drunk in the nearest saloon spending their liberty in maudlin mateyness interspersed with mindless violence. Ten days later London wakes up without his wallet, belt, or shoes, having seen no more of Japan than the saki bottle on the waterfront bar.

Having applauded the debunking honesty of *John Barleycorn*'s depictions of the male rites of drinking and his own early drinking career, one confronts the major problem. How should we take Jack London's assertions, which he makes three times in the first five pages, that drinker he may be, but 'I was no hereditary alcoholic . . . I have no constitutional predisposition for alcohol'? Hence in the scene-setting first chapter he insists that he is not writing 'the Memoirs of an Alcoholic' but 'Alcoholic Memoirs'. Is this the alcoholic's well-known 'denial' syndrome, or has London really mastered his demon? When Charmian tells 'a pleasantly jingled' Jack, again in the first chapter of *John Barleycorn*, 'You have shown yourself no alcoholic, no dipsomaniac, but merely an habitual drinker, one who has made John Barleycorn's acquaintance through long years of rubbing shoulders with him' is she to be believed? Or is she playing the part of the co-alcoholic 'enabler', the spouse who supports her partner in the consoling delusions which encourage his drinking? How should we take the last defiant assertion in these alcoholic memoirs?

No, I decided; I shall take my drink on occasion. With all the books on my shelves, with all the thoughts of the thinkers shaded by my particular temperament, I decided coolly and deliberately that I should continue to do what I had been trained to want to do. I would drink—but, oh, more skilfully, more discreetly, than ever before.

Is this self-delusion, or self-knowledge? It all boils down to the one question—was Jack London at the time of writing *John Barleycorn* an alcoholic?

If he were an alcoholic, one can see why, given the medical orthodoxies of the day, he would have been reluctant to admit it. To do so would be to label himself 'degenerate', a 'dipsomaniac', whose drinking originated in some genetic defect or bad blood. London is honest enough for most things, but not for that. Like the doctors of his age, he holds that 'comparatively few alcoholics are born in a generation. And by alcoholic I mean a man whose chemistry craves alcohol and drives him resistlessly to it'. To be 'alcoholic' as London sees it, is to be a congenital defective; to be subhuman; and to be so rare a phenomenon as almost to qualify for a freak show. 'Not one man in ten thousand', he claims, 'or in a hundred thousand, is a genuine, chemical dipsomaniac.'

Modern medicine sets the figure at one in ten adults, and tends—more charitably—to see alcoholism as a disease. And over the years, a series of influential biographers and commentators from their modern vantage point have diagnosed the Jack London who wrote *John Barleycorn* as a chronically sick man, dying of his addiction to the bottle. Irving Stone, for instance, claims that Jack 'often drank to numb the cyclical pain of his illegitimacy'. Jack's friend and young disciple, Upton Sinclair, claimed that in 1915, two years after promising in *John Barleycorn* to drink 'skilfully and discreetly' Jack was to be seen 'wandering about the bars of Oakland, dazed and disagreeably drunk'. The *ne plus ultra* of this line of interpretation is found in

Andrew Sinclair's 1977 biography, *Jack*. Andrew Sinclair pictures the author in his last years as one of the damned, destroying his body by self-administered overdoses of salvarsan—an arsenic compound, thought in the early twentieth century to be a remedy for syphilis. Sinclair's Jack London is a pathetic wreck of a man, fairly rotting apart at the time of writing *John Barleycorn*—his teeth oozing with pyorrhoea and poisoning his blood; his eyes infected with sties; his appendix chronically inflamed; his internal organs all malfunctioning. Sinclair's Jack is, allegedly, hooked on morphia, heroin and—above all—on alcohol; unable to abstain, even as the cocktail of drugs destroys his mind and body. To quote one typically gothic passage from *Jack*:

When Charmian's [first] baby did not survive [in June 1910], Jack set off on a long debauch. Throughout his heavy drinking of 1911 and 1912, his old nightmares and insomnia came back to him. In the opening chapters of *John Barleycorn*, the book he wrote to exorcise his shame, he recalled the delirium of his wine-drunk at the age of seven, when he had hunted his lost father through the cellars and dens of Chinatown. His new abuse of alcohol to kill the pain of his rotting kidneys and blocked bladder led to another form of nightmare which he called the White Logic . . . He knew this bleak clarity was the result of drink, but he could not give up the drug that stimulated his mind and soothed his physical ills.

This view of a disease-riddled Jack London, numbing his 'shame' and his 'pain' with alcohol, leads naturally to the assumption of suicide in 1916. From Irving Stone onwards, a commonly received view has been that Jack London killed himself by a deliberate or impulsively accidental morphine overdose and that the deed was hushed up by the family and compliant doctors who jointly conspired to deliver a verdict of death by uraemia (that is, kidney infection). The suicide hypothesis has been repeated so frequently and with such dramatic detail, that it is now put forward as incontrovertible literary-historical fact in such authoritative places as *The Norton Anthology of American Literature*.

Not surprisingly, London's family, descendants and partisan commentators have resented this image of Jack as debauched, diseased and suicidally depressive. And they are justified in being resentful. It is true that Jack London was probably embarrassed in the years of his fame by the fact that his parents had been joined only by common-law marriage, as who would not be? But there is no evidence that—as Stone claims—this drove him to drink excessively or even at all. Although he was a friend, Upton Sinclair actually saw very little of Jack London. Their relationship was conducted almost entirely by letters. Sinclair was a fanatic teetotaller, and his opinion of Jack (especially after his premature death) was coloured by the more lurid chapters of *John Barleycorn*. Upton Sinclair evidently never *himself* observed Jack staggering drunk in Oakland bars. Andrew Sinclair's hypotheses seem—in his not very clearly annotated biography—to depend heavily on meaningful marks (meaningful to Andrew Sinclair) in Jack's pamphlet collection. And it is extremely difficult to reconcile Sinclair's drugged and drunk zombie with the Jack London who wrote some two-score books after 1911 many of which—like *John Barleycorn*—show the author performing at his literary best. It is very odd if he were the debauchee portrayed by his unsympathetic biographers that none of the popular newspapers (most of which abominated Jack London as a socialist) picked the fact up. On close inspection, there is no reliable witness to any kind of substance abuse by London in his maturity. Russ Kingman, the most indefatigable of pro-Londonists, has actually investigated the author's bar bills (where they survive) and discovered them to be extremely modest. Kingman concludes that '*John Barleycorn* is as fictional as *The Call of the Wild* or *White Fang*.'

The defence of Jack's reputation has found a rallying

point in the 1988 three-volume *Letters of Jack London*. The editors (one of whom is the author's nearest descendant) defiantly assume that Jack had no problem with alcohol whatsoever. They simply ignore the issue out of consideration. 'Drinking' and 'alcohol' are not even mentioned in the volumes' index ('cigarettes' and 'diet' are). The editors of the *Letters* also reject indignantly the suicide hypothesis. As part and parcel of this corrective line, they implicitly dismiss *John Barleycorn* as so much fiction, a novel masquerading as autobiography. In their chronological summary of books published in 1913, *John Barleycorn* is pointedly excluded; presumably as a minor thing of no importance.

One the one side, then, is Jack London, debauchee; on the other, Jack London, paragon of sobriety. The truth is probably complex and rather untidy. And as regards Jack's alleged alcoholism, the truth almost certainly resides in the pages of *John Barleycorn*. However uncomfortable to his friends and admirers, these alcoholic memoirs must be confronted as fact not dismissed as fiction. Writing to a friendly prohibitionist in August 1915, Jack went so far as to claim that '*John Barleycorn* is frankly and truthfully autobiographical. There is no poetic license in it. It is a straight, true narrative of my personal experiences, and is toned *down*, not up.' If we have any respect for London at all, we must give some credit to such manifestly sincere assertions.

What then does this straight, true narrative tell us? From the testimony of *John Barleycorn* it seems a fair assumption that around the age of 16 Jack drank excessively, and probably did himself some physical damage. He notes with clinical accuracy the onset of 'shakes' and solitary morning drinking; his first prolonged alcoholic blackout (at the Hancock Fire Brigade's parade); his alcohol-induced suicide attempt when, after an epic three-week drunk, he stumbled overboard and gratefully allowed himself to be swept out through the Carquinez Straits to probable death. Any young man presenting to a modern doctor with these symptoms would be properly diagnosed as at risk from his drinking, and in urgent need of help.

But once he broke away from this waterfront drifter existence, Jack seems to have brought this excessive drinking under control easily enough. There were evidently many more interesting things to do than souse himself in rotgut. Thereafter, his heavy drinking restricted itself to occasional binges (such as the Bonin Islands episode), climaxing in the beer bust with University of California students around 1905, which he recalls in Chapter 27 as his last public drunkenness. It is clear that he continued to drink regularly, usually daily, but on the whole socially. There seems no reason to disbelieve Charmian's statement in her memoirs that in the ten years of their relationship she had never seen Jack *really* drunk—that is, incapable.

Nevertheless, there are good grounds for believing that around 1910, Jack took to solitary drinking in the mornings to help his writing. He describes the growth of this pernicious practice in Chapter 34 of *John Barleycorn.* He also describes how the habit grew insidiously. London offers a vivid description of his clandestine tippling which—if only temporarily—was clearly verging on the alcoholic:

I achieved a condition in which my body was never free from alcohol. Nor did I permit myself to be away from alcohol. If I traveled to out-of-the-way places, I declined to run the risk of finding them dry. I took a quart, or several quarts, along in my grip. In the past I had been amazed by other men guilty of this practice. Now I did it myself unblushingly. And when I got out with the fellows, I cast all rules by the board. I drank when they drank, what they drank, and in the same way they drank. I was carrying a beautiful alcoholic conflagration around with me. The thing fed on its own heat and flamed the fiercer. There was no time in all my waking time, that I didn't want a drink.

Again, anyone presenting to a modern doctor with these

symptoms would be seen at risk from his drinking. But, as he claims, London once more drew back from the brink and restored himself to normal drinking. The quart in the bag reverted to the sociable evening highballs and cocktails. And he performed this feat of recovery (as he again claims) by a heroic act of will. His success in thus controlling his alcohol intake predisposed Jack to the view that alcoholism is typically a failure of character or a socially-caused condition, not an organic disease. He asserts in *John Barleycorn* that 'drinking, as I deem it, is practically entirely a habit of mind. It is unlike tobacco, or cocaine, or morphine, or all the rest of the long list of drugs. The desire for alcohol is quite peculiarly mental in its origin. It is a matter of mental training and growth, and it is grown in social soil.' Few specialists (and probably few alcoholics) would agree with Jack London today. But he was generalizing from his own drinking career, not writing a medical treatise. He had himself twice gone into the lion's den and come out—if not unscathed—at least reasonably intact. It seems fair to conclude that Jack London came close enough to alcoholism to understand it intimately and that at some points in his life he was at least latently alcoholic. But his statement at the end of *John Barleycorn* that his drinking is no longer in 1913 any great problem to him is entirely credible.

II

Why, one may ask, did Jack London write *John Barleycorn*, with all its risks for his image and posthumous reputation? One reason was the agreement he signed with *Cosmopolitan* in 1912. That stipulated all *fiction* should go to the publisher for a fixed sum. London—who was never satisfied with his earnings—was thus motivated to write some non-fiction to make extra money. Travel books were a possibility, but they rarely became supersellers. What was needed was a non-fiction subject which would sell as greedily as a novel. The book of Jack London, with the demon rum as its hook, was an attractive formula in the circumstances. Thus, in a letter of 27 February 1913, we find the author informing a somewhat miffed editor of *Cosmopolitan* that *John Barleycorn* 'is not fiction . . . it is bare, bald, absolute fact'. At the same time, London was telling everyone who would listen to him (especially the Century Publishing Company) that his alcoholic memoir 'is bound to be a terrific winner.'

Commercial opportunism was, then, one main reason for London's writing the non-fictional *John Barleycorn*. But clearly many other motives combined to elicit such an extraordinarily self-revealing work. Men as preoccupied with their own masculine toughness as Jack London was do not lightly disclose their past weaknesses. In the first chapter he cites as a triggering factor the October 1911 suffrage amendment to the California Constitution which gave the vote to women in state elections. As he tells us, Jack cast his vote in favour of this amendment despite a long-standing opposition to the women's rights movement (which he thought unwomanly). He returns, 'pleasantly jingled', to Charmian at the ranch house and explains his paradoxical vote to his dutifully attentive wife. 'The wives and sisters and mothers will vote for prohibition', he tells her. Thus, the race will be forever protected from the poison of alcohol by a curtain of petticoats. London's thinking was prophetic. When women were enfranchised in Illinois in April 1914 their ballot box power promptly drove 1,000 Chicago saloons out of business. Votes were one way to bring about Prohibition. Propaganda was another. Underlying Jack's decision to write *John Barleycorn*, and quite apart from his commercial motives, was an idealistic intention to save America's young men from the dangers of alcohol. He wrote it, as Charmian noted in her diary, 'for Youth'. The fact that his wife was pregnant (with a son as he hoped) when he was making plans for *John Barleycorn* in mid-1912 must have influenced him. His son, he determined, should be protected from the temptations that had come so near to destroying the young Jack London. And in the interest of furthering Prohibition, Jack was evidently prepared to sacrifice his own good name with the American public. Let them know that he too had once been a drunkard, if that served in any way to close the saloons.

John Barleycorn was not, as the reader might suppose, begun in October 1911, on the day of the California Suffrage Amemdment. First notes for the book were not jotted down until the March–July 1912 voyage round the Horn to Seattle on the *Dirigo*. And the departure from Baltimore was preceded by a two-month stay in New York by Jack and Charmian. There are two quite contradictory accounts of this eve-of-sailing vacation. According to Andrew Sinclair and Richard O'Connor, it was the occasion of a massive bender on London's part, a 'wild maelstrom' in which all self-control (including faithfulness to his long-suffering mate) went overboard. 'He roistered night and day round the city with a pack of friends,' O'Connor records, 'he stopped writing and drank heavily, unable to resist the lure of being a literary lion. He went to boxing matches, he spent the nights on Broadway in smart saloons or with chorus girls. "Rome in its wildest days," he told a reporter, "could not compare with this city".' If we credit this lurid account, Jack London all but drank himself to death in New York in the first two months of 1912. On the verge of total physical collapse and suicidal remorse, he boarded the *Dirigo* in Baltimore. And as Andrew Sinclair tells us, '[Jack's] last acts on shore were to have himself shaved completely bald, and to be photographed standing by the grave of another literary debauchee, Edgar Allan Poe'.

The editors of the *Letters* offer a less Roman picture. 'While in New York,' they tersely note, 'the Londons

attended theater and symphony performances and parties
as well as shopping and meeting with friends and publishers.' There was no wild maelstrom; simply an out-of-town
couple from the West Coast letting their hair down a little
in the big city. Again any clinching evidence one way or
the other is lacking. But it is hard to believe that London
would have gone off the rails in the way that O'Connor
and Sinclair suggest. It is, however, quite likely that
London—with his reporter's instincts—witnessed some
strange goings-on in New York and that they gave him
the idea for writing his alcoholic memoirs.

The *Dirigo* was a dry vessel, and for five months London
was entirely abstinent. Judging by his wife's diaries, it
seems not to have caused him any great distress. Jack
and Charmian were the only passengers on board and
to get round regulations, they had to sign up as crew.
There were no comforts but no social distractions either.
Jack had always loved the sea and his mind and body
rebounded under the bracing *Dirigo* regime. He had
brought a number of writing chores with him (notably the
composition of his novel, *The Valley of the Moon*). But in
the ample spare time available on board he also thought
about *John Barleycorn* and began to scrawl ideas for this
'different' book. The earliest notes that have survived
are a few phrases indicting Barleycorn's 'cheats of sense
. . . snares of the flesh . . . lies of passion'. During the
voyage round the Horn and up the West Coast, he passed
onto Charmian other germinal ideas for *John Barleycorn*
for her to type up. But serious composition of the book
was reserved until they returned to Beauty Ranch in
September. When he set to writing, London wrote fast
and *John Barleycorn* was completed in January 1913. It
was published in August of the same year.

Despite the buoyant tone of *John Barleycorn*'s last
chapter, 1912–1913 were 'bad years' for Jack London,
possibly the worst of his life. Charmian miscarried in

August 1912, dashing Jack's hopes of a son. The building of Wolf House proved infinitely vexatious and then, when completed, the new structure burned down in August 1913 (arson was suspected, but never proved). Money troubles and copyright wrangles crowded in on the Londons. A late frost destroyed his fruit crops, hot summer winds burned his corn and locusts ate his eucalyptus trees. In July 1913 he was operated on for appendicitis and the operation—although successful—revealed the full extent of his nephritis-damaged kidneys.

Despite the general gloom of 1912–1913 Jack London had terrific hopes for *John Barleycorn*. As he told his publisher, it would be 'a killer, a winner' of a book. The *Saturday Evening Post* was infected by his authorial enthusiasm and gave him 15 cents a word for the American serial rights. The book publisher (Century) was rather stickier and was nervous about how 'different' *John Barleycorn* was from the run of Jack London's previous books. Jack had some difficulty screwing an $11,000 advance out of the firm. But he was adept at handling publishers (good, in fact, at any kind of man-to-man struggle) and eventually he got his cash. *John Barleycorn* probably earned London about $25,000 from all sources.

In the event, *John Barleycorn* was a mixed success. It was a definite hit in its serial form. But, as Charmian records, the serialization which ended in May killed the volume-form issue in August 1913 and there was 'no phenomenal book sale'. But the book made a lot of headlines and in 1914 inspired a six-reel film by Hobart Bosworth. This must have been gratifying; but *John Barleycorn's* appeal was not entirely of the kind that London hoped for. It did not, for instance, entirely restore his reputation with the discriminating critics who on the whole thought he had written too much too fast (an average three books a year). Reviewers, while applauding the 'naked' and 'brutal' honesty of the work, tended, on mature reflection, to take *John Barleycorn* as clinching evidence that London had destroyed himself as a writer. The confessions in the book explained what many affected to see as a palpable coarsening in his writing over recent years. This view was expressed most succinctly by his socialist 'comrade' André Tridon, writing in the *New Review*: 'I knew that there was something the matter with London's stuff. His vocabulary was apparently gone, his imagination seemed to be failing him, he repeated himself frightfully, his stories were becoming as safe as those of any popular novelist. Read *John Barleycorn* and you will soon enough discover what ails him.' This, needless to say, was not why Jack wanted his public to read his alcoholic memoirs. (It is, however, a mark of Jack's wonderful good nature that in subsequent correspondence with his critic he could write: 'André Tridon, I like you' and invite the man down to his ranch for some feasting and 'wordy battles'.)

But while *John Barleycorn* did little for London with the literary mandarins of his time, it was welcome ammunition for the growing Prohibitionist lobby. Jack London's scrapbooks retain some of the propaganda leaflets and fliers that were spawned from *John Barleycorn*. One, circulated in San Francisco in 1913, shows a wistful lad on the outside flap with the question 'How will your vote effect [*sic*] this Boy?' On the back is the photograph of a sodden tramp ('a saloon product') and the grim epitaph 'How Somebody's Vote effected Somebody's Boy'. In between is sandwiched the first chapter of *John Barleycorn*, as serialized by the *Post*. London also evidently gave the formidably energetic Women's Christian Temperance Union permission to use extracts of *John Barleycorn*, which they did, for years after, in pursuit of their goal of state-wide closing down of the saloons.

Doubtless, London's description of drinking debauches among seamen was a factor in rendering the US Navy dry in April 1914. This decision (which is still in force) was greeted with bellows of protest from bibulous old salts that 'under this tyrannous rule we send splendid fleets to sea with their officers tutored like schoolboys; chaperoned like schoolgirls.' Nevertheless, the US Navy was up with the times (as it was to be seventy years later, when—before any other branch of the armed service—it admitted women into its ranks). In the early decades of the century, national and even world-wide suppression of alcohol was seen as feasible legislation. *John Barleycorn* was duly translated as temperance propaganda immediately into a huge number of European languages.

Domestically in the United States, *John Barleycorn* added its considerable weight to the growing Prohibition or Anti-saloon crusade. Historically this crusade comprised three main forces: the Progressive Party, the Temperance Movement, and the Votes for Women pressure group. Combined, they were irresistible and succeeded in forcing on the legislature the passing of the Eighteenth Amendment (the Volstead Act) in January 1920. For thirteen years the United States of America was dry.

Prohibition was precisely the remedy that Jack proposed in *John Barleycorn*, although he did not live to see it. Merely make liquor unavailable, London had prophesied, and all desire for it will evaporate. The American saloon would go the way of bull baiting and witch burning. It was, of course, an experiment which went wrong. Far from solving the alcohol problem, Prohibition made it worse. As forbidden fruit, drink actually became more rather than less tempting to the young men (and women) who London thought would never want something put out of their reach. The licensed saloons had not been perfect, but they were preferable to the gang-operated speakeasies. The brewers were odious, but not diabolically evil like Al Capone or Dutch Shultz. Prohibition, America decided, was not the answer. The experiment of criminalizing a previously legal drug has never been tried again. As a blueprint for Prohibition, *John Barleycorn*'s reputation suffered after 1933. It was no longer taken seriously as a social document. In the words of one of his famous contemporaries, Jack London had seen the future, and it did not work.

III

The narrative of *John Barleycorn* is made up of three main components. It is, intermittently, an extended treatise on alcoholism; or, as London put it, an 'A to Z' of drinking. London was a close, if amateur, student of the medical literature of the day and his views on the disease were informed by the latest theory—such as it was. More valuably, he also offers the empirical record of his own drinking history with unprecedented candour.

Secondly, *John Barleycorn* is an exercise in autobiography. In this aspect, the book evidently absorbed London's earlier but unwritten 'Jack Liverpool', a work which he had conceived as something half-way between Tolstoy's *Confession* and the American super-tramp Josiah Flynt's *My Life*. Since he died before being able to write his full autobiography (provisionally entitled *Sailor on Horseback*) *John Barleycorn* remains the richest source we have for information on Jack London's childhood. (The first surviving private letters date from 1896, when Jack was 20 years old.) All biographies of London open with generous quotations and slices of paraphrase from *John Barleycorn*; not necessarily because biographers always trust London's unverifiable account of his early struggles, but because it is all that they have.

Thirdly, *John Barleycorn* is an extended meditation on pessimism, or alcohol induced melancholy. In particular its last five chapters make up an anatomy of what London calls 'The Long Sickness' and 'White Logic'. What he means by this last vivid but enigmatic phrase—with its overtones of the snowy Yukon wastes—is the suicidal clarity of thought (often misnamed 'depression') that afflicts the drinker in withdrawal. In this condition, he sees himself absolutely naked, stripped of all the 'vital lies', or what Ibsen in *The Wild Duck* calls life-lies; that is, the false consciousness that makes life liveable. From the purely experimental point-of-view, London was fascinated by what alcohol did to the mind and its powers to enlarge perception.

It is possible to grade *John Barleycorn* in terms of these three elements. In its first aspect, as a theoretical treatise, the work is vitiated by the age's primitive understanding of alcoholism, alcohol abuse, and alcohol addiction. In line with medical orthodoxy of 1913, London complacently trots out a host of vulgar errors; most egregiously that alcoholism is an extremely rare (indeed, almost non-existent) congenital condition. Time and again, London insists in *John Barleycorn* that the only true alcoholics are 'dipsomaniacs'—a numerically insignificant group of drinkers driven by 'chemical' needs. London's pharmacology in *John Barleycorn* is similarly primitive. He denies the addictive properties of alcohol, overlooking the evidence of his own withdrawal episodes and cravings as a younger man. He conceives alcohol as a stimulant; in fact it is a depressant drug, as Emil Kraepelin demonstrated at the University of Munich, in January 1914.

No-one today is going to read *John Barleycorn* as an 'A to Z' of drinking. But as autobiography, especially of London's first twenty years of life, the book is both indispensable and infuriating. It infuriates on a number of counts. Principally because of the gaps it leaves that can now never be filled. Thus we shall never know what happened to the blowsily voluptuous 'Oyster Queen' to whom on the roof of the *Razzle Dazzle* the boy-man Jack (apparently) surrendered his virginity. She warmed his bunk for a while, but then she slips out of the picture as do the other wharf rats with whom London made his piratical raids on the Company oyster beds. How, when, and why Jack broke with them is a story which is forever lost. As tantalizingly vague is London's account of his early relationship with his mother and his feelings about his true parentage (which is never mentioned in *John Barleycorn*).

Even where his descriptions of his growing up are fully detailed, they are sometimes less credible for what looks like self-serving hyperbole and exaggeration. It is hard to credit the Stakhanovite feats of manual work which Jack describes in the cannery, the jute factory and the electrical generating plant—more so in light of his apparent unwillingness to chain himself to a labouring job for any length of time, even when his family's survival largely depended on his wages. Jack was not prepared indefinitely to support his mother, step-father, and step-sister by mind-destroying manual toil at 10 cents an hour. It is a good thing for American literature that he wasn't. But it clearly worried him in later years and to justify what he saw as a dereliction of duty he plays up the hardness of the toil to the point where no human sinews could have stood it. One can't blame Jack for not staying a 'work beast' all his life but evidently he blamed himself.

Some biographers claim that London's account of his early years is occasionally tinged with retrospective black or rose. O'Connor, for example, claims that his family was never as poor in the early 1880s as London implies. O'Connor also notes that Jack's account of the saloon keeper Johnny Heinold's generosity with money seems still to have been affected by the many tots and schooners that Jack knocked back in the 'First and Last Chance Saloon'. According to O'Connor, the notion that 'the notably tight-fisted' Heinold would have loaned Jack $50 to continue his education 'aroused much sardonic laughter along the Oakland waterfront'. And certainly, things occurred on that waterfront that even the intrepid Jack

London dared not put in print. As he confessed to an admirer in September 1913: 'The only trouble, I must say, about *John Barleycorn*, is that I did not put in the whole truth . . . I did not dare put in the whole truth.'

This occasional unreliability of Jack's recollections is understandable enough as a psychological mechanism but infuriating in the absence of any other sources of information about his childhood. Nevertheless *John Barleycorn* is indispensable for putting on record—without extenuation—what we find nowhere else, namely London's emotional sensitivity. A striking example is the fourth chapter's description of the 7-year-old Jack's delirium, following too much wine at the neighbouring Italian rancho. The child is brought back, half conscious and raving:

One thing that had strongly impressed my young mind was the talk of my elders about the dens of iniquity in San Francisco's Chinatown. In my delirium I wandered deep beneath the ground through a thousand of these dens, and behind locked doors of iron I suffered and died a thousand deaths. And when I would come upon my father, seated at table in these subterranean crypts, gambling with Chinese for great stakes of gold, all my outrage gave vent in the vilest cursing. I would rise in bed, struggling against the detaining hands, and curse my father till the rafters rang. All the inconceivable filth a child running at large in a primitive countryside may hear men utter, was mine; and though I had never dared utter such oaths, they now poured from me.

It's an extraordinary and surreal episode, more so in the light of London's uncertain paternity (which father is he cursing—the true father who deserted him, or the false father who adopted him?) This child's nightmare tells us more about London than any number of pages describing how many tons of coal he could shovel, or how he could outsail any man on the San Franciso waters and outpunch any man in the Oakland bars. London adds, 'my brain was seared forever by that experience. Writing now, thirty years afterward, every vision is as distinct, as sharp-cut, every pain as vital and terrible, as on that night.' The quality of writing in this dream description is Dickensian, as is the stress which London lays on childhood trauma as the unexpungeable cargo that the adult mind must carry. It is, I think, a quality of writing which London only ever achieved or sustained in *John Barleycorn*.

It is as a meditation on alcohol induced pessimism that *John Barleycorn* is most unequivocally successful. We know that on the *Dirigo* he read William James's *The Varieties of Religious Experience*, because he made notes for *John Barleycorn* on its fly leaves and in its margins. Clearly enough, one of the things he aimed at in *John Barleycorn* was to create a 'Varieties of Alcoholic Experience'. London's copy of William James's book was published in New York (1902, reprinted 1911) and it is likely that he bought it just before leaving and read it for the first time on the voyage. Chapters such as James's 'The Sick Soul' and 'The Divided Self' clearly had a profound influence, especially on the last four chapters of *John Barleycorn*. He marked up his copy of *The Varieties of Religious Experience* extensively and in the margin of page 141 jotted down a sentence which is the key to *John Barleycorn*: 'The white logic that enables us to see through all the vital lies whereby we live.' The phrase 'vital lies' (which recurs in *John Barleycorn*) is borrowed from Violet Paget's book, responding to William James, *Vital Lies: Studies of some Varieties of Recent Obscurantism*. London's copy of this book was published in New York, 1912, and was also evidently read for the first time on the *Dirigo*. On the rear pastedown of his copy of James's *Varieties*, London noted cryptically another crucial shorthand key to *John Barleycorn*: '491-2-3-95–Barleycorn. See Saltus's *Philosophy of Disenchantment* for the whole list of the disenchanted thinkers.'

London's thought had long been steeped in a Schopenhauerian melancholy and rhetoric. It is evident that in the unusual lucidity induced by the five months on the *Dirigo* he was able to study and think methodically, probably for the first time in many years. James's book was what he principally studied and thought about. And the *Varieties* sharpened Jack's ideas and enabled him to weave his twin obsessions with drink and disenchantment into a thoroughgoing philosophy of pessimism. This philosophy is articulated in the last meditative sections of *John Barleycorn*.

For London, the essence of consciousness is a deep, irresistible world weariness; the product not of clouded but of unnaturally clear mental vision. It begins with a melancholia which he terms 'The Long Sickness' and climaxes with the more acutely distressing 'White Logic'. London anatomises this condition by means of dramatic dialogues. At its simplest, the debate is between the divided self of Jack London, in the style of Tennyson's poem *The Two Voices*. One Jack London, the optimist, points to the author's wealth, fame and achievements: 'not a hundred men in a million have been as happy as I.' The other, pessimistic Jack London, retorts with *contemptus mundi* and *memento mori* arguments. Like Webster, he sees the skull beneath the skin: 'I am aware that within this disintegrating body which has been dying since I was born I carry a skeleton; that under the rind of flesh which is called my face is a bony, noseless death's head.'

After this somewhat schizoid exchange, a more complex series of dialogues are played out in Chapters 35–38. The first is between Jack and John Barleycorn, now a much more menacing figure than the drinking companion of the early chapters. Barleycorn hands over to his ally, White Logic, 'the argent messenger of truth beyond truth, the antithesis of life, cruel and bleak as interstellar space, pulseless and frozen as absolute zero, dazzling with the frost of irrefragable logic and unforgettable fact'. The drinker, London suggests, creates for himself a mental state of such relentless clarity that the cosmic meaninglessness of life is unbearably persuasive. Terror plays no part in this; boredom does. The drinker realises that the real reason that he drinks is not to make himself 'good company' but to make other people bearable. Without drink, they would be what Sartre calls them—hell. The drinker thus sees himself for what he is, an unsocial animal temporarily and artificially habilitated by 'social drinking'.

.Finally (in Chapter 36, thirty-six being the years London had lived) White Logic gives way to a yet more fearful adversary, the 'Noseless One', death. Death—more particularly death by suicide—stands in the relationship of corollary to White Logic, just as White Logic stands in the relationship of inevitable consequence to John Barleycorn. Or to put it more simply in terms of the drinking sequence: having drunk for some years the drinker will, in the awful clearmindedness of his withdrawal phase, be afflicted with rational pessimism. He will 'see through' the shams of his life. In this condition, he will inexorably be driven to kill himself; not out of hangover remorse or pain (real as these are) but because alcohol has proved to him, beyond any contradiction, that continuing to live is irrational. The question that remains ambiguously posed at the end of *John Barleycorn* is whether the literary artist should pursue this dangerous knowledge as an act of creative duty. Must he drink the poisoned cup, like the poet in Keats's *Hyperion*, accepting the bargain that the price of supreme vision is self-destruction? In the last chapter London sidesteps this question, leaving the strong impression that it is something he is not prepared to discuss publicly in print. Suicide, we understand, is a private matter.

There are any number of reasons for reading *John Barleycorn*; not least the sheer infectious zest of its

writing. The book deserves to be instated as a classic of
American autobiography. In terms of London's remarkable
life, the early chapters are among the most self-revealing
things the author wrote. The later chapters are among
the most thoughtful things he ever wrote. But *John
Barleycorn* also requires a more careful reading than it
has traditionally received. Too often London's supporters
have neglected the book out of existence, downgrading it
as mere fiction so as to protect their man's reputation.
London's critics and those who would see him as more
glamorously depraved than he was have misread the book
as a confession of alcoholism. *John Barleycorn* is a more
complex, rewarding and, above all, enjoyable text than
either party allows.

NOTE ON THE TEXT

IT was Jack London's habit to squirrel away ideas for his books well in advance of writing them and it is likely that his alcoholic memoirs were in his mind as a future project long before 1912. There were, however, two events which triggered the writing of *John Barleycorn*. The first was the contract which London signed with *Cosmopolitan* in 1912, guaranteeing them all his future fiction for a fixed sum. This naturally inclined London towards non-fiction, as a supplementary source of revenue.

The other direct inspiration for writing *John Barley-corn* was the Londons' two months in New York, over the months January and February 1912 during which Jack evidently witnessed scenes of metropolitan debauchery. This vacation was followed by five months on board the *Dirigo*—a 'dry' vessel. During the voyage round the Horn from Baltimore to Seattle, London's main literary task was the composition of his agrarian idealistic novel, *The Valley of the Moon*, which he started on 8 March, a few days after the *Dirigo* left port. But, as Charmian recorded in her ship's diary, the relaxed timetable of the voyage allowed the Londons plentiful time for reading, together and separately. By 3 April Charmian noted that Jack was 'stuffing himself with books. What a library he travels with. Books he has never found time before to investigate.' Together, the couple read Richard Le Gallienne's translation of the *Rubaiyat of Omar Khayyam* (a poem in praise of wine) on 8 March. And on 7 April, she recalls them reading (him for the first time) Edwin Arnold's similarly philo-Oriental poem, *The Light of Asia*. On the rear endpapers of this book, London scrawled some notes about the destructiveness of alcohol ('cheats of sense ... snares of the flesh') under the headnote 'Barleycorn'.

These notes (which are reproduced in Hamilton's *The Tools of my Trade*, p. 55) evidently represent the stirrings of first thoughts for *John Barleycorn*.

On 16 April Charmian noted in her diary:

Jack is swinging along steadily (his habit!) on *Valley of the Moon*; but I think he has in mind his 'alcoholic memoirs', *John Barleycorn*, for an early opus. Anyway, he has me copying out all his little scribbled notes of years past, for J. B. And I am finding them very interesting indeed. He is all for youth being deprived of the chance to learn a taste for alcohol. The object of this book, more or less autobiographical (with the artist touch of exaggeration of his own case in order to point his moral) is to make the world a better place for YOUTH.

Jack continued supplying Charmian with snippets of ideas for *John Barleycorn*, to be typed up with the 1,000 words of his novel which he produced daily with religious regularity. Again on 14 June she notes: 'I copied up a big bunch of John Barleycorn notes.' These notes have not survived, but in the Huntington archive there are a couple of sheets of hastily pencilled memoranda on 'drinking' which must have been of the kind Charmian typed. They comprise scrappy observations on the different drinking habits of the rich and the poor, and on the specific costs of actual rounds of drinks (London was fanatic about the authenticity of such details). Other notes survive scrawled on margins, flyleaves or endpapers of the books which Jack took on the *Dirigo* with him. (Specifically in Paul Bourget's novel *Cosmopolis*; William James's *The Varieties of Religious Experience*; Josiah Flynt [Willard's] *My Life*. See Hamilton, pp. 73, 169, 293.)

On 1 July Charmian made a further entry in her diary which indicates that Jack had by now come to his resolution to continue moderate drinking once they returned ashore:

I know now that Jack, facing the writing of *John Barleycorn*, intends to drink moderately in the future, just to prove to an unbelieving public that he is the opposite of an 'alcoholic', that he is not afraid of being an alcoholic, and never was an alcoholic. Perhaps he is right; but I feel a trifle dashed.

It is clear from this that Jack had not yet started writing *John Barleycorn*, although also clear that the book's main arguments were firmly established in his head.

The Londons made harbour at Seattle on 26 July. On 7 September, writing from his ranch at Glen Ellen, London told William Ellsworth of the Century publishing company that: 'I am at present at work on *John Barleycorn*, which will be 50,000 or 60,000 words long . . . *The Saturday Evening Post* is giving me 15 cents a word for it, for American serial rights.' The primary purpose of this letter (quoted in *The Letters of Jack London*, II:1082) was to interest Ellsworth's company in buying the volume-form rights to *John Barleycorn*. They were indeed interested, but declined to make a definite offer until the work was finished. (It was a constant matter of apprehension with them that the book was dangerously 'different' from what the public had come to expect from Jack London.)

London finished writing *John Barleycorn* on 13 January 1913. On 10 January the Century Company had sent him $1,000 advance, and a contract for the book (20 per cent royalty) which he eventually signed and returned on 30 January. The manuscript of *John Barleycorn* comprises 669 pages in the author's boyish hand, written on plain quarto paper in fountain pen. London wrote fast and fluently, with relatively few corrections or additions. From time to time he queried his (admittedly slightly uncertain) spelling with the note '(spl?)'. It is clear from various spontaneous changes in the manuscript that the surviving manuscript of *John Barleycorn* is a first and final draft, evidently done in the author's usual 1,000 (or ten quarto sheets) a morning bursts. This would suggest that London began writing *John Barleycorn* in early November 1912.

The manuscript was duly given to a professional typist who marked the manuscript pages as he or she completed them. This typescript came to 161 pages, and contains virtually no errors (unlike Charmian's less sure keyboard work). One of the purposes of the typing up was to allow an exact word count, which is entered at the head of the copy as 66,896 words. At 15 cents a word, this meant that London received $10,034 for the serial rights.

The top copy of the typescript was evidently sent to the *Saturday Evening Post* (a carbon remains in the Huntington archive). The *Post* was a 5 cent illustrated weekly, whose contents were printed in narrow columns. The short sections of *John Barleycorn* which appear as rather abrupt and abbreviated chapters in book form were clearly designed for the weekly's layout. The instalments were all handsomely and profusely illustrated by H. T. Dunn.

John Barleycorn was serialized in eight sections of around 8,000 words each. The first instalment (chapters 1–5) appeared on 15 March 1913; the second (chapters 6–9) on 22 March; the third (chapters 10–14) on 29 March; the fourth (chapters 15–18) on 5 April; the fifth (chapters 19–23) on 12 April; the sixth (chapters 24–9) on 19 April; the seventh (chapters 30–5) on 26 April; the eighth (chapters 36–9) on 3 May. The first instalment was the opening item in the *Post*'s table of contents. Thereafter, *John Barleycorn* was serialized in the middle of the paper, around page 22.

In August 1913 the Century Company brought out their one-volume edition of *John Barleycorn* (embellished with eight of Dunn's illustrations), at $1.30. In England, Mills and Boon brought out a 6 shilling edition of the book in summer 1914, but its thunder was entirely stolen by the outbreak of the First World War. In America in 1914, Hobart Bosworth's Progressive Motion Picture Company (which had earlier produced the successful film of London's *Sea Wolf*) brought out a six-reel silent film of *John Barleycorn*, starring Elmer Clifton and Viola Barry.

The text reproduced here follows the 1913 Century edition which differs only in minor details from that in the *Saturday Evening Post*.

SELECT BIBLIOGRAPHY

THE best collection of Jack London's works is the two-volume Library of America set (1982), edited by Donald Pizer. The previously standard *Letters from Jack London* (1965), edited by King Hendricks and Irving Shepard has been superseded by the three-volume *Jack London Letters*, edited by Earle Labor, Robert Leitz, and I. Milo Shepard and published by Stanford University Press in 1988. Among various bibliographies, most useful are: Dale L. Walker and James E. Sisson III's *The Fiction of Jack London; a Chronological Bibliography* (1972) and *Jack London, A Bibliography* (1906, revised 1973) by Hensley C. Woodbridge, John London, and George H. Tweney. There are numerous critical biographies, many with their individual biases. Charmian London's *The Book of Jack London* (1921) is very close to its subject, but also very protective of his reputation. The daughter Joan London's *Jack London and his Times* (1939) is, by contrast, very frank (and surprisingly dismissive of *John Barleycorn*). Irving Stone's *Sailor on Horseback* (1938) ushered in a new era of unrestrained London biography and is dismissed by the editors of the recent *Letters* as a 'biographical novel'. Joseph Noel's *Footloose in Arcadia* (1940) is anecdotal, spiteful and not trustworthy. Richard O'Connor's *Jack London, A Biography* (1964) provides a clear narrative, although it is not always sympathetic to Jack. Franklin Walker's *Jack London and the Klondike* (1966) is amazingly informative and detailed, although it only covers in depth a year of the writer's diverse life. Andrew Sinclair's *Jack* (1977) is an influential modern critical biography; among much else, it dwells at great length on London's physical ailments. Robert Barltrop's *Jack London, the Man, the Writer, the Rebel* (1976) offers more of the political background to the writing. David Mike Hamilton's *The Tools of my Trade* (1986) is an invaluable exposition of London's thought, as reflected by annotations in his vast personal library. Russ Kingman's *A Pictorial Life of Jack London* (1979) vividly reconstructs the author's life around a photograph narrative and offers a reliable account of London's life and career.

A CHRONOLOGY OF LONDON'S LIFE AND WORKS

1876 Born John Griffith Chaney 12 January in San Francisco; the son of Flora Wellman and her common-law husband (1874–75), William Henry Chaney, 'a footloose astrologer'. On 7 September 1876, Wellman marries John London, whose name the young Jack adopts.

1878 The London family moves to Oakland, where John London runs a grocery store.

1881 John London's grocery business fails and the family leases a 20-acre 'ranch' in Alameda, where in 1882 Jack first attends grade school.

1882 The London family moves down the San Francisco peninsula to a 75-acre ranch, between Pedro Point and Moss Beach.

1884 The London family moves to another farm near Livermore, where John London builds ambitious facilities for rearing chickens. This fails.

1886 The London family returns to Oakland, where Flora runs an unsuccessful boarding house. Jack works as a newspaper delivery boy and at other odd jobs. He also uses the Oakland Public Library extensively under the tutelage of Ina Coolbrith.

1891 Jack graduates from Cole Grammar School (eighth grade). In the summer he works at a local cannery. Some months later with a borrowed $300 he buys the sloop *Razzle Dazzle* and sets up as an oyster pirate in San Francisco Bay.

1892 Jack serves as an deputy officer in the Fish Patrol in Benicia for the best part of a year.

1893 On his seventeenth birthday, Jack enlists as a boat-puller on the sealing schooner *Sophia Sutherland*, and spends seven months at sea in northern waters, off Japan. On his return in August, during an industrial depression, he works in a jute mill for 10 cents an hour. His essay 'Typhoon off the Coast of Japan' wins a prize for young writers run by the *San Francisco Morning Call*.

1894 Early in the year Jack works shovelling coal at the power plant of the Oakland, San Leandro and Haywards Electric

Railway. In April, Jack joins C. T. Kelly's division of Jacob Coxey's Army of the Unemployed, which intends to march on Washington. In May, in Hannibal Missouri, Jack deserts the bedraggled remnants of Kelly's Army and strikes out for himself across the eastern USA. In late June, he is sentenced to thirty days in Erie County Penitentiary, for vagrancy at the Niagara Falls. He works his passage back to Oakland, via Vancouver, as a coal stoker on the SS *Umatilla*. Out of this experience, Jack was later to write *The Road* (1907).

1895 Jack returns to Oakland High School. The school paper, the *Aegis*, publishes some of his fiction. Falls in love with Mabel Applegarth (the Ruth Morse of *Martin Eden*) who encourages his ambition to enter the University of California.

1896 Joins the Socialist Labor Party. Briefly attends a cramming academy at Alameda. Helped to study by his future wife, Bessie (Mae) Maddern. He takes his university entrance exams in August and passes. Meanwhile London has been attacked in the newspapers as Oakland's 'boy socialist'.

1897 In February leaves the University of California at Berkeley after only one semester. Begins to write seriously. Works for some time as an assistant in the Belmont Academy steam laundry. In July 1897, Jack persuades his stepsister Eliza to finance his expedition to the Yukon, to mine for gold.

1898 In July, Jack returns from the Yukon, still poor and sick with scurvy. Takes up serious writing again at his mother's encouragement. John London having died in October 1897, Jack is now the family breadwinner.

1899 In January, Jack sells his first story, 'To the Man on Trail' to the *Overland Monthly* for $5. During the course of the year he publishes some twenty-four stories and essays. In winter meets Anna Strunsky, with whom he falls in love.

1900 In April, Houghton Mifflin publishes Jack's first volume of short stories, *The Son of the Wolf*. In the same month, he marries Bessie Mae Maddern. They set up home in Oakland, initially with Jack's mother and nephew.

1901 In January the Londons' first daughter, Joan, is born. In July, Jack stands unsuccessfully as Social Democrat mayor of Oakland. Publishes *The God of his Fathers*.

1902 In the summer, Jack travels to the East End of London, where he undertakes six weeks investigation into social conditions. Later publishes *The People of the Abyss* (1903) from the experience. In October, the Londons have a second daughter, Becky. Jack publishes his first novel, *A Daughter of the Snows* and *The Cruise of the Dazzler*.

1903 *The Call of the Wild* published by Macmillan. Becomes a bestseller. Jack separates from his wife, having fallen in love with Charmian Kittredge. Buys a sloop, the *Spray*. Publishes *The Kempton-Wace Letters* with Anna Strunsky.

1904 From January to June Jack is in Korea as a war correspondent for Hearst newspapers. *The Sea-Wolf* published in November and is another bestseller. Bessie sues for divorce in June on grounds of desertion, naming Anna Strunsky. Publishes *The Faith of Men*.

1905 Jack again stands unsuccessfully as Social Democrat mayor of Oakland. He marries Charmian Kittredge in November. Honeymoons in the West Indies. Buys property and 129 acres in the Sonoma Valley which later becomes a portion of the larger Beauty Ranch. Lectures at American universities and publishes his sociological essays, *War of the Classes*, *Tales of the Fish Patrol* and the novel *The Game*.

1906 London lectures extensively on political topics in January and February. Begins building the 45-foot yacht, the *Snark*. Publishes *White Fang*, *Scorn of Women* and *Moon-Face and Other Stories*. Writes on the San Francisco earthquake for *Collier's Magazine*.

1907 In April, Jack and Charmian set out from San Francisco in the *Snark* for a voyage through the South Seas. By late December, they are in Tahiti. *Before Adam*, *Love of Life* and *The Road* published.

1908 The Londons travel to the Samoan Islands (May), Fiji (June) and on to Australia by November. Jack treated in Sydney for multiple ailments. He makes further purchases of land around the Glen Ellen area, in Sonoma County. *The Iron Heel* published.

1909 The Londons return in early summer by tramp steamer to New Orleans. Arrive home in Glen Ellen in August. Jack still recuperating from illnesses contracted on the *Snark* voyage in late October. *Martin Eden* published.

1910 Establishes himself and his family at the Beauty Ranch, now almost 1,000 acres in extent. Charmian's newborn daughter dies. Publishes *Revolution*, *Lost Face*, *Theft* and *Burning Daylight*. Plans construction of Wolf House.

1911 Jack and Charmian take a sailing trip in San Francisco Bay in April and a four-horse driving trip through northern California and Oregon, from June to September. Publishes *South Sea Tales*, *The Cruise of the Snark*, *Adventure* and *When God Laughs*.

1912 Over January–February, Jack and Charmian are in New York, on vacation. In early March, they leave Baltimore on the *Dirigo*, a four-masted barque, for a voyage round the Horn. In late July they arrive in Seattle, and return to Beauty Ranch in early August. On 12 August, Charmian has a miscarriage. Jack has planned *John Barleycorn* on the sea trip and begins writing it in November. Publishes *A Son of the Sun*, *Smoke Bellew* and *The House of Pride*. Jack is now earning $70,000 a year.

1913 Publishes *John Barleycorn* in the *Saturday Evening Post*, March–May. Wolf House burns down on 22 August. Publishes *The Abysmal Brute*, *Valley of the Moon* and *The Night-Born*.

1914 From April to June, Jack covers the Mexican Revolution for *Collier's Magazine*. Assignment cut short by attack of dysentery, complicating his already chronic ill health. Publishes *The Mutiny of the Elsinore*, *The Strength of the Strong*.

1915 Travels to Hawaii, February–July. Publishes *The Scarlet Plague*, *The Star Rover*.

1916 Spends the first half of the year semi-invalid in Hawaii. Resigns from the Socialist Party in March. Dies 22 November, either from acute kidney failure or from a self-administered overdose (possibly accidental) of morphine. *The Acorn-Planter*, *The Little Lady of the Big House* and *The Turtles of Tasman* published in 1916; *The Human Drift*, *Jerry of the Islands*, *Michael Brother of Jerry*, *On the Makaloa Mat* and *The Red One* published in 1917; *Hearts of Three* published in 1920; *Dutch Courage* published in 1922; *The Assassination Bureau* published in 1963.

ACKNOWLEDGEMENTS

I am grateful to Mr I. Milo Shepard and the Jack London estate for permission to use material still in copyright and for permission to examine manuscript material held at the Huntington Library. My thanks are also due to the Huntington Library for giving me access to their London archive and to Alan Jutzi for guiding me through its voluminous contents. David Mike Hamilton made many useful suggestions which I have been glad to incorporate. I owe a special debt of gratitude to Russ Kingman—who probably knows more about Jack London than any person living. Despite profound differences of opinion with me on the factuality of *John Barleycorn* (a work which he reads as more novel than memoir), Mr Kingman has corrected scores of errors in my typescript. Those that remain are, of course, wholly mine. But I am glad to acknowledge Mr Kingman's generous-spirited assistance, even to a scholar with whom he is in disagreement.

JOHN BARLEYCORN

CHAPTER I

IT all came to me one election day. It was on a warm California afternoon, and I had ridden down into the Valley of the Moon* from the ranch to the little village to vote yes and no to a host of proposed amendments to the Constitution of the State of California.* Because of the warmth of the day I had had several drinks before casting my ballot, and divers drinks after casting it. Then I had ridden up through the vine-clad hills and rolling pastures of the ranch and arrived at the farmhouse in time for another drink and supper.

'How did you vote on the suffrage amendment?' Charmian* asked.

'I voted for it.'

She uttered an exclamation of surprise. For be it known, in my younger days, despite my ardent democracy,* I had been opposed to woman suffrage. In my later and more tolerant years I had been unenthusiastic in my acceptance of it as an inevitable social phenomenon.

'Now just why did you vote for it?' Charmian asked.

I answered. I answered at length. I answered indignantly. The more I answered, the more indignant I became. (No; I was not drunk. The horse I had ridden was well-named 'The Outlaw'. I'd like to see any drunken man ride her.)

And yet—how shall I say?—I was lighted up, I was feeling 'good', I was pleasantly jingled.

'When the women get the ballot, they will vote for prohibition,' I said. 'It is the wives, and sisters, and mothers, and they only, who will drive the nails into the coffin of John Barleycorn—'

'But I thought you were a friend to John Barleycorn,' Charmian interpolated.

'I am. I was. I am not. I never am. I am never less his friend than when he is with me and when I seem most his friend. He is the king of liars. He is the frankest truth-sayer. He is the august companion with whom one walks with the gods. He is also in league with the Noseless One. His way leads to truth naked, and to death. He gives clear vision, and muddy dreams. He is the enemy of life, and the teacher of wisdom beyond life's vision. He is a red-handed killer, and he slays youth.'

And Charmian looked at me, and I knew she wondered where I had got it.

I continued to talk. As I say, I was lighted up. In my brain every thought was at home. Every thought, in its little cell, crouched ready-dressed at the door, like prisoners at midnight waiting a jail-break. And every thought was a vision, bright-imaged, sharp-cut, unmistakable. My brain was illuminated by the clear, white light of alcohol. John Barleycorn was on a truth-telling rampage, giving away the choicest secrets on himself. And I was his spokesman. There moved the multitudes of memories of my past life, all orderly arranged like soldiers in some vast review. It was mine to pick and choose. I was a lord of thought, the master of my vocabulary and of the totality of my experience, unerringly capable of selecting my data and building my exposition. For so John Barleycorn tricks and lures, setting the maggots of intelligence gnawing, whispering his fatal intuitions of truth, flinging purple passages into the monotony of one's days.

I outlined my life to Charmian, and expounded the make-up of my constitution. I was no hereditary alcoholic. I had been born with no organic, chemical predisposition toward alcohol. In this matter I was normal in my generation. Alcohol was an acquired taste. It had been painfully acquired. Alcohol had been a dreadfully repugnant thing—more nauseous than any physic. Even now I did not like the taste of it. I drank it only for its 'kick'. And from the age of five to that of twenty-five, I had not learned to care for its kick. Twenty years of unwilling apprenticeship had been required to make me, in the heart and the deeps of me, desirous of alcohol.

I sketched my first contacts with alcohol, told of my first intoxications and revulsions, and pointed out always the one thing that in the end had won me over—namely, the accessibility of alcohol. Not only had it always been accessible, but every interest of my developing life had drawn me to it. A newsboy on the streets, a sailor, a miner, a wanderer in far lands, always where men came together to exchange ideas, to laugh and boast and dare, to relax, to forget the dull toil of tiresome nights and days, always they came together over alcohol. The saloon was the place of congregation. Men gathered to it as primitive men gathered about the fire of the squatting-place or the fire at the mouth of the cave.

I reminded Charmian of the canoe-houses from which she had been barred in the South Pacific,* where the kinky-haired cannibals escaped from their womenkind and feasted and drank by themselves, the sacred precincts taboo to women under pain of death. As a youth, by way of the saloon I had escaped from the narrowness of women's influence into the wide free world of men. All ways led to the saloon. The thousand roads of romance and adventure drew together in the saloon, and thence led out and on over the world.

'The point is,' I concluded my sermon, 'that it is the accessibility of alcohol that has given me my taste for alcohol. I did not care for it. I used to laugh at it. Yet here I am, at the last, possessed with the drinker's desire. It took twenty years to implant that desire; and for ten years more that desire has grown. And the effect of satisfying that desire is anything but good. Temperamentally I am wholesome-hearted and merry. Yet when I walk with

John Barleycorn I suffer all the damnation of intellectual
pessimism.

'—But,' I hastened to add (I always hasten to add),
'—John Barleycorn must have his due. He does tell the
truth. That is the curse of it. The so-called truths of life
are not true. They are the vital lies* by which life lives,
and John Barleycorn gives them the lie.'

'Which does not make toward life,' Charmian said.

'Very true,' I answered. 'And that is the perfectest
hell of it. John Barleycorn makes toward death. That
is why I voted for the amendment to-day. I read back
in my life and saw how the accessibility of alcohol had
given me the taste for it. You see, comparatively few
alcoholics are born in a generation. And by alcoholic I
mean a man whose chemistry craves alcohol and drives
him resistlessly to it. The great majority of habitual
drinkers are born not only without desire for alcohol but
with actual repugnance toward it. Not the first, nor the
twentieth, nor the hundredth drink, succeeded in giving
them the liking. But they learned, just as men learn to
smoke; though it is far easier to learn to smoke than
to learn to drink. They learned because alcohol was so
accessible. The women know the game. They pay for
it—the wives and sisters and mothers. And when they
come to vote they will vote for prohibition. And the best
of it is that there will be no hardship worked on the
coming generation. Not having access to alcohol, not being
predisposed toward alcohol, it will never miss alcohol.
It will mean life more abundant for the manhood of
the young boys born and growing up—ay, and life more
abundant for the young girls born and growing up to share
the lives of the young men.'

'Why not write all this up for the sake of the young men
and women coming?' Charmian asked. 'Why not write it
so as to help the wives and sisters and mothers to the way
they should vote?'

'The "Memoirs of an Alcoholic".' I sneered—or, rather, John Barleycorn sneered; for he sat with me there at table in my pleasant, philanthropic jingle, and it is a trick of John Barleycorn to turn the smile to a sneer without an instant's warning.

'No,' said Charmian, ignoring John Barleycorn's roughness as so many women have learned to do. 'You have shown yourself no alcoholic, no dipsomaniac, but merely an habitual drinker, one who has made John Barleycorn's acquaintance through long years of rubbing shoulders with him. Write it up and call it "Alcoholic Memoirs".'

CHAPTER II

AND, ere I begin, I must ask the reader to walk with me in all sympathy; and, since sympathy is merely understanding, begin by understanding me and whom and what I write about. In the first place, I am a seasoned drinker. I have no constitutional predisposition for alcohol. I am not stupid. I am not a swine. I know the drinking game from A to Zed, and I have used my judgment in drinking. I never have to be put to bed. Nor do I stagger. In short, I am a normal, average man; and I drink in the normal, average way, as drinking goes. And this is the very point: I am writing of the effects of alcohol on the normal, average man. I have no word to say for or about the microscopically unimportant excessivist, the dipsomaniac.*

There are, broadly speaking, two types of drinkers. There is the man whom we all know, stupid, unimaginative, whose brain is bitten numbly by numb maggots; who walks generously with wide-spread, tentative legs, falls frequently in the gutter, and who sees, in the extremity of his ecstasy, blue mice and pink elephants. He is the type that gives rise to the jokes in the funny papers.

The other type of drinker has imagination, vision. Even when most pleasantly jingled he walks straight and naturally, never staggers nor falls, and knows just where he is and what he is doing. It is not his body but his brain that is drunken. He may bubble with wit, or expand with good fellowship. Or he may see intellectual specters and phantoms that are cosmic and logical and that take the forms of syllogisms. It is when in this condition that he strips away the husks of life's healthiest illusions and gravely considers the iron collar of necessity welded about the neck of his soul. This is the hour of John Barleycorn's subtlest power. It is easy for any man to roll in the gutter. But it is a terrible ordeal for a man to stand upright on his two legs unswaying, and decide that in all the universe he finds for himself but one freedom, namely, the anticipating of the day of his death. With this man this is the hour of the white logic (of which more anon), when he knows that he may know only the laws of things—the meaning of things never. This is his danger hour. His feet are taking hold of the path that leads down into the grave.

All is clear to him. All these baffling head-reaches after immortality are but the panics of souls frightened by the fear of death, and cursed with the thrice-cursed gift of imagination. They have not the instinct for death; they lack the will to die when the time to die is at hand. They trick themselves into believing they will outwit the game and win a future, leaving the other animals to the darkness of the grave or the annihilating heats of the crematory. But he, this man in the hour of his white logic, knows that they trick and outwit themselves. The one event happeneth to all alike. There is no new thing under the sun, not even that yearned-for bauble of feeble souls—immortality. But he knows, *he* knows, standing upright on his two legs unswaying. He is compounded of meat and wine and sparkle, of sun-mote and world-dust, a frail mechanism made to run for a span, to be tinkered at by doctors of divinity and doctors of physic, and to be flung into the scrap-heap at the end.

Of course, all this is soul-sickness,* life-sickness. It is the penalty the imaginative man must pay for his friendship with John Barleycorn. The penalty paid by the stupid man is simpler, easier. He drinks himself into sottish unconsciousness. He sleeps a drugged sleep, and, if he dream, his dreams are dim and inarticulate. But to the imaginative man, John Barleycorn sends the pitiless, spectral syllogisms of the white logic. He looks upon life and all its affairs with the jaundiced eye of a pessimistic

German philosopher.* He sees through all illusions. He
transvalues all values. God is bad, truth is a cheat, and life
is a joke. From his calm-mad heights, with the certitude of
a god, he beholds all life as evil. Wife, children, friends—
in the clear, white light of his logic they are exposed as
frauds and shams. He sees through them, and all that
he sees is their frailty, their meagerness, their sordidness,
their pitifulness. No longer do they fool him. They are
miserable little egotisms, like all the other little humans,
fluttering their May-fly life-dance of an hour. They are
without freedom. They are puppets of chance. So is he.
He realizes that. But there is one difference. He sees; he
knows. And he knows his one freedom: he may anticipate
the day of his death. All of which is not good for a man
who is made to live and love and be loved. Yet suicide,
quick or slow, a sudden spill or a gradual oozing away
through the years, is the price John Barleycorn exacts. No
friend of his ever escapes making the just, due payment.

CHAPTER III

I WAS five years old the first time I got drunk. It was
on a hot day, and my father* was plowing in the field. I
was sent from the house, half a mile away, to carry to him
a pail of beer. 'And be sure you don't spill it,' was the
parting injunction.

It was, as I remember it, a lard pail, very wide across
the top, and without a cover. As I toddled along, the beer
slopped over the rim upon my legs. And as I toddled, I
pondered. Beer was a very precious thing. Come to think
of it, it must be wonderfully good. Else why was I never
permitted to drink of it in the house? Other things kept
from me by the grown-ups I had found good. Then this,
too, was good. Trust the grown-ups. They knew. And
anyway, the pail was too full. I was slopping it against
my legs and spilling it on the ground. Why waste it? And
no one would know whether I had drunk or spilled it.

I was so small that in order to negotiate the pail, I
sat down and gathered it into my lap. First I sipped the
foam. I was disappointed. The preciousness evaded me.
Evidently it did not reside in the foam. Besides, the taste
was not good. Then I remembered seeing the grown-ups
blow the foam away before they drank. I buried my face
in the foam and lapped the solid liquid beneath. It wasn't
good at all. But still I drank. The grown-ups knew what
they were about. Considering my diminutiveness, the size
of the pail in my lap, and my drinking out of it with my
breath held and my face buried to the ears in foam, it was
rather difficult to estimate how much I drank. Also, I was
gulping it down like medicine, in nauseous haste to get the
ordeal over.

I shuddered when I started on, and decided that the

good taste would come afterward. I tried several times more in the course of that long half-mile. Then, astounded by the quantity of beer that was lacking, and remembering having seen stale beer made to foam afresh, I took a stick and stirred what was left till it foamed to the brim.

And my father never noticed. He emptied the pail with the wide thirst of the sweating plowman, returned it to me, and started up the plow. I endeavored to walk beside the horses. I remember tottering and falling against their heels in front of the shining share, and that my father hauled back on the lines so violently that the horses nearly sat down on me. He told me afterward that it was by only a matter of inches that I escaped disembowelling. Vaguely, too, I remember, my father carried me in his arms to the trees on the edge of the field, while all the world reeled and swung about me and I was aware of deadly nausea mingled with an appalling conviction of sin.

I slept the afternoon away under the trees, and when my father roused me at sundown it was a very sick little boy that got up and dragged wearily homeward. I was exhausted, oppressed by the weight of my limbs, and in my stomach was a harp-like vibration that extended to my throat and brain. My condition was like that of one who had gone through a battle with poison. In truth, I had been poisoned.

In the weeks and months that followed I had no more interest in beer than in the kitchen stove after it had burned me. The grown-ups were right. Beer was not for children. The grown-ups didn't mind it; but neither did they mind taking pills and castor oil. As for me, I could manage to get along quite well without beer. Yes, and to the day of my death I could have managed to get along quite well without it. But circumstance decreed otherwise. At every turn in the world in which I lived, John Barleycorn beckoned. There was no escaping him.

All paths led to him. And it took twenty years of contact, of exchanging greetings and passing on with my tongue in my cheek, to develop in me a sneaking liking for the rascal.

CHAPTER IV

MY next bout with John Barleycorn occurred when I was seven. This time my imagination was at fault, and I was frightened into the encounter. Still farming, my family had moved to a ranch on the bleak sad coast of San Mateo County south of San Francisco.* It was a wild, primitive countryside in those days; and often I heard my mother pride herself that we were old American stock and not immigrant Irish and Italians like our neighbors. In all our section there was only one other old American family.

One Sunday morning found me, how or why I cannot now remember, at the Morrisey ranch. A number of young people had gathered there from the nearer ranches. Besides, the oldsters had been there, drinking since early dawn, and, some of them, since the night before. The Morriseys were a huge breed, and there were many strapping great sons and uncles, heavy-booted, big-fisted, rough-voiced.

Suddenly there were screams from the girls and cries of 'Fight!' There was a rush. Men hurled themselves out of the kitchen. Two giants, flush-faced, with graying hair, were locked in each other's arms. One was Black Matt, who, everybody said, had killed two men in his time. The women screamed softly, crossed themselves, or prayed brokenly, hiding their eyes and peeping through their fingers. But not I. It is a fair presumption that I was the most interested spectator. Maybe I would see that wonderful thing, a man killed. Anyway, I would see a man-fight. Great was my disappointment. Black Matt and Tom Morrisey merely held on to each other and lifted their clumsy-booted feet in what seemed a grotesque, elephantine dance. They were too drunk to fight. Then the peacemakers got hold of them and led them back to cement the new friendship in the kitchen.

Soon they were all talking at once, rumbling and roaring as big-chested open-air men will when whisky has whipped their taciturnity. And I, a little shaver of seven, my heart in my mouth, my trembling body strung tense as a deer's on the verge of flight, peered wonderingly in at the open door and learned more of the strangeness of men. And I marveled at Black Matt and Tom Morrisey, sprawled over the table, arms about each other's necks, weeping lovingly.

The kitchen-drinking continued, and the girls outside grew timorous. They knew the drink game, and all were certain that something terrible was going to happen. They protested that they did not wish to be there when it happened, and some one suggested going to a big Italian rancho four miles away, where they could get up a dance. Immediately they paired off, lad and lassie, and started down the sandy road. And each lad walked with his sweetheart—trust a child of seven to listen and to know the love affairs of his countryside. And behold, I, too, was a lad with a lassie. A little Irish girl of my own age had been paired off with me. We were the only children in this spontaneous affair. Perhaps the oldest couple might have been twenty. There were chits of girls, quite grown up, of fourteen and sixteen, walking with their fellows. But we were uniquely young, this little Irish girl and I, and we walked hand in hand, and, sometimes, under the tutelage of our elders, with my arm around her waist. Only that wasn't comfortable. And I was very proud, on that bright Sunday morning, going down the long bleak road among the sandhills. I, too, had my girl, and was a little man.

The Italian rancho was a bachelor establishment. Our visit was hailed with delight. The red wine was poured in tumblers for all, and the long dining-room was partly cleared for dancing. And the young fellows drank and danced with the girls to the strains of an accordeon. To

me that music was divine. I had never heard anything
so glorious. The young Italian who furnished it would
even get up and dance, his arms around his girl, playing
the accordeon behind her back. All of which was very
wonderful for me, who did not dance, but who sat at a
table and gazed wide-eyed at the amazingness of life. I
was only a little lad, and there was so much of life for me
to learn. As the time passed, the Irish lads began helping
themselves to the wine, and jollity and high spirits reigned.
I noted that some of them staggered and fell down in the
dances, and that one had gone to sleep in a corner. Also,
some of the girls were complaining and wanting to leave,
and others of the girls were titteringly complacent, willing
for anything to happen.

When our Italian hosts had offered me wine in a general
sort of way, I had declined. My beer experience had been
enough for me, and I had no inclination to traffic further
in the stuff nor in anything related to it. Unfortunately,
one young Italian, Peter, an impish soul, seeing me sitting
solitary, stirred by a whim of the moment, half-filled a
tumbler with wine and passed it to me. He was sitting
across the table from me. I declined. His face grew stern,
and he insistently proffered the wine. And then terror
descended upon me—a terror which I must explain.

My mother had theories. First, she steadfastly maintained that brunettes and all the tribe of dark-eyed
humans were deceitful. Needless to say, my mother was a
blond.* Next, she was convinced that the dark-eyed Latin
races were profoundly sensitive, profoundly treacherous,
and profoundly murderous. Again and again, drinking in
the strangeness and the fearsomeness of the world from
her lips, I had heard her state that if one offended an
Italian, no matter how slightly and unintentionally, he was
certain to retaliate by stabbing one in the back. That was
her particular phrase—'stab you in the back'.

Now, although I had been eager to see Black Matt kill

Tom Morrisey that morning, I did not care to furnish to the dancers the spectacle of a knife sticking in *my* back. I had not yet learned to distinguish between facts and theories. My faith was implicit in my mother's exposition of the Italian character. Besides, I had some glimmering inkling of the sacredness of hospitality. Here was a treacherous, sensitive, murderous Italian, offering me hospitality. I had been taught to believe that if I offended him he would strike at me with a knife precisely as a horse kicked out when one got too close to its heels and worried it. Then, too, this Italian, Peter, had those terrible black eyes I had heard my mother talk about. They were eyes different from the eyes I knew, from the blues and grays and hazels of my own family, from the pale and genial blues of the Irish. Perhaps Peter had had a few drinks. At any rate his eyes were brilliantly black and sparkling with deviltry. They were the mysterious, the unknown, and who was I, a seven-year-old, to analyze them and know their prankishness? In them I visioned sudden death, and I declined the wine half-heartedly. The expression in his eyes changed. They grew stern and imperious as he shoved the tumbler of wine closer.

What could I do? I have faced real death since in my life, but never have I known the fear of death as I knew it then. I put the glass to my lips, and Peter's eyes relented. I knew he would not kill me just then. That was a relief. But the wine was not. It was cheap, new wine, bitter and sour, made of the leavings and scrapings of the vineyards and the vats, and it tasted far worse than beer. There is only one way to take medicine, and that is to take it. And that is the way I took that wine. I threw my head back and gulped it down. I had to gulp again and hold the poison down, for poison it was to my child's tissues and membranes.

Looking back now, I can realize that Peter was astounded. He half-filled a second tumbler and shoved it

across the table. Frozen with fear, in despair at the fate
which had befallen me, I gulped the second glass down like
the first. This was too much for Peter. He must share the
infant prodigy he had discovered. He called Dominick, a
young mustached Italian, to see the sight. This time it was
a full tumbler that was given me. One will do anything to
live. I gripped myself, mastered the qualms that rose in
my throat, and downed the stuff.

Dominick had never seen an infant of such heroic
caliber. Twice again he refilled the tumbler, each time to
the brim, and watched it disappear down my throat. By
this time my exploits were attracting attention. Middle-
aged Italian laborers, old-country peasants who did not
talk English and who could not dance with the Irish girls,
surrounded me. They were swarthy and wild-looking; they
wore belts and red shirts; and I knew they carried knives;
and they ringed me around like a pirate chorus. And Peter
and Dominick made me show off for them.

Had I lacked imagination, had I been stupid, had I
been stubbornly mulish in having my own way, I should
never have got in this pickle. And the lads and lassies were
dancing, and there was no one to save me from my fate.
How much I drank I do not know. My memory of it is of an
age-long suffering of fear in the midst of a murderous crew,
and of an infinite number of glasses of red wine passing
across the bare boards of a wine-drenched table and going
down my burning throat. Bad as the wine was, a knife in
the back was worse, and I must survive at any cost.

Looking back with the drinker's knowledge, I know
now why I did not collapse stupefied upon the table.
As I have said, I was frozen, I was paralyzed, with fear.
The only movement I made was to convey that never-
ending procession of glasses to my lips. I was a poised and
motionless receptacle for all that quantity of wine. It lay
inert in my fear-inert stomach. I was too frightened, even,
for my stomach to turn. So all that Italian crew looked

on and marveled at the infant phenomenon that downed wine with the *sang-froid* of an automaton. It is not in the spirit of braggadocio that I dare to assert they had never seen anything like it.

The time came to go. The tipsy antics of the lads had led a majority of the soberer-minded lassies to compel a departure. I found myself at the door, beside my little maiden. She had not had my experience, so she was sober. She was fascinated by the titubations of the lads who strove to walk beside their girls, and began to mimic them. I thought this a great game, and I, too, began to stagger tipsily. But she had no wine to stir up, while my movements quickly set the fumes rising to my head. Even at the start, I was more realistic than she. In several minutes I was astonishing myself. I saw one lad, after reeling half a dozen steps, pause at the side of the road, gravely peer into the ditch, and gravely, and after apparent deep thought, fall into it. To me this was excruciatingly funny. I staggered to the edge of the ditch, fully intending to stop on the edge. I came to myself, in the ditch, in process of being hauled out by several anxious-faced girls.

I didn't care to play at being drunk any more. There was no more fun in me. My eyes were beginning to swim, and with wide-open mouth I panted for air. A girl led me by the hand on either side, but my legs were leaden. The alcohol I had drunk was striking my heart and brain like a club. Had I been a weakling of a child, I am confident that it would have killed me. As it was, I know I was nearer death than any of the scared girls dreamed. I could hear them bickering among themselves as to whose fault it was; some were weeping—for themselves, for me, and for the disgraceful way their lads had behaved. But I was not interested. I was suffocating, and I wanted air. To move was agony. It made me pant harder. Yet those girls persisted in making me walk, and it was four miles home. Four miles! I remember my swimming eyes saw a small bridge across the road an infinite distance away. In fact, it was not a hundred feet distant. When I reached it, I sank down and lay on my back panting. The girls tried to lift me, but I was helpless and suffocating. Their cries of alarm brought Larry, a drunken youth of seventeen, who proceeded to resuscitate me by jumping on my chest. Dimly I remember this, and the squalling of the girls as they struggled with him and dragged him away. And then I knew nothing, though I learned afterward that Larry wound up under the bridge and spent the night there.

When I came to, it was dark. I had been carried unconscious for four miles and been put to bed. I was a sick child, and, despite the terrible strain on my heart and tissues, I continually relapsed into the madness of delirium. All the content of the terrible and horrible in my child's mind spilled out. The most frightful visions were realities to me. I saw murders committed, and I was pursued by murderers. I screamed and raved and fought. My sufferings were prodigious. Emerging from such delirium, I would hear my mother's voice: 'But the child's brain. He will lose his reason.' And sinking back into delirium, I would take the idea with me and be immured in madhouses, and be beaten by keepers, and surrounded by screeching lunatics.

One thing that had strongly impressed my young mind was the talk of my elders about the dens of iniquity in San Francisco's Chinatown. In my delirium I wandered deep beneath the ground through a thousand of these dens, and behind locked doors of iron I suffered and died a thousand deaths. And when I would come upon my father, seated at table in these subterranean crypts, gambling with Chinese for great stakes of gold, all my outrage gave vent in the vilest cursing. I would rise in bed, struggling against the detaining hands, and curse my father till the rafters rang. All the inconceivable filth a child running at large in a primitive countryside may hear men utter, was mine; and though I had never dared utter such oaths, they now poured from me, at the top of my lungs, as I cursed my father sitting there underground and gambling with long-haired, long-nailed Chinamen.

It is a wonder that I did not burst my heart or brain that night. A seven-year-old child's arteries and nerve-centers are scarcely fitted to endure the terrific paroxysms that convulsed me. No one slept in the thin, frame farmhouse that night when John Barleycorn had his will of me. And Larry, under the bridge, had no delirium like mine. I am confident that his sleep was stupefied and dreamless, and that he awoke next day merely to heaviness and moroseness, and that if he lives to-day he does not remember that night, so passing was it as an incident. But my brain was seared forever by that experience. Writing now, thirty years afterward, every vision is as distinct, as sharp-cut, every pain as vital and terrible, as on that night.

I was sick for days afterward, and I needed none of my mother's injunctions to avoid John Barleycorn in the future. My mother had been dreadfully shocked. She held that I had done wrong, very wrong, and that I had gone contrary to all her teaching. And how was I, who was never allowed to talk back,* who lacked the very words with which to express my psychology—how was I to tell my mother that it was her teaching that was directly responsible for my drunkenness? Had it not been for her theories about dark eyes and Italian character, I should never have wet my lips with the sour, bitter wine. And not until man-grown did I tell her the true inwardness of that disgraceful affair.

In those after-days of sickness, I was confused on some points, and very clear on others. I felt guilty of sin, yet smarted with a sense of injustice. It had not been my fault; yet I had done wrong. But very clear was my resolution never to touch liquor again. No mad dog was ever more afraid of water than was I of alcohol.

Yet the point I am making is that this experience, terrible as it was, could not in the end deter me from forming John Barleycorn's cheek-by-jowl acquaintance. All about me, even then, were the forces moving me toward him. In the first place, barring my mother, ever extreme in her views, it seemed to me all the grown-ups looked upon the affair with tolerant eyes. It was a joke, something funny that had happened. There was no shame attached. Even the lads and lassies giggled and snickered over their part in the affair, narrating with gusto how Larry had jumped on my chest and slept under the bridge, how So-and-So had slept out in the sandhills that night, and what had happened to the other lad who fell in the ditch. As I say, so far as I could see, there was no shame anywhere. It had been something ticklishly, devilishly fine—a bright and gorgeous episode in the monotony of life and labor on that bleak, fog-girt coast.

The Irish ranchers twitted me good-naturedly on my exploit, and patted me on the back until I felt that I had done something heroic. Peter and Dominick and the other Italians were proud of my drinking prowess. The face of morality was not set against drinking. Besides, everybody drank. There was not a teetotaler in the community. Even the teacher of our little country school, a graying man of fifty, gave us vacations on the occasions when he wrestled with John Barleycorn and was thrown. Thus there was no spiritual deterrence. My loathing for alcohol was purely physiological. I didn't like the damned stuff.

CHAPTER V

THIS physical loathing for alcohol I have never got over. But I have conquered it. To this day I re-conquer it every time I take a drink. The palate never ceases to rebel, and the palate can be trusted to know what is good for the body. But men do not knowingly drink for the effect alcohol produces on the body. What they drink for is the brain-effect; and if it must come through the body, so much the worse for the body.

And yes, despite my physical loathing for alcohol, the brightest spots in my child life were the saloons. Sitting on the heavy potato wagons, wrapped in fog, feet stinging from inactivity, the horses plodding slowly along the deep road through the sandhills, one bright vision made the way never too long. The bright vision was the saloon at Colma,* where my father, or whoever drove, always got out to get a drink. And I got out to warm by the great stove and get a soda cracker. Just one soda cracker, but a fabulous luxury. Saloons were good for something. Back behind the plodding horses, I would take an hour in consuming that one cracker. I took the smallest of nibbles, never losing a crumb, and chewed the nibble till it became the thinnest and most delectable of pastes. I never voluntarily swallowed this paste. I just tasted it, and went on tasting it, turning it over with my tongue, spreading it on the inside of one cheek, then on the inside of the other cheek, until, at the end, it eluded me and in tiny drops and oozelets slipped and dribbled down my throat. Horace Fletcher had nothing on me when it came to soda crackers.*

I liked saloons. Especially I liked the San Francisco saloons. They had the most delicious dainties for the taking—strange breads and crackers, cheeses, sausages, sardines—wonderful foods that I never saw on our meager home-table. And once, I remember, a barkeeper mixed me a sweet temperance drink of syrup and soda water. My father did not pay for it. It was the barkeeper's treat, and he became my ideal of a good, kind man. I dreamed day dreams of him for years. Although I was seven years old at the time, I can see him now with undiminished clearness, though I never laid eyes on him but that one time. The saloon was south of Market Street in San Francisco. It stood on the west side of the street. As you entered, the bar was on the left. On the right, against the wall, was the free-lunch counter. It was a long, narrow room, and at the rear, beyond the beer kegs on tap, were small round tables and chairs. The barkeeper was blue-eyed, and had fair, silky hair peeping out from under a black silk skull-cap. I remember he wore a brown Cardigan jacket, and I know precisely the spot, in the midst of the array of bottles, from which he took the bottle of red-colored syrup. He and my father talked long, and I sipped my sweet drink and worshiped him. And for years afterward I worshiped the memory of him.

Despite my two disastrous experiences, here was John Barleycorn, prevalent and accessible everywhere in the community, luring and drawing me. Here were connotations of the saloon making deep indentations in a child's mind. Here was a child, forming its first judgments of the world, finding the saloon a delightful and desirable place. Stores, nor public buildings, nor all the dwellings of men ever opened their doors to me and let me warm by their fires or permitted me to eat the food of the gods from narrow shelves against the wall. Their doors were ever closed to me; the saloon's doors were ever open. And always and everywhere I found saloons, on highway and byway, up narrow alleys and on busy thoroughfares, bright-lighted and cheerful, warm in winter and in summer

dark and cool. Yes, the saloon was a mighty fine place, and
it was more than that.

By the time I was ten years old, my family had
abandoned ranching and gone to live in the city.* And
here, at ten, I began on the streets as a newsboy. One
of the reasons for this was that we needed the money.*
Another reason was that I needed the exercise. I had
found my way to the free public library,* and was reading
myself into nervous prostration. On the poor-ranches on
which I had lived there had been no books. In ways truly
miraculous, I had been lent four books, marvelous books,
and them I had devoured. One was the life of Garfield;*
the second, Paul du Chaillu's African travels;* the third,
a novel by Ouida with the last forty pages missing;* and
the fourth, Irving's 'Alhambra'.* This last had been lent
me by a school-teacher. I was not a forward child. Unlike
Oliver Twist, I was incapable of asking for more. When I
returned the 'Alhambra' to the teacher I hoped she would
lend me another book. And because she did not—most
likely she deemed me unappreciative—I cried all the way
home on the three-mile tramp from the school to the
ranch. I waited and yearned for her to lend me another
book. Scores of times I nerved myself almost to the point
of asking her, but never quite reached the necessary pitch
of effrontery.

And then came the city of Oakland, and on the shelves
of that free-library I discovered all the great world beyond
the skyline. Here were thousands of books as good as my
four wonder-books, and some were even better. Libraries
were not concerned with children in those days, and I
had strange adventures. I remember, in the catalogue,
being impressed by the title, 'The Adventures of Peregrine
Pickle'.* I filled an application blank and the librarian
handed me the collected and entirely unexpurgated works
of Smollet in one huge volume. I read everything, but
principally history and adventure, and all the old travels

and voyages. I read mornings, afternoons, and nights. I read in bed, I read at the table, I read as I walked to and from school, and I read at recess while the other boys were playing. I began to get the 'jerks'. To everybody I replied: 'Go away. You make me nervous.'

And so, at ten, I was out on the streets, a newsboy. I had no time to read. I was busy getting exercise and learning how to fight, busy learning forwardness, and brass and bluff. I had an imagination and a curiosity about all things that made me plastic. Not least among the things I was curious about was the saloon. And I was in and out of many a one. I remember, in those days, on the east side of Broadway between Sixth and Seventh, from corner to corner, there was a solid block of saloons.

In the saloons life was different. Men talked with great voices, laughed great laughs, and there was an atmosphere of greatness. Here was something more than common every-day where nothing happened. Here life was always very live, and, sometimes, even lurid, when blows were struck, and blood was shed, and big policemen came shouldering in. Great moments, these, for me, my head filled with all the wild and valiant fighting of the gallant adventures on sea and land. There were no big moments when I trudged along the street throwing my papers in at doors. But in the saloons, even the sots, stupefied, sprawling across the tables or in the sawdust, were objects of mystery and wonder.

And more, the saloons were right. The city fathers sanctioned them and licensed them. They were not the terrible places I heard boys deem them who lacked my opportunities to know. Terrible they might be, but then that only meant they were terribly wonderful, and it is the terribly wonderful that a boy desires to know. In the same way pirates, and shipwrecks, and battles were terrible; and what healthy boy wouldn't give his immortal soul to participate in such affairs?

Besides, in saloons I saw reporters, editors, lawyers, judges, whose names and faces I knew. They put the seal of social approval on the saloon. They verified my own feeling of fascination in the saloon. They, too, must have found there that something different, that something beyond, which I sensed and groped after. What it was, I did not know; yet there it must be, for there men focused like buzzing flies about a honey pot. I had no sorrows, and the world was very bright, so I could not guess that what these men sought was forgetfulness of jaded toil and stale grief.

Not that I drank at that time. From ten to fifteen I rarely tasted liquor, but I was intimately in contact with drinkers and drinking places. The only reason I did not drink was because I didn't like the stuff. As the time passed, I worked as boy-helper on an ice-wagon, set up pins in a bowling-alley with a saloon attached, and swept out saloons at Sunday picnic grounds.

Big jovial Josie Harper ran a road-house at Telegraph Avenue and Thirty-ninth Street. Here for a year I delivered an evening paper, until my route was changed to the water-front and tenderloin of Oakland. The first month, when I collected Josie Harper's bill, she poured me a glass of wine. I was ashamed to refuse, so I drank it. But after that I watched the chance when she wasn't around so as to collect from her barkeeper.

The first day I worked in the bowling-alley, the barkeeper, according to custom, called us boys up to have a drink after we had been setting up pins for several hours. The others asked for beer. I said I'd take ginger ale. The boys snickered, and I noticed the barkeeper favored me with a strange, searching scrutiny. Nevertheless he opened a bottle of ginger ale. Afterward, back in the alleys, in the pauses between games, the boys enlightened me. I had offended the barkeeper. A bottle of ginger ale cost the saloon ever so much more than a glass of steam beer;* and

it was up to me, if I wanted to hold my job, to drink beer.
Besides, beer was food. I could work better on it. There
was no food in ginger ale. After that, when I couldn't sneak
out of it, I drank beer and wondered what men found in it
that was so good. I was always aware that I was missing
something.

What I really liked in those days was candy. For five
cents I could buy five 'cannon-balls'—big lumps of the
most delicious lastingness. I could chew and worry a single
one for an hour. Then there was a Mexican who sold big
slabs of brown chewing-taffy for five cents each. It required
a quarter of a day properly to absorb one of them. And
many a day I made my entire lunch off of one of those
slabs. In truth, I found food there, but not in beer.

CHAPTER VI

BUT the time was rapidly drawing near when I was to begin my second series of bouts with John Barleycorn. When I was fourteen, my head filled with the tales of the old voyagers, my vision with tropic isles and far sea-rims, I was sailing a small centerboard skiff* around San Francisco Bay and on the Oakland Estuary. I wanted to go to sea. I wanted to get away from monotony and the commonplace. I was in the flower of my adolescence, a-thrill with romance and adventure, dreaming of wild life in the wild man-world. Little I guessed how all the warp and woof of that man-world was entangled with alcohol.

So, one day, as I hoisted sail on my skiff, I met Scotty. He was a husky youngster of seventeen, a runaway apprentice, he told me, from an English ship in Australia. He had just worked his way on another ship to San Francisco; and now he wanted to see about getting a berth on a whaler. Across the estuary, near where the whalers lay, was lying the sloop-yacht *Idler.* The caretaker was a harpooner who intended sailing next voyage on the whale ship *Bonanza.* Would I take him, Scotty, over in my skiff to call upon the harpooner?

Would I? Hadn't I heard the stories and rumors about the *Idler?*—the big sloop that had come up from the Sandwich Islands where it had been engaged in smuggling opium. And the harpooner who was caretaker! How often had I seen him and envied him his freedom. He never had to leave the water. He slept aboard the *Idler* each night, while I had to go home upon the land to go to bed. The harpooner was only nineteen years old (and I have never had anything but his own word that he was a harpooner); but he had been too shining and glorious a personality for me ever to address as I paddled around

the yacht at a wistful distance. Would I take Scotty, the
runaway sailor, to visit the harpooner, on the opium-
smuggler *Idler?* Would I!

The harpooner came on deck to answer our hail, and
invited us aboard. I played the sailor and the man,
fending off the skiff so that it would not mar the yacht's
white paint, dropping the skiff astern on a long painter,
and making the painter fast with two nonchalant half-
hitches. We went below. It was the first sea-interior I
had ever seen. The clothing on the wall smelled musty.
But what of that? Was it not the sea-gear of men?—
leather jackets lined with corduroy, blue coats of pilot
cloth, sou'westers, sea-boots, oilskins. And everywhere
was in evidence the economy of space—the narrow bunks,
the swinging tables, the incredible lockers. There were
the tell-tale compass, the sea-lamps in their gimbals, the
blue-backed charts carelessly rolled and tucked away, the
signal-flags in alphabetical order, and a mariner's dividers
jammed into the woodwork to hold a calendar. At last I
was living. Here I sat, inside my first ship, a smuggler,
accepted as a comrade by a harpooner and a runaway
English sailor who said his name was Scotty.

The first thing that the harpooner, aged nineteen, and
the sailor, aged seventeen, did to show that they were
men, was to behave like men. The harpooner suggested the
eminent desirableness of a drink, and Scotty searched his
pockets for dimes and nickels. Then the harpooner carried
away a pink flask to be filled in some blind pig, for there
were no licensed saloons in that locality. We drank the
cheap rotgut out of tumblers. Was I any the less strong,
and the less valiant, than the harpooner and the sailor?
They were men. They proved it by the way they drank.
Drink was the badge of manhood. So I drank with them,
drink by drink, raw and straight, though the damned
stuff couldn't compare with a stick of chewing taffy or
a delectable 'cannonball'. I shuddered and swallowed my

gorge with every drink, though I manfully hid all such symptoms.

Divers times we filled the flask that afternoon. All I had was twenty cents, but I put it up like a man, though with secret regret at the enormous store of candy it could have bought. The liquor mounted in the heads of all of us, and the talk of Scotty and the harpooner was upon running the Easting down,* gales off the Horn and pamperos off the Plate, lower topsail breezes, southerly busters, North Pacific gales, and of smashed whaleboats in the Arctic ice.

'You can't swim in that ice water,' said the harpooner confidentially to me. 'You double up in a minute and go down. When a whale smashes your boat, the thing to do is to get your belly across an oar, so that when the cold doubles you you'll float.'

'Sure,' I said, with a grateful nod and an air of certitude that I, too, would hunt whales and be in smashed boats in the Arctic Ocean. And, truly, I registered his advice as singularly valuable information, and filed it away in my brain, where it persists to this day.

But I couldn't talk—at first. Heavens! I was only fourteen, and had never been on the ocean in my life. I could only listen to the two sea-dogs, and show my manhood by drinking with them, fairly and squarely, drink and drink.

The liquor worked its will with me; the talk of Scotty and the harpooner poured through the pent space of the *Idler's* cabin and through my brain like great gusts of wide, free wind; and in imagination I lived my years to come and rocked over the wild, mad, glorious world on multitudinous adventures.

We unbent. Our inhibitions and taciturnities vanished. We were as if we had known each other for years and years, and we pledged ourselves to years of future voyagings together. The harpooner told of misadventures and secret shames. Scotty wept over his poor old mother in

Edinburg—a lady, he insisted, gently born—who was in reduced circumstances, who had pinched herself to pay the lump sum to the ship-owners for his apprenticeship, whose sacrificing dream had been to see him a merchantman officer and a gentleman, and who was heartbroken because he had deserted his ship in Australia and joined another as a common sailor before the mast. And Scotty proved it. He drew her last sad letter from his pocket and wept over it as he read it aloud. The harpooner and I wept with him, and swore that all three of us would ship on the whaleship *Bonanza*, win a big pay-day, and, still together, make a pilgrimage to Edinburg and lay our store of money in the dear lady's lap.

And, as John Barleycorn heated his way into my brain, thawing my reticence, melting my modesty, talking through me and with me and as me, my adopted twin brother and *alter ego*, I, too, raised my voice to show myself a man and an adventurer, and bragged in detail and at length of how I had crossed San Francisco Bay in my open skiff in a roaring southwester when even the schooner sailors doubted my exploit. Further, I—or John Barleycorn, for it was the same thing—told Scotty that he might be a deep sea sailor and know the last rope on the great deep sea ships, but that when it came to small-boat sailing I could beat him hands down and sail circles around him.

The best of it was that my assertion and brag were true. With reticence and modesty present, I could never have dared tell Scotty my small-boat estimate of him. But it is ever the way of John Barleycorn to loosen the tongue and babble the secret thought.

Scotty, or John Barleycorn, or the pair, was very naturally offended by my remarks. Nor was I loath. I could whip any runaway sailor seventeen years old. Scotty and I flared and raged like young cockerels, until the harpooner poured another round of drinks to enable us to forgive and make up. Which we did, arms around each other's necks, protesting vows of eternal friendship—just like Black Matt and Tom Morrisey, I remembered, in the ranch kitchen in San Mateo. And remembering, I knew that I was at last a man—despite my meager fourteen years—a man as big and manly as those two strapping giants who had quarreled and made up on that memorable Sunday morning of long ago.

By this time the singing stage was reached, and I joined Scotty and the harpooner in snatches of sea songs and chanties. It was here, in the cabin of the *Idler*, that I first heard 'Blow the Man Down', 'Flying Cloud', and 'Whisky, Johnny, Whisky'. Oh, it was brave. I was beginning to grasp the meaning of life. Here was no commonplace, no Oakland Estuary, no weary round of throwing newspapers at front doors, delivering ice, and setting up ninepins. All the world was mine, all its paths were under my feet, and John Barleycorn, tricking my fancy, enabled me to anticipate the life of adventure for which I yearned.

We were not ordinary. We were three tipsy young gods, incredibly wise, gloriously genial, and without limit to our powers. Ah!—and I say it now, after the years— could John Barleycorn keep one at such a height, I should never draw a sober breath again. But this is not a world of free freights. One pays according to an iron schedule—for every strength the balanced weakness; for every high a corresponding low; for every fictitious god-like moment an equivalent time in reptilian slime. For every feat of telescoping long days and weeks of life into mad, magnificent instants, one must pay with shortened life, and, oft-times, with savage usury added.

Intenseness and duration are as ancient enemies as fire and water. They are mutually destructive. They cannot co-exist. And John Barleycorn, mighty necromancer though he be, is as much a slave to organic chemistry as we mortals are. We pay for every nerve Marathon we run,

nor can John Barleycorn intercede and fend off the just
payment. He can lead us to the heights, but he cannot
keep us there, else would we all be devotees. And there is
no devotee but pays for the mad dances John Barleycorn
pipes.

Yet the foregoing is all in after-wisdom spoken. It was
no part of the knowledge of the lad, fourteen years old,
who sat in the *Idler's* cabin between the harpooner and
the sailor, the air rich in his nostrils with the musty smell
of men's sea-gear, roaring in chorus: 'Yankee ship come
down de ribber—Pull, my bully boys, pull!'

We grew maudlin, and all talked and shouted at once.
I had a splendid constitution, a stomach that would
digest scrap-iron, and I was still running my Marathon
in full vigor when Scotty began to fail and fade. His talk
grew incoherent. He groped for words and could not find
them, while the ones he found his lips were unable to
form. His poisoned consciousness was leaving him. The
brightness went out of his eyes, and he looked as stupid
as were his efforts to talk. His face and body sagged as
his consciousness sagged. (A man cannot sit upright save
by an act of will). Scotty's reeling brain could not control
his muscles. All his correlations were breaking down. He
strove to take another drink, and feebly dropped the
tumbler on the floor. Then, to my amazement, weeping
bitterly, he rolled into a bunk on his back and immediately
snored off to sleep.

The harpooner and I drank on, grinning in a superior
way to each other over Scotty's plight. The last flask was
opened, and we drank it between us, to the accompani-
ment of Scotty's stertorous breathing. Then the harpooner
faded away into his bunk, and I was left alone, unthrown,
on the field of battle.

I was very proud, and John Barleycorn was proud with
me. I could carry my drink, into unconsciousness. And I
was still on my two feet, upright, making my way on deck

to get air into my scorching lungs. It was in this bout on the *Idler* that I discovered what a good stomach and a strong head I had for drink—a bit of knowledge that was to be a source of pride in succeeding years, and that ultimately I was to come to consider a great affliction. The fortunate man is the one who cannot take more than a couple of drinks without becoming intoxicated. The unfortunate wight is the one who can take many glasses without betraying a sign; who *must* take numerous glasses in order to get the 'kick'.

The sun was setting when I came on the *Idler's* deck. There were plenty of bunks below. I did not need to go home. But I wanted to demonstrate to myself how much I was a man. There lay my skiff astern. The last of a strong ebb was running out in channel in the teeth of an ocean breeze of forty miles an hour. I could see the stiff whitecaps, and the suck and run of the current was plainly visible in the face and trough of each one.

I set sail, cast off, took my place at the tiller, the sheet in my hand, and headed across channel. The skiff heeled over and plunged into it madly. The spray began to fly. I was at the pinnacle of exaltation. I sang 'Blow the Man Down' as I sailed. I was no boy of fourteen, living the mediocre ways of the sleepy town called Oakland. I was a man, a god, and the very elements rendered me allegiance as I bitted them to my will.

The tide was out. A full hundred yards of soft mud intervened between the boat wharf and the water. I pulled up my centerboard, ran full tilt into the mud, took in sail, and, standing in the stern as I had often done at low tide, I began to shove the skiff with an oar. It was then that my correlations began to break down. I lost my balance and pitched headforemost into the ooze. Then, and for the first time, as I floundered to my feet covered with slime, the blood running down my arms from a scrape against a barnacled stake, I knew that I was drunk. But what of it?

Across the channel two strong sailormen lay unconscious in their bunks where I had drunk them. I *was* a man. I was still on my legs, if they *were* knee deep in mud. I disdained to get back into the skiff. I waded through the mud, shoving the skiff before me and yammering the chant of my manhood to the world.

I paid for it. I was sick for a couple of days, meanly sick, and my arms were painfully poisoned from the barnacle scratches. For a week I could not use them, and it was a torture to put on and take off my clothes.

I swore, 'Never again!' The game wasn't worth it. The price was too stiff. I had no moral qualms. My revulsion was purely physical. No exalted moments were worth such hours of misery and wretchedness. When I got back to my skiff, I shunned the *Idler*. I would cross the opposite side of the channel to go around her. Scotty had disappeared. The harpooner was still about, but him I avoided. Once, when he landed on the boat-wharf, I hid in a shed so as to escape seeing him. I was afraid he would propose some more drinking, maybe have a flask full of whisky in his pocket.

And yet—and here enters the necromancy of John Barleycorn—that afternoon's drunk on the *Idler* had been a purple passage flung into the monotony of my days. It was memorable. My mind dwelt on it continually. I went over the details, over and over again. Among other things, I had got into the cogs and springs of men's actions. I had seen Scotty weep about his own worthlessness and the sad case of his Edinburg mother who was a lady. The harpooner had told me terribly wonderful things of himself. I had caught a myriad enticing and inflammatory hints of a world beyond my world, and for which I was certainly as fitted as the two lads who had drunk with me. I had got behind men's souls. I had got behind my own soul and found unguessed potencies and greatnesses.

Yes, that day stood out above all my other days. To

this day it so stands out. The memory of it is branded in my brain. But the price exacted was too high. I refused to play and pay, and returned to my cannonballs and taffy-slabs. The point is that all the chemistry of my healthy, normal body drove me away from alcohol. The stuff didn't agree with me. It was abominable. But despite this, circumstance was to continue to drive me toward John Barleycorn, to drive me again and again, until, after long years, the time should come when I would look up John Barleycorn in every haunt of men—look him up and hail him gladly as benefactor and friend. And detest and hate him all the time. Yes, he is a strange friend, John Barleycorn.

CHAPTER VII

I WAS barely turned fifteen, and working long hours in a cannery.* Month in and month out, the shortest day I ever worked was ten hours. When to ten hours of actual work at a machine is added the noon hour; the walking to work and walking home from work; the getting up in the morning, dressing, and eating; the eating at night, undressing, and going to bed, there remains no more than the nine hours out of the twenty-four required by a healthy youngster for sleep. Out of those nine hours, after I was in bed and ere my eyes drowsed shut, I managed to steal a little time for reading.

But many a night I did not knock off work until midnight. On occasion I worked eighteen and twenty hours on a stretch. Once I worked at my machine for thirty-six consecutive hours. And there were weeks on end when I never knocked off work earlier than eleven o'clock, got home and in bed at half after midnight, and was called at half-past five to dress, eat, walk to work, and be at my machine at seven o'clock whistle blow.

No moments here to be stolen for my beloved books. And what had John Barleycorn to do with so strenuous, Stoic toil of a lad just turned fifteen? He had everything to do with it. Let me show you. I asked myself if this were the meaning of life—to be a work-beast? I knew of no horse in the city of Oakland that worked the hours I worked. If this were living, I was entirely unenamored of it. I remembered my skiff, lying idle and accumulating barnacles at the boat-wharf; I remembered the wind that blew every day on the bay, the sunrises and sunsets I never saw; the bite of the salt air in my nostrils, the bite of the salt water on my flesh when I plunged overside; I remembered all the beauty and the wonder and the sense-delights of the world denied me. There was only one way to escape my deadening toil. I must get out and away on the water. I

must earn my bread on the water. And the way of the
water led inevitably to John Barleycorn. I did not know
this. And when I did learn it, I was courageous enough
not to retreat back to my bestial life at the machine.

I wanted to be where the winds of adventure blew.
And the winds of adventure blew the oyster pirate sloops
up and down San Francisco Bay, from raided oyster-beds
and fights at night on shoal and flat, to markets in the
morning against city wharves, where peddlers and saloon-
keepers came down to buy. Every raid on an oyster-bed
was a felony. The penalty was state imprisonment, the
stripes and the lockstep. And what of that? The men in
stripes worked a shorter day than I at my machine. And
there was vastly more romance in being an oyster pirate
or a convict than in being a machine slave. And behind
it all, behind all of me with youth a-bubble, whispered
Romance, Adventure.

So I interviewed my Mammy Jennie,* my old nurse at
whose black breast I had sucked. She was more prosperous
than my folks. She was nursing sick people at a good
weekly wage. Would she lend her 'white child' the money?
Would she? What she had was mine.

Then I sought out French Frank, the oyster pirate,
who wanted to sell, I had heard, his sloop, the *Razzle
Dazzle.* I found him lying at anchor on the Alameda side of
the estuary, near the Webster Street bridge, with visitors
aboard, whom he was entertaining with afternoon wine.
He came on deck to talk business. He was willing to sell.
But it was Sunday. Besides, he had guests. On the morrow
he would make out the bill of sale and I could enter
into possession. And in the meantime I must come below
and meet his friends. They were two sisters, Mamie and
Tess; a Mrs. Hadley, who chaperoned them; 'Whisky' Bob,
a youthful oyster pirate of sixteen; and 'Spider' Healey,
a black-whiskered wharf-rat of twenty. Mamie, who was
Spider's niece, was called the Queen of the Oyster Pirates,

and, on occasion, presided at their revels. French Frank
was in love with her, though I did not know it at the time;
and she steadfastly refused to marry him.

French Frank poured a tumbler of red wine from a big
demijohn to drink to our transaction. I remembered the
red wine of the Italian rancho, and shuddered inwardly.
Whisky and beer were not quite so repulsive. But the
Queen of the Oyster Pirates was looking at me, a part-
emptied glass in her own hand. I had my pride. If I was
only fifteen, at least I could not show myself any less a man
than she. Besides, there were her sister, and Mrs. Hadley,
and the young oyster pirate, and the whiskered wharf-rat,
all with glasses in their hands. Was I a milk and water
sop? No; a thousand times no, and a thousand glasses no.
I downed the tumblerful like a man.

French Frank was elated by the sale, which I had bound
with a twenty-dollar goldpiece. He poured more wine.
I had learned my strong head and stomach, and I was
certain I could drink with them in a temperate way and
not poison myself for a week to come. I could stand as
much as they; and besides, they had already been drinking
for some time.

We got to singing. Spider sang 'The Boston Burglar'
and 'Black Lulu'. The Queen sang 'Then I Wisht I were
a Little Bird'. And her sister Tess sang 'Oh, Treat My
Daughter Kind-i-ly'. The fun grew fast and furious. I
found myself able to miss drinks without being noticed
or called to account. Also, standing in the companionway,
head and shoulders out and glass in hand, I could fling
the wine overboard.

I reasoned something like this: It is a queerness of these
people that they like this vile-tasting wine. Well, let them.
I cannot quarrel with their tastes. My manhood, according
to their queer notions, must compel me to appear to like
this wine. Very well. I shall so appear. But I shall drink
no more than is unavoidable.

And the Queen began to make love to me, the latest recruit to the oyster pirate fleet, and no mere hand, but a master and owner. She went upon deck to take the air, and took me with her. She knew, of course, but I never dreamed, how French Frank was raging down below. Then Tess joined us, sitting on the cabin; and Spider, and Bob; and at the last, Mrs. Hadley and French Frank. And we sat there, glasses in hand, and sang, while the big demijohn went around; and I was the only strictly sober one.

And I enjoyed it as no one of them was able to enjoy it. Here, in this atmosphere of bohemianism, I could not but contrast the scene with my scene of the day before, sitting at my machine, in the stifling, shut-in air, repeating, endlessly repeating, at top speed, my series of mechanical motions. And here I sat now, glass in hand, in warm-glowing camaraderie, with the oyster pirates, adventurers who refused to be slaves to petty routine, who flouted restrictions and the law, who carried their lives and their liberty in their hands. And it was through John Barleycorn that I came to join this glorious company of free souls, unashamed and unafraid.

And the afternoon sea breeze blew its tang into my lungs, and curled the waves in mid-channel. Before it came the scow schooners, wing-and-wing, blowing their horns for the drawbridges to open. Red-stacked tugs tore by, rocking the *Razzle Dazzle* in the waves of their wake. A sugar bark towed from the 'boneyard' to sea.* The sun-wash was on the crisping water, and life was big. And Spider sang:

> 'Oh, it's Lulu, black Lulu, my darling,
>   Oh, it's where have you been so long?
> Been layin' in jail,
> A-waitin' for bail,
>   Till my bully comes rollin' along.'

There it was, the smack and slap of the spirit of revolt, of adventure, of romance, of the things forbidden and done defiantly and grandly. And I knew that on the morrow I would not go back to my machine at the cannery. To-morrow I would be an oyster pirate,* as free a freebooter as the century and the waters of San Francisco Bay would permit. Spider had already agreed to sail with me as my crew of one, and, also, as cook while I did the deck work. We would outfit our grub and water in the morning, hoist the big mainsail (which was a bigger piece of canvas than any I had ever sailed under), and beat our way out the estuary on the first of the sea breeze and the last of the ebb. Then we would slack sheets, and on the first of the flood run down the bay to the Asparagus Islands, where we would anchor miles off shore. And at last my dream would be realized: I would sleep upon the water. And next morning I would wake upon the water; and thereafter all my days and nights would be on the water.

And the Queen asked me to row her ashore in my skiff, when at sunset French Frank prepared to take his guests ashore. Nor did I catch the significance of his abrupt change of plan when he turned the task of rowing his skiff over to Whisky Bob, himself remaining on board the sloop. Nor did I understand Spider's grinning side-remark to me: 'Gee! There's nothin' slow about *you*.' How could it possibly enter my boy's head that a grizzled man of fifty should be jealous of me?

CHAPTER VIII

We met by appointment, early Monday morning, to complete the deal, in Johnny Heinhold's 'Last Chance'*— a saloon, of course, for the transactions of men. I paid the money over, received the bill of sale, and French Frank treated. This struck me as an evident custom, and a logical one—the seller, who receives the money, to wet a piece of it in the establishment where the trade was consummated. But to my surprise, French Frank treated the house. He and I drank, which seemed just; but why should Johnny Heinhold, who owned the saloon and waited behind the bar, be invited to drink? I figured it immediately that he made a profit on the very drink he drank. I could, in a way, considering that they were friends and shipmates, understand Spider and Whisky Bob being asked to drink; but why should the longshoremen, Bill Kelly and Soup Kennedy, be asked?

Then there was Pat, the Queen's brother, making a total of eight of us. It was early morning and all ordered whisky. What could I do, here in this company of big men, all drinking whisky? 'Whisky,' I said, with the careless air of one who had said it a thousand times. And such whisky! I tossed it down. A-r-r-r-gh! I can taste it yet.

And I was appalled at the price French Frank had paid—eighty cents. *Eighty cents!* It was an outrage to my thrifty soul. Eighty cents—the equivalent of eight long hours of my toil at the machine, gone down our throats and gone like that, in a twinkling, leaving only a bad taste in my mouth. There was no discussion but that French Frank was a waster.

I was anxious to be gone, out into the sunshine, out over the water to my glorious boat. But all hands lingered.

Even Spider, my crew, lingered. No hint broke through my obtuseness of why they lingered. I have often thought since of how they must have regarded me, the newcomer being welcomed into their company, standing at bar with them, and not standing for a single round of drinks.

French Frank, who, unknown to me, had swallowed his chagrin since the day before, now that the money for the *Razzle Dazzle* was in his pocket began to behave curiously toward me. I sensed the change in his attitude, saw the forbidding glitter in his eyes, and wondered. The more I saw of men, the queerer they became. Johnny Heinhold leaned across the bar and whispered in my ear: 'He's got it in for you. Watch out.'

I nodded comprehension of his statement, and acquiescence in it, as a man should nod who knows all about men. But secretly I was perplexed. Heavens! How was I, who had worked hard and read books of adventure, and who was only fifteen years old, who had not dreamed of giving the Queen of the Oyster Pirates a second thought, and who did not know that French Frank was madly and Latinly in love with her—how was I to guess that I had done him shame? And how was I to guess that the story of how the Queen had thrown him down on his own boat, the moment I hove in sight, was already the gleeful gossip of the waterfront? And by the same token, how was I to guess that her brother Pat's offishness with me was anything else than temperamental gloominess of spirit?

Whisky Bob got me aside a moment. 'Keep your eyes open,' he muttered. 'Take my tip. French Frank's ugly. I'm going up river with him to get a schooner for oystering. When he gets down on the beds, watch out. He says he'll run you down. After dark, any time he's around, change your anchorage and douse your riding light. Savve?'

Oh, certainly, I savve'd. I nodded my head, and as one man to another thanked him for his tip; and drifted back to the group at the bar. No; I did not treat. I never dreamed that I was expected to treat. I left with Spider, and my ears burn now as I try to surmise the things they must have said about me.

I asked Spider, in an off-hand way, what was eating French Frank. 'He's crazy jealous of you,' was the answer. 'Do you think so?' I stalled, and dismissed the matter as not worth thinking about.

But I leave it to any one—the swell of my fifteen-years-old manhood at learning that French Frank, the adventurer of fifty, the sailor of all the seas of all the world, was jealous of me—and jealous over a girl most romantically named the Queen of the Oyster Pirates. I had read of such things in books, and regarded them as personal probabilities of a distant maturity. Oh, I felt a rare young devil, as we hoisted the big mainsail that morning, broke out anchor, and filled away close-hauled on the three-mile beat to windward out into the bay.

Such was my escape from the killing machine-toil, and my introduction to the oyster pirates. True, the introduction had begun with drink, and the life promised to continue with drink. But was I to stay away from it for such reason? Wherever life ran free and great, there men drank. Romance and adventure seemed always to go down the street locked arm in arm with John Barleycorn. To know the two, I must know the third. Or else I must go back to my free-library books and read of the deeds of other men and do no deeds of my own save slave for ten cents an hour at a machine in a cannery.

No; I was not to be deterred from this brave life on the water by the fact that the water-dwellers had queer and expensive desires for beer and wine and whisky. What if their notions of happiness included the strange one of seeing me drink? When they persisted in buying the stuff and thrusting it upon me, why, I would drink it. It was the price I would pay for their comradeship. And I didn't have to get drunk. I had not got drunk the Sunday afternoon

I arranged to buy the *Razzle Dazzle*, despite the fact that none of the rest was sober. Well, I could go on into the future that way, drinking the stuff when it gave them pleasure that I should drink it, but carefully avoiding over-drinking.

CHAPTER IX

GRADUAL as was my development as a heavy drinker among the oyster pirates, the real heavy drinking came suddenly and was the result, not of desire for alcohol, but of an intellectual conviction.

The more I saw of the life, the more I was enamored of it. I can never forget my thrills, the first night I took part in a concerted raid, when we assembled on board the *Annie*—rough men, big and unafraid, and weazened wharf rats, some of them ex-convicts, all of them enemies of the law and meriting jail, in sea-boots and sea-gear, talking in gruff, low voices, and 'Big' George with revolvers strapped about his waist to show that he meant business.

Oh, I know, looking back, that the whole thing was sordid and silly. But I was not looking back in those days when I was rubbing shoulders with John Barleycorn and beginning to accept him. The life was brave and wild, and I was living the adventure I had read so much about.

Nelson, 'Young Scratch' they called him to distinguish him from 'Old Scratch', his father, sailed in the sloop *Reindeer*, partners with one 'Clam'. Clam was a dare-devil, but Nelson was a reckless maniac. He was twenty years old, with the body of a Hercules. When he was shot in Benicia, a couple of years later, the coroner said he was the greatest-shouldered man he had ever seen laid on a slab.

Nelson could not read nor write. He had been 'dragged' up by his father on San Francisco Bay, and boats were second nature with him. His strength was prodigious, and his reputation along the waterfront for violence was anything but savory. He had Berserker rages and did mad, terrible things. I made his acquaintance the first cruise of the *Razzle Dazzle*, and saw him sail the *Reindeer* in a blow and dredge oysters all around the rest of us as we lay at two anchors, troubled with fear of going ashore.

He was some man, this Nelson; and when, passing by the Last Chance saloon, he spoke to me, I felt very proud. But try to imagine my pride when he promptly asked me in to have a drink. I stood at bar and drank a glass of beer with him, and talked manfully of oysters, and boats, and of the mystery of who had put the load of buckshot through the *Annie's* mainsail.

We talked and lingered at the bar. It seemed to me strange that we lingered. We had had our beer. But who was I to lead the way outside when great Nelson chose to lean against the bar? After a few minutes, to my surprise, he asked me to have another drink, which I did. And still we talked, and Nelson evinced no intention of leaving the bar.

Bear with me while I explain the way of my reasoning and of my innocence. First of all, I was very proud to be in the company of Nelson, who was the most heroic figure among the oyster pirates and bay adventurers. Unfortunately for my stomach and mucous membranes, Nelson had a strange quirk of nature that made him find happiness in treating me to beer. I had no moral disinclination for beer, and just because I didn't like the taste of it and the weight of it was no reason I should forego the honor of his company. It was his whim to drink beer, and to have me drink beer with him. Very well, I would put up with the passing discomfort.

So we continued to talk at bar, and to drink beer ordered and paid for by Nelson. I think, now, when I look back upon it, that Nelson was curious. He wanted to find out just what kind of a gink I was. He wanted to see how many times I'd let him treat without offering to treat in return.

After I had drunk half-a-dozen glasses, my policy of temperateness in mind, I decided that I had had enough for that time. So I mentioned that I was going aboard the *Razzle Dazzle*, then lying at the city wharf a hundred yards away.

I said good-by to Nelson, and went on down the wharf. But John Barleycorn, to the extent of six glasses, went with me. My brain tingled and was very much alive. I was uplifted by my sense of manhood. I, a truly-true oyster pirate, was going aboard my own boat after hobnobbing in the Last Chance with Nelson, the greatest oyster pirate of us all. Strong in my brain was the vision of us leaning against the bar and drinking beer. And curious it was, I decided, this whim of nature that made men happy in spending good money for beer for a fellow like me who didn't want it.

As I pondered this, I recollected that several times other men, in couples, had entered the Last Chance, and first one, then the other, had treated to drinks. I remembered, on the drunk on the Idler, how Scotty and the harpooner and myself had raked and scraped dimes and nickels with which to buy the whisky. Then came my boy code: when on a day a fellow gave another a 'cannonball' or a chunk of taffy, on some other day he would expect to receive back a cannonball or a chunk of taffy.

That was why Nelson had lingered at the bar. Having bought a drink, he had waited for me to buy one. *I had let him buy six drinks and never once offered to treat.* And he was the great Nelson! I could feel myself blushing with shame. I sat down on the stringer-piece* of the wharf and buried my face in my hands. And the heat of my shame burned up my neck and into my cheeks and forehead. I have blushed many times in my life, but never have I experienced so terrible a blush as that one.

And sitting there on the stringer-piece in my shame, I

did a great deal of thinking and transvaluing of values. I
had been born poor. Poor I had lived. I had gone hungry
on occasion. I had never had toys nor playthings like
other children. My first memories of life were pinched
by poverty. The pinch of poverty had been chronic.* I
was eight years old when I wore my first little undershirt
actually sold in a store across the counter. And then it
had been only one little undershirt. When it was soiled I
had to return to the awful home-made things until it was
washed. I had been so proud of it that I insisted on wearing
it without any outer garment. For the first time I mutinied
against my mother—mutinied myself into hysteria, until
she let me wear the store undershirt so all the world could
see.

Only a man who has undergone famine can properly
value food; only sailors and desert-dwellers know the
meaning of fresh water. And only a child, with a child's
imagination, can come to know the meaning of things it
has been long denied. I early discovered that the only
things I could have were those I got for myself. My meager
childhood developed meagerness. The first things I had
been able to get for myself had been cigarette pictures,
cigarette posters, and cigarette albums.* I had not had
the spending of the money I earned, so I traded 'extra'
newspapers for these treasures. I traded duplicates with
the other boys, and circulating, as I did, all about town,
I had greater opportunities for trading and acquiring.

It was not long before I had complete every series issued
by every cigarette manufacturer—such as the Great Race
Horses, Parisian Beauties, Women of All Nations, Flags of
All Nations, Noted Actors, Champion Prize Fighters, etc.
And each series I had three different ways: in the card from
the cigarette package, in the poster, and in the album.

Then I began to accumulate duplicate sets, duplicate
albums. I traded for other things that boys valued and

which they usually bought with money given them by
their parents. Naturally, they did not have the keen sense
of values that I had, who was never given money to
buy anything. I traded for postage stamps, for minerals,
for curios, for birds' eggs, for marbles (I had a more
magnificent collection of agates than I have ever seen any
other boy possess—and the nucleus of the collection was
a handful worth at least three dollars which I had kept as
security for twenty cents I loaned to a messenger-boy who
was sent to reform school before he could redeem them).

I'd trade anything and everything for anything else, and
turn it over in a dozen more trades until it was transmuted
into something that was worth something. I was famous as
a trader. I was notorious as a miser. I could even make a
junk man weep when I had dealings with him. Other boys
called me in to sell for them their collections of bottles,
rags, old iron, grain and gunny sacks, and five-gallon oil-
cans—ay, and gave me a commission for doing it.

And this was the thrifty, close-fisted boy, accustomed
to slave at a machine for ten cents an hour, who sat on
the stringer-piece and considered the matter of beer at
five cents a glass and gone in a moment with nothing to
show for it. I was now with men I admired. I was proud
to be with them. Had all my pinching and saving brought
me the equivalent of one of the many thrills which had
been mine since I came among the oyster pirates? Then
what was worth while—money or thrills? These men had
no horror of squandering a nickel, or many nickels. They
were magnificently careless of money, calling up eight men
to drink whisky at ten cents a glass, as French Frank had
done. Why, Nelson had just spent sixty cents on beer for
the two of us.

Which was it to be? I was aware that I was making a
grave decision. I was deciding between money and men,
between niggardliness and romance. Either I must throw

overboard all my old values of money and look upon it as something to be flung about wastefully, or I must throw overboard my comradeship with those men whose peculiar quirks made them care for strong drink.

I retraced my steps up the wharf to the Last Chance where Nelson still stood outside. 'Come on and have a beer,' I invited. Again we stood at bar and drank and talked, but this time it was I who paid—ten cents! A whole hour of my labor at a machine for a drink of something I didn't want and which tasted rotten. But it wasn't difficult. I had achieved a concept. Money no longer counted. It was comradeship that counted. 'Have another,' I said. And we had another, and I paid for it. Nelson, with the wisdom of the skilled drinker, said to the barkeeper, 'Make mine a small one, Johnny.' Johnny nodded and gave him a glass that contained only a third as much as the glasses we had been drinking. Yet the charge was the same—five cents.

By this time I was getting nicely jingled, so such extravagance didn't hurt me much. Besides, I was learning. There was more in this buying of drinks than mere quantity. I got my finger on it. There was a stage when the beer didn't count at all, but just the spirit of comradeship of drinking together. And, ha!—another thing! I, too, could call for small beers and minimize by two-thirds the detestable freightage with which comradeship burdened one.

'I had to go aboard to get some money,' I remarked casually, as we drank, in the hope Nelson would take it as an explanation of why I had let him treat six consecutive times.

'Oh, well, you didn't have to do that,' he answered. 'Johnny'll trust a fellow like you—won't you, Johnny?'

'Sure,' Johnny agreed, with a smile.

'How much you got down against me?' Nelson queried.

Johnny pulled out the book he kept behind the bar, found Nelson's page, and added up the account of several dollars. At once I became possessed with a desire to have a page in that book. Almost it seemed the final badge of manhood.

After a couple more drinks, for which I insisted on paying, Nelson decided to go. We parted true comradely, and I wandered down the wharf to the *Razzle Dazzle*. Spider was just building the fire for supper.

'Where'd you get it?' he grinned up at me through the open companion.

'Oh, I've been with Nelson,' I said carelessly, trying to hide my pride.

Then an idea came to me. Here was another one of them. Now that I had achieved my concept, I might as well practice it thoroughly. 'Come on,' I said, 'up to Johnny's and have a drink.'

Going up the wharf, we met Clam coming down. Clam was Nelson's partner, and he was a fine, brave, handsome, mustached man of thirty—everything, in short, that his nickname did not connote. 'Come on,' I said, 'and have a drink.' He came. As we turned into the Last Chance, there was Pat, the Queen's brother, coming out.

'What's your hurry?' I greeted him. 'We're having a drink. Come on along.' 'I've just had one,' he demurred. 'What of it?—we're having one now,' I retorted. And Pat consented to join us, and I melted my way into his good graces with a couple of glasses of beer. Oh! I was learning things that afternoon about John Barleycorn. There was more in him than the bad taste when you swallowed him. Here, at the absurd cost of ten cents, a gloomy, grouchy individual, who threatened to become an enemy, was made into a good friend, even genial, his looks were kindly, and our voices mellowed together as we talked water-front and oyster-bed gossip.

'Small beer for me, Johnny,' I said, when the others had ordered schooners. Yet I said it like the accustomed drinker, carelessly, casually, as a sort of spontaneous thought that had just occurred to me. Looking back, I am confident that the only one there who guessed I was a tyro at bar-drinking was Johnny Heinhold.

'Where'd he get it?' I overheard Spider confidentially ask Johnny.

'Oh, he's been sousin' here with Nelson all afternoon,' was Johnny's answer.

I never let on that I'd heard, but *proud?* Ay, even the barkeeper was giving me commendation as a man. *'He's been sousin' here with Nelson all afternoon.'* Magic words! The accolade delivered by a barkeeper with a beer glass!

I remembered that French Frank had treated Johnny the day I bought the *Razzle Dazzle*. The glasses were filled, and we were ready to drink. 'Have something yourself, Johnny,' I said, with an air of having intended to say it all the time but of having been a trifle remiss because of the interesting conversation I had been holding with Clam and Pat.

Johnny looked at me with quick sharpness, divining, I am positive, the strides I was making in my education, and poured himself whisky from his private bottle. This hit me for a moment on my thrifty side. He had taken a ten-cent drink when the rest of us were drinking five-cent drinks! But the hurt was only for a moment. I dismissed it as ignoble, remembered my concept, and did not give myself away.

'You'd better put me down in the book for this,' I said, when we had finished the drink. And I had the satisfaction of seeing a fresh page devoted to my name and a charge penciled for a round of drinks amounting to thirty cents. And I glimpsed, as through a golden haze, a future wherein that page would be much-charged, and crossed off, and charged again.

I treated a second time around, and then, to my amazement, Johnny redeemed himself in that matter of the ten-cent drink. He treated us a round from behind the bar, and I decided that he had arithmetically evened things up handsomely.

'Let's go around to the St. Louis House,'* Spider suggested, when we got outside. Pat, who had been shoveling coal all day, had gone home, and Clam had gone upon the *Reindeer* to cook supper.

So around Spider and I went to the St. Louis House— my first visit—a huge barroom, where perhaps fifty men, mostly longshoremen, were congregated. And there I met Stew Kennedy for the second time, and Bill Kelly. And Smith, of the *Annie*, drifted in—he of the belt-buckled revolvers. And Nelson showed up. And I met others, including the Vigy brothers, who ran the place, and, chiefest of all, Joe Goose, with the wicked eyes, the twisted nose, and the flowered vest, who played the harmonica like a roystering angel and went on the most atrocious tears that even the Oakland water-front could conceive of and admire.

As I bought drinks–others treated as well–the thought flickered across my mind that Mammy Jennie wasn't going to be repaid much on her loan out of that week's earnings of the *Razzle Dazzle*. 'But what of it?' I thought, or rather, John Barleycorn thought it for me. 'You're a man and you're getting acquainted with men. Mammy Jennie doesn't need the money as promptly as all that. She isn't starving. You know that. She's got other money in bank. Let her wait, and pay her back gradually.'

And thus it was I learned another trait of John Barleycorn. He inhibits morality. Wrong conduct that it is impossible for one to do sober, is done quite easily when one is not sober. In fact, it is the only thing one can do, for John Barleycorn's inhibition rises like a wall between one's immediate desires and long-learned morality.

I dismissed my thought of debt to Mammy Jennie and proceeded to get acquainted at the trifling expense of some trifling money and a jingle that was growing unpleasant. Who took me on board and put me to bed that night I do not know, but I imagine it must have been Spider.

CHAPTER X

AND so I won my manhood's spurs. My status on the water-front and with the oyster pirates became immediately excellent. I was looked upon as a good fellow, as well as no coward. And somehow, from the day I achieved that concept sitting on the stringer-piece of the Oakland City Wharf, I have never cared much for money. No one has ever considered me a miser since, while my carelessness of money is a source of anxiety and worry to some that know me.

So completely did I break with my parsimonious past that I sent word home to my mother to call in the boys of the neighborhood and give to them all my collections. I never even cared to learn what boys got what collections. I was a man, now, and I made a clean sweep of everything that bound me to my boyhood.

My reputation grew. When the story went around the water-front of how French Frank had tried to run me down with his schooner, and of how I had stood on the deck of the *Razzle Dazzle*, a cocked double-barreled shotgun in my hands, steering with my feet and holding her to her course, and compelled him to put up his wheel and keep away, the water-front decided that there was something to me despite my youth. And I continued to show what was in me. There were the times I brought the *Razzle Dazzle* in with a bigger load of oysters than any other two-man craft; there was the time when we raided far down in Lower Bay and mine was the only craft back at daylight to the anchorage off Asparagus Island; there was the Thursday night we raced for market and I brought the *Razzle Dazzle* in without a rudder, first of the fleet, and skimmed the cream of the Friday morning trade; and there was the time I brought her in from Upper Bay under a jib, when

Scotty burned my mainsail.* (Yes; it was Scotty of the
Idler adventure. Irish had followed Spider on board the
Razzle Dazzle, and Scotty, turning up, had taken Irish's
place.)

But the things I did on the water only partly counted.
What completed everything and won for me the title of
'Prince of the Oyster Beds', was that I was a good fellow
ashore with my money, buying drinks like a man. I little
dreamed that the time would come when the Oakland
water-front, which had shocked me at first, would be
shocked and annoyed by the deviltry of the things I did.

But always the life was tied up with drinking. The
saloons are poor men's clubs. Saloons are congregating
places. We engaged to meet one another in saloons. We
celebrated our good fortune or wept our grief in saloons.
We got acquainted in saloons.

Can I ever forget the afternoon I met 'Old Scratch',
Nelson's father? It was in the Last Chance. Johnny
Heinhold introduced us. That Old Scratch was Nelson's
father was noteworthy enough. But there was more to it
than that. He was owner and master of the scow-schooner
Annie Mine, and some day I might ship as a sailor with
him. Still more, he was romance. He was a blue-eyed,
yellow-haired, raw-boned Viking, big-bodied and strong-
muscled despite his age. And he had sailed the seas in
ships of all nations in the old savage sailing days.

I had heard many weird tales about him, and worshiped
him from a distance. It took the saloon to bring us
together. Even so, our acquaintance might have been no
more than a handgrip and a word—he was a laconic old
fellow—had it not been for the drinking.

'Have a drink,' I said, with promptitude, after the pause
which I had learned good form in drinking dictates. Of
course, while we drank our beer, which I had paid for, it
was incumbent on him to listen to me and to talk to me.
And Johnny, like a true host, made the tactful remarks

that enabled us to find mutual topics of conversation. And of course, having drunk my beer, Captain Nelson must now buy beer in turn. This led to more talking, and Johnny drifted out of the conversation to wait on other customers.

The more beer Captain Nelson and I drank the better we got acquainted. In me he found an appreciative listener, who, by virtue of book-reading, knew much about the sea-life he had lived. So he drifted back to his wild young days, and spun many a rare yarn for me, while we downed beer, treat by treat, all through a blessed summer afternoon. And it was only John Barleycorn that made possible that long afternoon with the old sea dog.

It was Johnny Heinhold who secretly warned me across the bar that I was getting pickled and advised me to take small beers. But as long as Captain Nelson drank large beers, my pride forbade anything else than large beers. And not until the skipper ordered his first small beer did I order one for myself. Oh, when we came to a lingering fond farewell, I was drunk. But I had the satisfaction of seeing Old Scratch as drunk as I. My youthful modesty scarcely let me dare believe that the hardened old bucaneer was even drunker.

And afterwards, from Spider, and Pat, and Clam, and Johnny Heinhold, and others, came the tips that Old Scratch liked me and had nothing but good words for the fine lad I was. Which was the more remarkable, because he was known as a savage, cantankerous old cuss who never liked anybody. (His very nickname, 'Scratch', arose from a Berserker trick of his, in fighting, of tearing off his opponent's face.) And that I had won to his friendship, all thanks were due to John Barleycorn. I have given the incident merely as an example of the multitudinous lures and draws and services by which John Barleycorn wins his followers.

CHAPTER XI

AND still there arose in me no desire for alcohol, no chemical demand. In years and years of heavy drinking, drinking did not beget the desire. Drinking was the way of the life I led, the way of the men with whom I lived. While away on my cruises on the bay, I took no drink along; and while out on the bay the thought of the desirableness of a drink never crossed my mind. It was not until I tied the *Razzle Dazzle* up to the wharf and got ashore in the congregating places of men, where drink flowed, that the buying of drinks for other men, and the accepting of drinks from other men, devolved upon me as a social duty and a manhood rite.

Then, too, there were the times, lying at the city wharf or across the estuary on the sandpit, when the Queen, and her sister, and her brother Pat, and Mrs. Hadley came aboard. It was my boat. I was host, and I could only dispense hospitality in the terms of their understanding of it. So I would rush Spider, or Irish, or Scotty, or whoever was my crew, with the can for beer and the demijohn for red wine. And again, lying at the wharf disposing of my oysters, there were dusky twilights when big policemen and plain clothes men stole on board. And because we lived in the shadow of the police, we opened oysters and fed them to them with squirts of pepper sauce, and rushed the growler* or got stronger stuff in bottles.

Drink as I would, I couldn't come to like John Barleycorn. I valued him extremely well for his associations, but not for the taste of him. All the time I was striving to be a man amongst men, and all the time I nursed secret and shameful desires for candy. But I would have died before I'd let anybody guess it. I used to indulge in lonely debauches, on nights when I knew my crew was going to sleep ashore. I would go up to the Free Library, exchange my books, buy a quarter's worth of all sorts of candy that chewed and lasted, sneak aboard the *Razzle Dazzle*, lock myself in the cabin, go to bed, and lie there long hours of bliss, reading and chewing candy. And those were the only times I felt that I got my real money's worth. Dollars and dollars, across the bar, couldn't buy the satisfaction that twenty-five cents did in a candy store. As my drinking grew heavier, I began to note more and more that it was in the drinking bouts the purple passages occurred. Drunks were always memorable. At such times things happened. Men like Joe Goose dated existence from drunk to drunk. The longshoremen all looked forward to their Saturday night drunk. We of the oyster boats waited until we had disposed of our cargoes before we got really started, though a scattering of drinks and a meeting of a chance friend sometimes precipitated an accidental drunk.

In ways, the accidental drunks were the best. Stranger and more exciting things happened at such times. As, for instance, the Sunday when Nelson and French Frank and Captain Spink stole the stolen salmon boat from Whisky Bob and Nicky the Greek. Changes had taken place in the personnel of the oyster boats. Nelson had got into a fight with Bill Kelly on the *Annie* and was carrying a bullet-hole through his left hand. Also, having quarreled with Clam and broken partnership, Nelson had sailed the *Reindeer*, his arm in a sling, with a crew of two deep-water sailors, and he had sailed so madly as to frighten them ashore. Such was the tale of his recklessness they spread, that no one on the water-front would go out with Nelson. So the *Reindeer*, crewless, lay across the estuary at the sandpit. Beside her lay the *Razzle Dazzle* with a burned mainsail and with Scotty and me on board. Whisky Bob had fallen out with French Frank and gone on a raid 'up river' with Nicky the Greek.

The result of this raid was a brand new Columbia River

salmon boat, stolen from an Italian fisherman. We oyster pirates were all visited by the searching Italian, and we were convinced, from what we knew of their movements, that Whisky Bob and Nicky the Greek were the guilty parties. But where was the salmon boat? Hundreds of Greek and Italian fishermen, up river and down bay, had searched every slough and tule patch for it. When the owner despairingly offered a reward of fifty dollars, our interest increased and the mystery deepened.

One Sunday morning, old Captain Spink paid me a visit. The conversation was confidential. He had just been fishing in his skiff in the old Alameda ferry slip. As the tide went down, he had noticed a rope tied to a pile under water and leading downward. In vain he had tried to heave up what was fast on the other end. Farther along, to another pile, was a similar rope, leading downward and unheavable. Without doubt, it was the missing salmon boat. If we restored it to its rightful owner there was fifty dollars in it for us. But I had queer ethical notions about honor amongst thieves, and declined to have anything to do with the affair.

But French Frank had quarreled with Whisky Bob, and Nelson was also an enemy. (Poor Whisky Bob!—without viciousness, good-natured, generous, born weak, raised poorly, with an irresistible chemical demand for alcohol, still prosecuting his vocation of bay pirate, his body was picked up, not long afterward, beside a dock where it had sunk full of gunshot wounds.) Within an hour after I had rejected Captain Spink's proposal, I saw him sail down the estuary on board the *Reindeer* with Nelson. Also, French Frank went by on his schooner.

It was not long ere they sailed back up the estuary, curiously side by side. As they headed in for the sandpit, the submerged salmon boat could be seen, gunwales awash and held up from sinking by ropes fast to the schooner and the sloop. The tide was half out, and they sailed squarely in on the sand, grounding in a row with the salmon boat in the middle.

Immediately Hans, one of French Frank's sailors, was into a skiff and pulling rapidly for the north shore. The big demijohn in the sternsheets told his errand. They couldn't wait a moment to celebrate the fifty dollars they had so easily earned. It is the way of the devotees of John Barleycorn. When good fortune comes, they drink. When they have no fortune they drink to the hope of good fortune. If fortune be ill, they drink to forget it. If they meet a friend, they drink. If they quarrel with a friend and lose him, they drink. If their love-making be crowned with success, they are so happy they needs must drink. If they be jilted, they drink for the contrary reason. And if they haven't anything to do at all, why they take a drink, secure in the knowledge that when they have taken a sufficient number of drinks the maggots will start crawling in their brains and they will have their hands full with things to do. When they are sober they want to drink; and when they have drunk they want to drink more.

Of course, as fellow comrades, Scotty and I were called in for the drinking. We helped to make a hole in that fifty dollars not yet received. The afternoon, from just an ordinary, common, summer, Sunday afternoon, became a gorgeous, purple afternoon. We all talked and sang and ranted and bragged, and ever French Frank and Nelson sent more drinks around. We lay in full sight of the Oakland water-front, and the noise of our revels attracted friends. Skiff after skiff crossed the estuary and hauled up on the sandpit, while Hans' work was cut out for him— ever to row back and forth for more supplies of booze.

Then Whisky Bob and Nicky the Greek arrived, sober, indignant, outraged in that their fellow pirates had raised their plant. French Frank, aided by John Barleycorn, orated hypocritically about virtue and honesty, and, despite his fifty years, got Whisky Bob out on the sand

and proceded to lick him. When Nicky the Greek jumped in with a short-handled shovel to Whisky Bob's assistance, short work was made of him by Hans. And of course, when the bleeding remnants of Bob and Nicky were sent packing in their skiff, the event must needs be celebrated in further carousal.

By this time, our visitors being numerous, we were a large crowd compounded of many nationalities and diverse temperaments, all aroused by John Barleycorn, all restraints cast off. Old quarrels revived, ancient hates flared up. Fight was in the air. And whenever a longshoreman remembered something against a scow-schooner sailor, or vice versa, or an oyster pirate remembered or was remembered, a fist shot out and another fight was on. And every fight was made up in more rounds of drinks, wherein the combatants, aided and abetted by the rest of us, embraced each other and pledged undying friendship.

And of all times, Soup Kennedy selected this time to come and retrieve an old shirt of his, left aboard the *Reindeer* from the trip he sailed with Clam. He had espoused Clam's side of the quarrel with Nelson. Also, he had been drinking in the St. Louis House, so that it was John Barleycorn who led him to the sandpit in quest of his old shirt. A few words started the fray. He locked with Nelson in the cockpit of the *Reindeer*, and in the mix-up barely escaped being brained by an iron bar wielded by irate French Frank—irate because a two-handed man had attacked a one-handed man. (If the *Reindeer* still floats, the dent of the iron bar remains in the hard-wood rail of her cockpit.)

But Nelson pulled his bandaged hand, bullet-perforated, out of its sling, and, held by us, wept and roared his Berserker belief that he could lick Soup Kennedy one-handed. And we let them loose on the sand. Once, when it looked as if Nelson were getting the worst of it, French Frank and John Barleycorn sprang unfairly into the fight.

Scotty protested and reached for French Frank, who whirled upon him and fell on top of him in a pummeling clinch after a sprawl of twenty feet across the sand. In the course of separating these two, half-a-dozen fights started amongst the rest of us. These fights were finished, one way or the other, or we separated them with drinks, while all the time Nelson and Soup Kennedy fought on. Occasionally we returned to them and gave advice, such as, when they lay exhausted in the sand, unable to strike a blow, 'Throw sand in his eyes'. And they threw sand in each other's eyes, recuperated and fought on to successive exhaustions.

And now, of all this that is squalid, and ridiculous, and bestial, try to think what it meant to me, a youth not yet sixteen, burning with the spirit of adventure, fancy-filled with tales of bucaneers and sea-rovers, sacks of cities and conflicts of armed men, and imagination-maddened by the stuff I had drunk. It was life raw and naked, wild and free—the only life of that sort which my birth in time and space permitted me to attain. And more than that. It carried a promise. It was the beginning. From the sandpit the way led out through the Golden Gate to the vastness of adventure of all the world, where battles would be fought, not for old shirts and over stolen salmon boats, but for high purposes and romantic ends.

And because I told Scotty what I thought of his letting an old man like French Frank get away with him, we, too, brawled and added to the festivity of the sandpit. And Scotty threw up his job as crew, and departed in the night with a pair of blankets belonging to me. During the night, while the oyster pirates lay stupefied in their bunks, the schooner and the *Reindeer* floated on the high water and swung about to their anchors. The salmon boat, still filled with rocks and water, rested on the bottom.

In the morning, early, I heard wild cries from the *Reindeer*, and tumbled out in the chill gray to see a spectacle that made the water-front laugh for days. The beautiful salmon boat lay on the hard sand, squashed flat as a pancake, while on it were perched French Frank's schooner and the *Reindeer*. Unfortunately two of the *Reindeer's* planks had been crushed in by the stout oak stem of the salmon boat. The rising tide had flowed through the hole and just awakened Nelson by getting into his bunk with him. I lent a hand, and we pumped the *Reindeer* out and repaired the damage.

Then Nelson cooked breakfast, and while we ate we considered the situation. He was broke. So was I. The fifty dollars' reward would never be paid for that pitiful mess of splinters on the sand beneath us. He had a wounded hand and no crew. I had a burned mainsail and no crew. 'What d'ye say you and me?' Nelson queried. 'I'll go you,' was my answer. And thus I became partners with 'Young Scratch' Nelson, the wildest, maddest of them all. We borrowed the money for an outfit of grub from Johnny Heinhold, filled our water-barrels, and sailed away that day for the oyster-beds.

CHAPTER XII

NOR have I ever regretted those months of mad deviltry
I put in with Nelson. He *could* sail, even if he did
frighten every man that sailed with him. To steer to miss
destruction by an inch or an instant was his joy. To do
what everybody else did not dare attempt to do was his
pride. Never to reef down was his mania, and in all the
time I spent with him, blow high or low, the *Reindeer* was
never reefed. Nor was she ever dry. We strained her open
and sailed her open and sailed her open continually. And
we abandoned the Oakland water-front and went wider
afield for our adventures.

And all this glorious passage in my life was made
possible for me by John Barleycorn. And this is my
complaint against John Barleycorn. Here I was, thirsting
for the wild life of adventure, and the only way for me to
win to it was through John Barleycorn's mediation. It was
the way of the men who lived the life. Did I wish to live
the life, I must live it the way they did. It was by virtue of
drinking that I gained that partnership and comradeship
with Nelson. Had I drunk only the beer he paid for, or
had I declined to drink at all, I should never have been
selected by him as a partner. He wanted a partner who
would meet him on the social side, as well as the work
side, of life.

I abandoned myself to the life, and developed the
misconception that the secret of John Barleycorn lay
in going on mad drunks, rising through the successive
stages that only an iron constitution could endure to
final stupefaction and swinish unconsciousness. I did not
like the taste, so I drank for the sole purpose of getting
drunk, of getting hopelessly, helplessly drunk. And I, who
had saved and scraped, traded like a Shylock and made

junkmen weep; I, who had stood aghast when French Frank, at a single stroke, spent eighty cents for whisky for eight men; I turned myself loose with a more lavish disregard for money than any of them.

I remember going ashore one night with Nelson. In my pocket was one hundred and eighty dollars. It was my intention, first, to buy me some clothes, after that some drinks. I needed the clothes. All I possessed were on me, and they were as follows: a pair of sea-boots that providentially leaked the water out as fast as it ran in, a pair of fifty-cent overalls, a forty-cent cotton shirt, and a sou'wester. I had no hat, so I had to wear the sou'wester, and it will be noted that I have listed neither underclothes nor socks. I didn't own any.

To reach the stores where clothes could be bought, we had to pass a dozen saloons. So I bought me the drinks first. I never got to the clothing stores. In the morning, broke, poisoned, but contented, I came back on board, and we set sail. I possessed only the clothes I had gone ashore in, and not a cent remained of the one hundred and eighty dollars. It might well be deemed impossible, by those who have never tried it, that in twelve hours a lad can spend all of one hundred and eighty dollars for drinks. I know otherwise.

And I had no regrets. I was proud. I had shown them I could spend with the rest of them. Amongst strong men I had proved myself strong. I had clinched again, as I had often clinched, my right to the title of 'Prince'. Also, my attitude may be considered, in part, as a reaction from my childhood's meagerness and my childhood's excessive toil.

Possibly my inchoate thought was: Better to reign among booze-fighters, a prince, than to toil twelve hours a day at a machine for ten cents an hour. There are no purple passages in machine toil. But if the spending of one hundred and eighty dollars in twelve hours isn't a purple passage, then I'd like to know what is.

Oh, I skip much of the details of my trafficking with John Barleycorn during this period, and shall only mention events that will throw light on John Barleycorn's ways. There were three things that enabled me to pursue this heavy drinking: first, a magnificent constitution far better than the average; second, the healthy, open-air life on the water; and third, the fact that I drank irregularly. While out on the water, we never carried any drink along.

The world was opening up to me. Already I knew several hundred miles of the waterways of it, and of the towns and cities and fishing hamlets on the shores. Came the whisper to range farther. I had not found it yet. There was more behind. But even this much of the world was too wide for Nelson. He wearied for his beloved Oakland water-front, and when he elected to return to it we separated in all friendliness.

I now made the old town of Benicia, on the Carquinez Straits, my headquarters.* In a cluster of fisherman's arks, moored in the tules on the water-front, dwelt a congenial crowd of drinkers and vagabonds, and I joined them. I had longer spells ashore, between fooling with salmon fishing and making raids up and down bay and rivers as a deputy fish patrolman,* and I drank more and learned more about drinking. I held my own with any one, drink for drink; and often drank more than my share to show the strength of my manhood. When, on a morning, my unconscious carcass was disentangled from the nets on the drying-frames, whither I had stupidly, blindly crawled the night before; and when the water-front talked it over with many a giggle and laugh and another drink, I was proud indeed. It was an exploit.

And when I never drew a sober breath, on one stretch, for three solid weeks, I was certain I had reached the top. Surely, in that direction, one could go no farther. It was

time for me to move on. For always, drink or sober, at
the back of my consciousness something whispered that
this carousing and bay-adventuring was not all of life.
This whisper was my good fortune. I happened to be so
made that I could hear it calling, always calling, out and
away over the world. It was not canniness on my part. It
was curiosity, desire to know, an unrest and a seeking for
things wonderful that I seemed somehow to have glimpsed
or guessed. What was this life for, I demanded, if this were
all? No; there was something more, away and beyond.
(And, in relation to my much later development as a
drinker, this whisper, this promise of the things at the
back of life, must be noted, for it was destined to play a
dire part in my later wrestlings with John Barleycorn.)

But what gave immediacy to my decision to move on,
was a trick John Barleycorn played me—a monstrous,
incredible trick that showed abysses of intoxication hith-
erto undreamed. At one o'clock in the morning, after a
prodigious drunk, I was tottering aboard a sloop at the
end of the wharf, intending to go to sleep. The tides sweep
through Carquinez Straits as in a mill-race, and the full
ebb was on when I stumbled overboard. There was nobody
on the wharf, nobody on the sloop. I was borne away by
the current. I was not startled. I thought the misadventure
delightful. I was a good swimmer, and in my inflamed
condition the contact of the water with my skin soothed
me like cool linen.

And then John Barleycorn played me his maniacal
trick. Some maundering fancy of going out with the tide
suddenly obsessed me. I had never been morbid. Thoughts
of suicide had never entered my head. And now that they
entered, I thought it fine, a splendid culmination, a perfect
rounding off of my short but exciting career. I, who had
never known girl's love, nor woman's love, nor the love of
children; who had never played in the wide joy-fields of
art, nor climbed the star-cool heights of philosophy, nor

seen with my eyes more than a pin-point's surface of the gorgeous world; I decided that this was all, that I had seen all, lived all, been all, that was worth while, and that now was the time to cease. This was the trick of John Barleycorn, laying me by the heels of my imagination and in a drug-dream dragging me to death.

Oh, he was convincing. I had really experienced all of life, and it didn't amount to much. The swinish drunkenness in which I had lived for months (this was accompanied by the sense of degradation and the old feeling of conviction of sin) was the last and best, and I could see for myself what it was worth. There were all the broken-down old bums and loafers I had bought drinks for. That was what remained of life. Did I want to become like them? A thousand times no; and I wept tears of sweet sadness over my glorious youth going out with the tide. (And who has not seen the weeping-drunk, the melancholic drunk? They are to be found in all the barrooms, if they can find no other listener telling their sorrows to the barkeeper, who is paid to listen.)

The water was delicious. It was a man's way to die. John Barleycorn changed the tune he played in my drink-maddened brain. Away with tears and regret. It was a hero's death, and by the hero's own hand and will. So I struck up my death-chant and was singing it lustily, when the gurgle and splash of the current-riffles in my ears reminded me of my more immediate situation.

Below the town of Benicia, where the *Solano* wharf projects, the straits widen out into what bay-farers call the 'Bight of Turner's Shipyard'.* I was in the shore-tide that swept under the *Solano* wharf and on into the bight. I knew of old the power of the suck which developed when the tide swung around the end of Dead Man's Island and drove straight for the wharf. I didn't want to go through those piles. It wouldn't be nice, and I might lose an hour in the bight on my way out with the tide.

I undressed in the water and struck out with a strong, single-overhand stroke, crossing the current at right angles. Nor did I cease until, by the wharf-lights, I knew I was safe to sweep by the end. Then I turned over and rested. The stroke had been a telling one, and I was a little time in recovering my breath.

I was elated, for I had succeeded in avoiding the suck. I started to raise my death-chant again—a purely extemporized farrago of a drug-crazed youth. 'Don't sing ... yet,' whispered John Barleycorn. 'The *Solano* runs all night.* There are railroad men on the wharf. They will hear you, and come out in a boat and rescue you, and you don't want to be rescued.' I certainly didn't. What? Be robbed of my hero's death? Never. And I lay on my back in the starlight, watching the familiar wharf-lights go by, red and green and white, and bidding sad, sentimental farewell to them, each and all.

When I was well clear, in mid-channel, I sang again. Sometimes I swam a few strokes, but in the main I contented myself with floating and dreaming long drunken dreams. Before daylight, the chill of the water and the passage of the hours had sobered me sufficiently to make me wonder what portion of the Straits I was in, and also to wonder if the turn of the tide wouldn't catch me and take me back ere I had drifted out into San Pablo Bay.

Next I discovered that I was very weary and very cold, and quite sober, and that I didn't in the least want to be drowned. I could make out the Selby Smelter on the Contra Costa shore* and the Mare Island* lighthouse. I started to swim for the Solano shore, but was too weak and chilled, and made so little headway, and at the cost of so painful effort that I gave it up and contented myself with floating, now and then giving a stroke to keep my balance in the tide-rips which were increasing their commotion on the surface of the water. And I knew fear. I was sober, now, and I didn't want to die. I discovered scores of reasons for living. And the more reasons I discovered, the more liable it seemed that I was going to drown anyway.

Daylight, after I had been four hours in the water, found me in a parlous condition in the tide-rips off Mare Island light, where the swift ebbs from Vallejo Straits and Carquinez Straits were fighting with each other, and where, at that particular moment, they were fighting the flood tide setting up against them from San Pablo Bay. A stiff breeze had sprung up, and the crisp little waves were persistently lapping into my mouth, and I was beginning to swallow salt water. With my swimmer's knowledge, I knew the end was near. And then the boat came—a Greek fisherman running in for Vallejo; and again I had been saved from John Barleycorn by my constitution and physical vigor.

And in passing, let me note that this maniacal trick John Barleycorn played me is nothing uncommon. An absolute statistic of the percentage of suicides due to John Barleycorn would be appalling. In my case, healthy, normal, young, full of the joy of life, the suggestion to kill myself was unusual; but it must be taken into account that it came on the heels of a long carouse, when my nerves and brain were fearfully poisoned, and that the dramatic, romantic side of my imagination, drink-maddened to lunacy, was delighted with the suggestion. And yet, the older, more morbid drinkers, more jaded with life and disillusioned, who kill themselves, do so usually after a long debauch, when their nerves and brains are thoroughly poison-soaked.

CHAPTER XIII

SO I left Benicia, where John Barleycorn had nearly got me, and ranged wider afield* in pursuit of the whisper from the back of life to come and find. And wherever I ranged, the way lay along alcohol-drenched roads. Men still congregated in saloons. They were the poorman's clubs, and they were the only clubs to which I had access. I could get acquainted in saloons. I could go into a saloon and talk with any man. In the strange towns and cities I wandered through, the only place for me to go was the saloon. I was no longer a stranger in any town the moment I had entered a saloon.

And right here let me break in with experiences no later than last year.* I harnessed four horses to a light trap, took Charmian along, and drove for three months and a half over the wildest mountain parts of California and Oregon. Each morning I did my regular day's work of writing fiction. That completed, I drove on through the middle of the day and the afternoon to the next stop. But the irregularity of occurrence of stopping places, coupled with widely varying road conditions, made it necessary to plan, the day before, each day's drive and my work. I must know when I was to start driving in order to start writing in time to finish my day's output. Thus, on occasion, when the drive was to be long, I would be up and at my writing by five in the morning. On easier driving days I might not start writing till nine o'clock.

But how to plan? As soon as I arrived in a town, and put the horses up, on the way from the stable to the hotel I dropped into the saloons. First thing, a drink—oh, I wanted the drink, but also it must not be forgotten that, because of wanting to know things, it was in this very way I had learned to want a drink. Well, the first thing, a drink.

'Have something yourself,' to the barkeeper. And then, as we drink, my opening query about roads and stopping-places on ahead.

'Let me see,' the barkeeper will say, 'there's the road across Tarwater Divide. That used to be good. I was over it three years ago. But it was blocked this spring—Say, I'll tell you what. I'll ask Jerry—' And the barkeeper turns and addresses some men sitting at a table or leaning against the bar farther along, and who may be Jerry, or Tom, or Bill. 'Say, Jerry, how about the Tarwater road? You was down to Wilkins last week.'

And while Bill or Jerry or Tom is beginning to unlimber his thinking and speaking apparatus, I suggest that he join us in the drink. Then discussions arise about the advisability of this road or that, what the best stopping places may be, what running time I may expect to make, where the best trout streams are, and so forth, in which other men join, and which are punctuated with more drinks.

Two or three more saloons, and I accumulate a warm jingle and come pretty close to knowing everybody in town, all about the town, and a fair deal about the surrounding country. I know the lawyers, editors, business men, local politicians, and the visiting ranchers, hunters, and miners, so that by evening, when Charmian and I stroll down the main street and back, she is astounded by the number of my acquaintances in that totally strange town.

And thus is demonstrated a service John Barleycorn renders, a service by which he increases his power over men. And over the world, wherever I have gone, during all the years, it has been the same. It may be a cabaret in the Latin Quarter, a café in some obscure Italian village, a boozing-ken in sailor-town, and it may be up at the club over Scotch and soda; but always it will be where John Barleycorn makes fellowship that I get immediately

in touch, and meet, and know. And in the good days
coming, when John Barleycorn will have been banished
out of existence along with the other barbarians, some
other institution than the saloon will have to obtain, some
other congregating place of men where strange men and
stranger men may get in touch, and meet, and know.

But to return to my narrative. When I turned my back
on Benicia, my way led through saloons. I had developed
no moral theories against drinking, and I disliked as much
as ever the taste of the stuff. But I had grown respectfully
suspicious of John Barleycorn. I could not forget that trick
he had played on me—on *me*, who did not want to die.
So I continued to drink, and to keep a sharp eye on John
Barleycorn, resolved to resist all future suggestions of self-
destruction.

In strange towns I made immediate acquaintances in
the saloons. When I hoboed, and hadn't the price of a
bed, a saloon was the only place that would receive me
and give me a chair by the fire. I could go into a saloon
and wash up, brush my clothes, and comb my hair. And
saloons were always so damnably convenient. They were
everywhere in my western country.

I couldn't go into the dwellings of strangers that way.
Their doors were not open to me; no seats were there
for me by their fires. Also, churches and preachers I had
never known. And from what I didn't know I was not
attracted toward them. Besides, there was no glamour
about them, no haze of romance, no promise of adventure.
They were the sort with whom things never happened.
They lived and remained always in the one place, creatures
of order and system, narrow, limited, restrained. They
were without greatness, without imagination, without
camaraderie. It was the good fellows, easy and genial,
daring, and, on occasion, mad, that I wanted to know—
the fellows, generous-hearted and handed, and not rabbit-
hearted.

And here is another complaint I bring against John Barleycorn. It is these good fellows that he gets—the fellows with the fire and the go in them, who have bigness, and warmness, and the best of the human weaknesses. And John Barleycorn puts out the fire, and soddens the agility, and, when he does not more immediately kill them or make maniacs of them, he coarsens and grossens them, twists and malforms them out of the original goodness and fineness of their natures.

Oh!—and I speak out of later knowledge—heaven forefend me from the most of the average run of male humans who are not good fellows—the ones cold of heart and cold of head who don't smoke, drink, nor swear, nor do much of anything else that is brave, and resentful, and stinging, because in their feeble fibers there has never been the stir and prod of life to well over its boundaries and be devilish and daring. One doesn't meet these in saloons, nor rallying to lost causes, nor flaming on the adventure-paths, nor loving as God's own mad lovers. They are too busy keeping their feet dry, conserving their heart-beats, and making unlovely life-successes of their spirit mediocrity.

And so I draw the indictment home to John Barleycorn. It is just these, the good fellows, the worth while, the fellows with the weakness of too much strength, too much spirit, too much fire and flame of fine devilishness, that he solicits and ruins. Of course, he ruins weaklings; but with them, the worst we breed, I am not here concerned. My concern is that it is so much of the best we breed whom John Barleycorn destroys. And the reason why these best are destroyed is because John Barleycorn stands on every highway and byway, accessible, law-protected, saluted by the policeman on the beat, speaking to them, leading them by the hand to the places where the good fellows and daring ones foregather and drink deep. With John Barleycorn out of the way, these daring ones would still be born, and they would do things instead of perishing.

Always I encountered the camaraderie of drink. I might be walking down the track to the water-tank to lie in wait for a passing freight-train, when I would chance upon a bunch of 'alki-stiffs'. An alki-stiff is a tramp who drinks druggist's alcohol. Immediately, with greeting and salutation, I am taken into the fellowship. The alcohol, shrewdly blended with water, is handed to me, and soon I am caught up in the revelry, with maggots crawling in my brain and John Barleycorn whispering to me that life is big, and that we are all brave and fine—free spirits sprawling like careless gods upon the turf and telling the two-by-four, cut-and-dried, conventional world to go hang.

CHAPTER XIV

BACK in Oakland from my wanderings, I returned to the water-front and renewed my comradeship with Nelson, who was now on shore all the time and living more madly than before. I, too, spent my time on shore with him, only occasionally going for cruises of several days on the bay to help out on short-handed scow-schooners.

The result was that I was no longer reinvigorated by periods of open-air abstinence and healthy toil. I drank every day, and whenever opportunity offered I drank to excess; for I still labored under the misconception that the secret of John Barleycorn lay in drinking to bestiality and unconsciousness. I became pretty thoroughly alcohol-soaked during this period. I practically lived in saloons; became a barroom loafer, and worse.

And right here was John Barleycorn getting me in a more insidious though no less deadly way than when he nearly sent me out with the tide. I had a few months still to run before I was seventeen; I scorned the thought of a steady job at anything; I felt myself a pretty tough individual in a group of pretty tough men; and I drank because these men drank and because I had to make good with them. I had never had a real boyhood, and in this, my precocious manhood, I was very hard and woefully wise. Though I had never known girl's love even, I had crawled through such depths that I was convinced absolutely that I knew the last word about love and life. And it wasn't a pretty knowledge. Without being pessimistic, I was quite satisfied that life was a rather cheap and ordinary affair.

You see, John Barleycorn was blunting me. The old stings and prods of the spirit were no longer sharp. Curiosity was leaving me. What did it matter what lay on the other side of the world? Men and women, without doubt, very much like the men and women I knew; marrying and giving in marriage and all the petty run of petty human concerns; and drinks, too. But the other side of the world was a long way to go for a drink. I had but to step to the corner and get all I wanted at Joe Vigy's. Johnny Heinhold still ran the Last Chance. And there were saloons on all the corners and between the corners.

The whispers from the back of life were growing dim as my mind and body soddened. The old unrest was drowsy. I might as well rot and die here in Oakland as anywhere else. And I should have so rotted and died and not in very long order either, at the pace John Barleycorn was leading me, had the matter depended wholly on him. I was learning what it was to have no appetite. I was learning what it was to get up shaky in the morning, with a stomach that quivered, with fingers touched with palsy, and to know the drinker's need for a stiff glass of whisky neat in order to brace up. (Oh! John Barleycorn is a wizard dopester. Brain and body, scorched and jangled and poisoned, return to be tuned up by the very poison that caused the damage.)

There is no end to John Barleycorn's tricks. He had tried to inveigle me into killing myself. At this period he was doing his best to kill me at a fairly rapid pace. But not satisfied with that, he tried another dodge. He very nearly got me, too, and right there I learned a lesson about him—became a wiser, a more skilful drinker. I learned there were limits to my gorgeous constitution, and that there were no limits to John Barleycorn. I learned that in a short hour or two he could master my strong head, my broad shoulders and deep chest, put me on my back, and with a devil's grip on my throat proceed to choke the life out of me.

Nelson and I were sitting in the Overland House. It was early in the evening, and the only reason we were there was because we were broke and it was election time. You see, in election time local politicians, aspirants for office, have a way of making the rounds of the saloons to get votes. One is sitting at a table, in a dry condition, wondering who is going to turn up and buy him a drink, or if his credit is good at some other saloon and if it's worth while to walk that far to find out, when suddenly the saloon doors swing wide and enters a bevy of well-dressed men, themselves usually wide and exhaling an atmosphere of prosperity and fellowship.

They have smiles and greetings for everybody—for you, without the price of a glass of beer in your pocket, for the timid hobo who lurks in the corner and who certainly hasn't a vote but who may establish a lodging-house registration. And do you know, when these politicians swing wide the doors and come in, with their broad shoulders, their deep chests, and their generous stomachs which cannot help making them optimists and masters of life, why, you perk right up. It's going to be a warm evening after all, and you know you'll get a souse started at the very least. And—who knows?—the gods may be kind, other drinks may come, and the night culminate in glorious greatness. And the next thing you know, you are lined up at the bar, pouring drinks down your throat and learning the gentlemen's names and the offices which they hope to fill.

It was during this period, when the politicians went their saloon rounds, that I was getting bitter bits of education and having illusions punctured—I, who had pored and thrilled over 'The Rail-Splitter',* and 'From Canal Boy to President'. Yes, I was learning how noble politics and politicians are.

Well, on this night, broke, thirsty, but with the drinker's faith in the unexpected drink, Nelson and I sat in the Overland House waiting for something to turn up, especially politicians. And there entered Joe Goose—he of the unquenchable thirst, the wicked eyes, the crooked nose, the flowered vest.

'Come on, fellows—free booze—all you want of it. I didn't want you to miss it.'

'Where?' we wanted to know.

'Come on. I'll tell you as we go along. We haven't a minute to lose.' And as we hurried up town, Joe Goose explained. 'It's the Hancock Fire Brigade. All you have to do is wear a red shirt and a helmet, and carry a torch. They're going down on a special train to Haywards to parade.'

(I think the place was Haywards. It may have been San Leandro or Niles.* And, to save me, I can't remember whether the Hancock Fire Brigade was a Republican or a Democratic organization. But anyway, the politicians who ran it were short of torch-bearers, and anybody who would parade could get drunk if he wanted to.)

'The town'll be wide open,' Joe Goose went on. 'Booze? It'll run like water. The politicians have bought the stocks of the saloons. There'll be no charge. All you got to do is walk right up and call for it. We'll raise hell.'

At the hall, on Eighth Street near Broadway, we got into the firemen's shirts and helmets, were equipped with torches, and, growling because we weren't given at least one drink before we started, were herded aboard the train. Oh, those politicians had handled our kind before. At Haywards there were no drinks either. Parade, first, and earn your booze, was the order of the night.

We paraded. Then the saloons were opened. Extra barkeepers had been engaged, and the drinkers jammed six deep before every drink-drenched and unwiped bar. There was no time to wipe the bar, nor wash glasses, nor do anything save fill glasses. The Oakland water-front can be real thirsty on occasion.

This method of jamming and struggling in front of the bar was too slow for us. The drink was ours. The politicians had bought it for us. We'd paraded and earned it, hadn't we? So we made a flank attack around the end

of the bar, shoved the protesting barkeepers aside, and
helped ourselves to bottles.

Outside, we knocked the necks of the bottles off against
the concrete curbs, and drank. Now Joe Goose and Nelson
had learned discretion with straight whisky, drunk in
quantity. I hadn't: I still labored under the misconception
that one was to drink all he could get—especially when it
didn't cost anything. We shared our bottles with others,
and drank a good portion ourselves, while I drank most of
all. And I didn't like the stuff. I drank it as I had drunk
beer at five, and wine at seven. I mastered my qualms and
downed it like so much medicine. And when we wanted
more bottles, we went into other saloons where the free
drink was flowing, and helped ourselves.

I haven't the slightest idea of how much I drank—
whether it was two quarts or five. I do know that I
began the orgy with half-pint draughts and with no water
afterward to wash the taste away and to dilute the whisky.

Now the politicians were too wise to leave the town
filled with drunks from the water-front of Oakland. When
train time came, there was a round-up of the saloons.
Already I was feeling the impact of the whisky. Nelson
and I were hustled out of a saloon, and found ourselves in
the very last rank of a disorderly parade. I struggled along
heroically, my correlations breaking down, my legs tottering under me, my head swimming, my heart pounding,
my lungs panting for air.

My helplessness was coming on so rapidly that my
reeling brain told me I would go down and out and
never reach the train if I remained at the rear of the
procession. I left the ranks and ran down a pathway beside
the road under broadspreading trees. Nelson pursued me,
laughing. Certain things stand out, as in memories of
nightmare. I remember those trees especially, and my
desperate running along under them, and how, every time
I fell, roars of laughter went up from the other drunks.

They thought I was merely antic drunk. They did not dream that John Barleycorn had me by the throat in a death-clutch. But I knew it. And I remember the fleeting bitterness that was mine as I realized that I was in a struggle with death and that these others did not know. It was as if I were drowning before a crowd of spectators who thought I was cutting up tricks for their entertainment.

And running there under the trees, I fell and lost consciousness. What happened afterward, with one glimmering exception, I had to be told. Nelson, with his enormous strength, picked me up and dragged me on and aboard the train. When he had got me into a seat, I fought and panted so terribly for air that even with his obtuseness he knew I was in a bad way. And right there, at any moment, I know now, I might have died. I often think it is the nearest to death I have ever been. I have only Nelson's description of my behavior to go by.

I was scorching up, burning alive internally, in an agony of fire and suffocation, and I wanted air. I madly wanted air. My efforts to raise a window were vain, for all the windows in the car were screwed down. Nelson had seen drink-crazed men, and thought I wanted to throw myself out. He tried to restrain me, but I fought on. I seized some man's torch and smashed the glass.

Now there were pro-Nelson and anti-Nelson factions on the Oakland water-front, and men of both factions, with more drink in them than was good, filled the car. My smashing of the window was the signal for the anti's. One of them reached for me, and dropped me, and started the fight, of all of which I have no knowledge save what was told me afterward, and a sore jaw next day from the blow that put me out. The man who struck me went down across my body, Nelson followed him, and they say there were few unbroken windows in the wreckage of the car that followed as the free-for-all fight had its course.

This being knocked cold and motionless was perhaps

the best thing that could have happened to me. My violent struggles had only accelerated my already dangerously accelerated heart, and increased the need for oxygen in my suffocating lungs.

After the fight was over and I came to, I did not come to myself. I was no more myself than a drowning man is who continues to struggle after he has lost consciousness. I have no memory of my actions, but I cried 'Air! Air!' so insistently, that it dawned on Nelson that I did not contemplate self-destruction. So he cleared the jagged glass from the window ledge and let me stick my head and shoulders out. He realized, partially, the seriousness of my condition, and held me by the waist to prevent me from crawling farther out. And for the rest of the run in to Oakland I kept my head and shoulders out, fighting like a maniac whenever he tried to draw me inside.

And here my one glimmering streak of true consciousness came. My sole recollection, from the time I fell under the trees until I awoke the following evening, is of my head out the window, facing the wind caused by the train, cinders striking and burning and blinding me, while I breathed with will. All my will was concentrated on breathing—on breathing the air in the hugest lung-full gulps I could, pumping the greatest amount of air into my lungs in the shortest possible time. It was that or death, and I was a swimmer and diver and I knew it; and in the most intolerable agony of prolonged suffocation, during those moments I was conscious, I faced the wind and the cinders and breathed for life.

All the rest is a blank. I came to the following evening, in a water-front lodging-house. I was alone. No doctor had been called in. And I might well have died there, for Nelson and the others, deeming me merely 'sleeping off my drunk', had let me lie there in a comatose condition for seventeen hours. Many a man, as every doctor knows, has died of the sudden impact of a quart or more of whisky.

Usually one reads of them so dying, strong drinkers, on account of a wager. But I didn't know . . . then. And so I learned; and by no virtue nor prowess, but simply through good fortune and constitution. Again my constitution had triumphed over John Barleycorn. I had escaped from another death-pit, dragged myself through another morass, and perilously acquired the discretion that would enable me to drink wisely for many another year to come.

Heavens! That was twenty years ago, and I am still very much and wisely alive; and I have seen much, done much, lived much, in that intervening score of years; and I shudder when I think how close a shave I ran, how near I was to missing that splendid fifth of a century that has been mine. And, oh, it wasn't John Barleycorn's fault that he didn't get me that night of the Hancock Fire Brigade.

CHAPTER XV

IT was during the early winter of 1892 that I resolved to go to sea. My Hancock Fire Brigade experience was very little responsible for this. I still drank and frequented saloons—practically lived in saloons. Whisky was dangerous, in my opinion, but not wrong. Whisky was dangerous, like other dangerous things in the natural world. Men died of whisky; but then, too, fishermen were capsized and drowned, hoboes fell under trains and were cut to pieces. To cope with winds and waves, railroad trains, and barrooms, one must use judgment. To get drunk after the manner of men was all right, but one must do it with discretion. No more quarts of whisky for me.

What really decided me to go to sea was that I had caught my first vision of the death-road which John Barleycorn maintains for his devotees. It was not a clear vision, however, and there were two phases of it, somewhat jumbled at the time. It struck me, from watching those with whom I associated, that the life we were living was more destructive than that lived by the average man.

John Barleycorn, by inhibiting morality, incited to crime. Everywhere I saw men doing, drunk, what they would never dream of doing sober. And this wasn't the worst of it. It was the penalty that must be paid. Crime was destructive. Saloon-mates I drank with, who were good fellows and harmless, sober, did most violent and lunatic things when they were drunk. And then the police gathered them in and they vanished from our ken. Sometimes I visited them behind the bars and said good-by ere they journeyed across the bay to put on the felon's stripes. And time and again I heard the one explanation: *If I hadn't been drunk I wouldn't a-done it.* And sometimes, under the spell of John Barleycorn, the most frightful things were done—things that shocked even my case-hardened soul.

The other phase of the death-road was that of the habitual drunkards, who had a way of turning up their toes without apparent provocation. When they took sick, even with trifling afflictions that any ordinary man could pull through, they just pegged out. Sometimes they were found unattended and dead in their beds; on occasion their bodies were dragged out of the water; and sometimes it was just plain accident, as when Bill Kelly, unloading cargo while drunk, had a finger jerked off, which, under the circumstances, might just as easily have been his head.

So I considered my situation and knew that I was getting into a bad way of living. It made toward death too quickly to suit my youth and vitality. And there was only one way out of this hazardous manner of living and that was to get out. The sealing-fleet was wintering in San Francisco Bay, and in the saloons I met skippers, mates, hunters, boat-steerers, and boat-pullers. I met the seal-hunter, Pete Holt, and agreed to be his boat-puller* and to sign on any schooner he signed on. And I had to have half-a-dozen drinks with Peter Holt there and then to seal our agreement.

And at once awoke all my old unrest that John Barleycorn had put to sleep. I found myself actually bored with the saloon-life of the Oakland water-front, and wondered what I had ever found fascinating in it. Also, with this death-road concept in my brain, I began to grow afraid that something would happen to me before sailing day, which was set for some time in January. I lived more circumspectly, drank less deeply, and went home more frequently. When drinking grew too wild, I got out. When Nelson was in his maniacal cups, I managed to get separated from him.

On the twelfth of January, 1893, I was seventeen, and the twentieth of January I signed before the shipping commissioner the articles of the *Sophie Sutherland*, a three topmast sealing schooner* bound on a voyage to the coast of Japan. And of course we had to drink on it. Joe Vigy cashed my advance note, and Pete Holt treated, and I treated, and Joe Vigy treated, and other hunters treated. Well, it was the way of men, and who was I, just turned seventeen, that I should decline the way of life of these fine, chesty, man-grown men?

CHAPTER XVI

THERE was nothing to drink on the *Sophie Sutherland*, and we had fifty-one days of glorious sailing, taking the southern passage in the northeast trades to Bonin Islands.* This isolated group, belonging to Japan, had been selected as the rendezvous of the Canadian and American sealing-fleets. Here they filled their water-barrels and made repairs before starting on the hundred days' harrying of the seal-herd along the northern coasts of Japan to Behring Sea.

Those fifty-one days of fine sailing and intense sobriety had put me in splendid fettle. The alcohol had been worked out of my system, and from the moment the voyage began I had not known the desire for a drink. I doubt if I even thought once about a drink. Often, of course, the talk in the forecastle turned on drink, and the men told of their more exciting or humorous drunks, remembering such passages more keenly, with greater delight, than all the other passages of their adventurous lives.

In the forecastle, the oldest man, fat and fifty, was Louis. He was a broken skipper. John Barleycorn had thrown him, and he was winding up his career where he had begun it, in the forecastle. His case made quite an impression on me. John Barleycorn did other things beside kill a man. He hadn't killed Louis. He had done much worse. He had robbed him of power and place and comfort, crucified his pride, and condemned him to the hardship of the common sailor that would last as long as his healthy breath lasted, which promised to be for a long time.

We completed our run across the Pacific, lifted the volcanic peaks, jungle-clad, of the Bonin Islands, sailed in among the reefs to the landlocked harbor, and let our anchor rumble down where lay a score or more of sea-gipsies like ourself. The scents of strange vegetation blew off the tropic land. Aborigines, in queer outrigger canoes, and Japanese, in queerer sampans, paddled about the bay and came aboard. It was my first foreign land; I had won to the other side of the world, and I would see all I had read in the books come true. I was wild to get ashore.

Victor and Axel, a Swede and a Norwegian, and I planned to keep together. (And so well did we, that for the rest of the cruise we were known as the 'Three Sports'.) Victor pointed out a pathway that disappeared up a wild canyon, emerged on a steep, bare lava-slope, and thereafter appeared and disappeared, ever climbing, among the palms and flowers. We would go over that path, he said, and we agreed, and we would see beautiful scenery, and strange native villages, and find Heaven alone knew what adventure at the end. And Axel was keen to go fishing. The three of us agreed to that, too. We would get a sampan, and a couple of Japanese fishermen who knew the fishing grounds, and we would have great sport. As for me, I was keen for anything.

And then, our plans made, we rowed ashore over the banks of living coral and pulled our boat up the white beach of coral sand. We walked across the fringe of beach under the cocoanut palms and into the little town, and found several hundred riotous seamen from all the world, drinking prodigiously, singing prodigiously, dancing prodigiously—and all on the main street to the scandal of a helpless handful of Japanese police.

Victor and Axel said we'd have a drink before we started on our long walk. Could I decline to drink with these two chesty shipmates? Drinking together, glass in hand, put the seal on comradeship. It was the way of life. Our teetotaler owner-captain was laughed at, and sneered at, by all of us because of his teetotalism. I didn't in the least want a drink, but I did want to be a good fellow and a good comrade. Nor did Louis' case deter me, as I poured the biting, scorching stuff down my throat. John Barleycorn had thrown Louis to a nasty fall, but I was young. My blood ran full and red; I had a constitution of iron; and—well, youth ever grins scornfully at the wreckage of age.

Queer, fierce, alcoholic stuff it was that we drank. There was no telling where or how it had been manufactured— some native concoction, most likely. But it was hot as fire, pale as water, and quick as death with its kick. It had been filled into empty 'square-face' bottles which had once contained Holland gin and which still bore the fitting legend: 'Anchor Brand'. It certainly anchored us. We never got out of the town. We never went fishing in the sampan. And though we were there ten days, we never trod that wild path along the lava-cliffs and among the flowers.

We met old acquaintances from other schooners, fellows we had met in the saloons of San Francisco before we sailed. And each meeting meant a drink; and there was much to talk about; and more drinks; and songs to be sung; and pranks and antics to be performed; until the maggots of imagination began to crawl, and it all seemed great and wonderful to me, these lusty, hard-bitten sea-rovers, of whom I made one, gathered in wassail on a coral strand. Old lines* about knights at table in the great banquet-halls, and of those above the salt and below the salt, and of Vikings feasting fresh from sea and ripe for battle, came to me; and I knew that the old times were not dead and that we belonged to that selfsame ancient breed.

By mid-afternoon Victor went mad with drink, and wanted to fight everybody and everything. I have since seen lunatics in the violent wards of asylums that seemed to behave in no wise different from Victor's way, save that perhaps he was more violent. Axel and I interfered as peace-makers, were roughed and jostled in the mix-ups, and finally, with infinite precaution and intoxicated cunning, succeeded in inveigling our chum down to the boat and in rowing him aboard our schooner.

But no sooner did Victor's feet touch the deck, than he began to clean up the ship. He had the strength of several men, and he ran amuck with it. I remember especially one man whom he got into the chain-boxes but failed to damage through inability to hit him. The man dodged and ducked, and Victor broke the knuckles of both his fists against the huge links of the anchor chain. By the time we dragged him out of that, his madness had shifted to the belief that he was a great swimmer, and the next moment he was overboard and demonstrating his ability by floundering like a sick porpoise and swallowing much salt water.

We rescued him, and by the time we got him below, undressed, and into his bunk, we were wrecks ourselves. But Axel and I wanted to see more of shore, and away we went, leaving Victor snoring. It was curious, the judgment passed on Victor by his shipmates, drinkers themselves. They shook their heads disapprovingly and muttered: 'A man like that oughtn't to drink.' Now Victor was the smartest sailor and best-tempered shipmate in the forecastle. He was an all-around splendid type of seaman; his mates recognized his worth, and respected him and liked him. Yet John Barleycorn metamorphosed him into a violent lunatic. And that was the very point these drinkers made. They knew that drink—and drink with a sailor is always excessive—made them mad, but only mildly mad. Violent madness was objectionable because it spoiled the fun of others and often culminated in tragedy. From their standpoint, mild madness was all right. But from the standpoint of the whole human race, is not all madness objectionable? And is there a greater maker of madness of all sorts than John Barleycorn?

But to return. Ashore, snugly ensconced in a Japanese

house of entertainment, Axel and I compared bruises, and over a comfortable drink talked of the afternoon's happenings. We liked the quietness of that drink and took another. A shipmate dropped in, several shipmates dropped in, and we had more quiet drinks. Finally, just as we had engaged a Japanese orchestra, and as the first strains of the *samisens* and *taikos* were rising, through the paper-walls came a wild howl from the street. We recognized it. Still howling, disdaining doorways, with bloodshot eyes and wildly waving muscular arms, Victor burst upon us through the fragile walls. The old amuck rage was on him, and he wanted blood, anybody's blood. The orchestra fled; so did we. We went through doorways, and we went through paper-walls—anything to get away.

And after the place was half wrecked, and we had agreed to pay the damage, leaving Victor partly subdued and showing symptoms of lapsing into a comatose state, Axel and I wandered away in quest of a quieter drinking-place. The main street was a madness. Hundreds of sailors rollicked up and down. Because the chief of police with his small force was helpless, the Governor of the colony had issued orders to the captains to have all their men on board by sunset.

What! To be treated in such fashion! As the news spread among the schooners, they were emptied. Everybody came ashore. Men who had had no intention of coming ashore, climbed into the boats. The unfortunate governor's *ukase* had precipitated a general debauch for all hands. It was hours after sunset, and the men wanted to see anybody try to put them on board. They went around inviting the authorities to try to put them on board. In front of the governor's house they were gathered thickest, bawling sea-songs, circulating square-faces, and dancing uproarious Virginia reels and old-country dances. The police, including the reserves, stood in little forlorn groups, waiting for the command the governor was too wise to issue. And I thought this saturnalia was great. It was like the old days of the Spanish Main come back. It was license; it was adventure. And I was part of it, a chesty sea-rover along with all these other chesty sea-rovers among the paper houses of Japan.

The governor never issued the order to clear the streets, and Axel and I wandered on from drink to drink. After a time, in some of the antics, getting hazy myself, I lost him. I drifted along, making new acquaintances, downing more drinks, getting hazier and hazier. I remember, somewhere, sitting in a circle with Japanese fishermen, kanaka boat-steerers from our own vessels, and a young Danish sailor fresh from cowboying in the Argentine and with a penchant for native customs and ceremonials. And with due and proper and most intricate Japanese ceremonial, we of the circle drank *sake*, pale, mild, and lukewarm, from tiny porcelain bowls.

And, later, I remember the runaway apprentices—boys of eighteen and twenty, of middle class English families, who had jumped their ships and apprenticeships in various ports of the world and drifted into the forecastles of the sailing schooners. They were healthy, smooth-skinned, clear-eyed, and they were young—youths like me, learning the way of their feet in the world of men. And they *were* men. No mild *sake* for them, but square-faces illicitly refilled with corrosive fire that flamed through their veins and burst into conflagrations in their heads. I remember a melting song they sang, the refrain of which was:

'Tis but a little golden ring,
I give it to thee with pride,
Wear it for your mother's sake
When you are on the tide.

They wept over it as they sang it, the graceless young scamps who had all broken their mothers' prides, and I sang with them, and wept with them, and luxuriated in the pathos and the tragedy of it, and struggled to make glimmering inebriated generalizations on life and romance. And one last picture I have, standing out very clear and bright in the midst of vagueness before and blackness afterward. We—the apprentices and I—are swaying and clinging to one another under the stars. We are singing a rollicking sea-song, all save one who sits on the ground and weeps; and we are marking the rhythm with waving square-faces. From up and down the street come far choruses of sea-voices similarly singing, and life is great, and beautiful, and romantic, and magnificently mad.

And next, after the blackness, I open my eyes in the early dawn to see a Japanese woman, solicitously anxious, bending over me. She is the port-pilot's wife, and I am lying in her doorway. I am chilled and shivering, sick with the after sickness of debauch. And I feel lightly clad. Those rascals of run-away apprentices! They have acquired the habit of running away. They have run away with my possessions. My watch is gone. My few dollars are gone. My coat is gone. So is my belt. And yes, my shoes.

And the foregoing is a sample of the ten days I spent in the Bonin Islands. Victor got over his lunacy, rejoined Axel and me, and after that we caroused somewhat more discreetly. And we never climbed that lava path among the flowers. The town and the square-faces were all we saw.

One who has been burned by fire must preach about the fire. I might have seen and healthily enjoyed a whole lot more of the Bonin Islands, if I had done what I ought to have done. But, as I see it, it is not a matter of what one ought to do, or ought not to do. It is what one *does* do. That is the everlasting, irrefragable fact. I did just what I did. I did what all those men did in the Bonin Islands. I did what millions of men over the world were doing at that particular point in time. I did it because the way led to it, because I was only a human boy, a creature of my environment, and neither an anemic nor a god. I was just human, and I was taking the path in the world that men took—men whom I admired, if you please; full-blooded men, lusty, breedy, chesty men, free spirits and anything but niggards in the way they foamed life away.

And the way was open. It was like an uncovered well in a yard where children play. It is small use to tell the brave little boys toddling their way along into knowledge of life that they mustn't play near the uncovered well. They *will* play near it. Any parent knows that. And we know that a certain percentage of them, the livest and most daring, will fall into the well. The thing to do— we all know it—is to cover up the well. The case is the same with John Barleycorn. All the no-saying and no-preaching in the world will fail to keep men, and youths growing into manhood, away from John Barleycorn when John Barleycorn is everywhere accessible, and where John Barleycorn is everywhere the connotation of manliness, and daring, and great-spiritedness.

The only rational thing for the twentieth century folk to do is to cover up the well; to make the twentieth century in truth the twentieth century, and to relegate to the nineteenth century and all the preceding centuries the things of those centuries, the witch-burnings, the intolerances, the fetiches, and, not least among such barbarisms, John Barleycorn.

CHAPTER XVII

NORTH we raced from the Bonin Islands to pick up the seal-herd, and north we hunted it for a hundred days into frosty, wintry weather and into and through vast fogs which hid the sun from us for a week at a time. It was wild and heavy work off the Siberian coast,* without a drink or thought of drink. Then we sailed south to Yokohama, with a big catch of skins in our salt and a heavy pay-day coming.

I was eager to be ashore and see Japan, but the first day was devoted to ship's work, and not until evening did we sailors land. And here, by the very system of things, by the way life was organized and men transacted affairs, John Barleycorn reached out and tucked my arm in his. The captain had given money for us to the hunters, and the hunters were waiting in a certain Japanese public house for us to come and get it. We rode to the place in rickshaws. Our own crowd had taken possession of it. Drink was flowing. Everybody had money, and everybody was treating. After the hundred days of hard toil and absolute abstinence, in the pink of physical condition, bulging with health, overspilling with spirits that had been long pent by discipline and circumstance, of course we would have a drink or two. And after that we would see the town.

It was the old story. There were so many drinks to be drunk, and as the warm magic poured through our veins and mellowed our voices and affections we knew it was no time to make invidious distinctions—to drink with this shipmate and to decline to drink with that shipmate. We were all shipmates who had been through stress and storm together, who had pulled and hauled on the same sheets and tackles, relieved one another's wheels, lain out side by side on the same jib-boom when she was plunging into it and looked to see who was missing when she cleared and lifted. So we drank with all, and all treated, and our voices rose, and we remembered a myriad kindly acts of comradeship, and forgot our fights and wordy squabbles, and knew one another for the best fellows in the world.

Well, the night was young when we arrived in that public house, and for all of that first night that public house was what I saw of Japan—a drinking place which was very like a drinking place at home or anywhere else over the world.

We lay in Yokohama harbor for two weeks, and about all we saw of Japan was its drinking places where sailors congregated. Occasionally, some one of us varied the monotony with a more exciting drunk. In such fashion I managed a real exploit by swimming off to the schooner one dark midnight and going soundly to sleep while the water-police searched the harbor for my body and brought my clothes out for identification.

Perhaps it was for things like that, I imagined, that men got drunk. In our little round of living what I had done was a noteworthy event. All the harbor talked about it. I enjoyed several days of fame among the Japanese boatmen and ashore in the pubs. It was a red letter event. It was an event to be remembered and narrated with pride. I remember it to-day, twenty years afterward, with a secret glow of pride. It was a purple passage, just as Victor's wrecking of the tea house in the Bonin Islands and my being looted by the runaway apprentices were purple passages.

The point is that the charm of John Barleycorn was still a mystery to me. I was so organically a non-alcoholic that alcohol itself made no appeal; the chemical reactions it produced in me were not satisfying because I possessed no need for such chemical satisfaction. I drank because the men I was with drank, and because my nature was

such that I could not permit myself to be less of a man
than other men at their favorite pastime. And I still had
a sweet tooth, and on privy occasions when there was no
man to see, bought candy and blissfully devoured it.

We hove up anchor to a jolly chanty, and sailed out of
Yokohama harbor for San Francisco. We took the northern
passage, and with the stout west wind at our back made
the run across the Pacific in thirty-seven days of brave
sailing.* We still had a big pay-day coming to us, and for
thirty-seven days, without a drink to addle our mental
processes, we incessantly planned the spending of our
money.

The first statement of each man—ever an ancient one
in homeward-bound forecastles—was: 'No boarding-house
sharks in mine.' Next, in parentheses, was regret at having
spent so much money in Yokohama. And after that, each
man proceeded to paint his favorite phantom. Victor, for
instance, said that immediately he landed in San Francisco
he would pass right through the water-front and the
Barbary Coast,* and put an advertisement in the papers.
His advertisement would be for board and room in some
simple working-class family. 'Then,' said Victor, 'I shall
go to some dancing-school for a week or two, just to meet
and get acquainted with the girls and fellows. Then I'll get
the run of the different dancing-crowds, and be invited to
their homes, and to parties, and all that, and with the
money I've got I can last out till next January when I'll
go sealing again.'

No; he wasn't going to drink. He knew the way of it,
particularly his way of it, wine in, wit out, and his money
would be gone in no time. He had his choice, based on
bitter experience, between three days' debauch among the
sharks and harpies of the Barbary Coast and a whole
winter of wholesome enjoyment and sociability, and there
wasn't any doubt of the way he was going to choose.

Said Axel Gunderson, who didn't care for dancing and

social functions: 'I've got a good pay-day. Now I can go
home. It is fifteen years since I've seen my mother and all
the family. When I pay off I shall send my money home to
wait for me. Then I'll pick a good ship bound for Europe,
and arrive there with another pay-day. Put them together,
and I'll have more money than ever in my life before. I'll
be a prince at home. You haven't any idea how cheap
everything is in Norway. I can make presents to everybody,
and spend my money like what would seem to them a
millionaire, and live a whole year there before I'd have to
go back to sea.'

'The very thing I'm going to do,' declared Red John.*
'It's three years since I've received a line from home and
ten years since I was there. Things are just as cheap in
Sweden, Axel, as in Norway, and my folks are real country
folks and farmers. I'll send my pay-day home and ship on
the same ship with you for around the Horn. We'll pick a
good one.'

And as Axel Gunderson and Red John painted the
pastoral delights and festive customs of their respective
countries, each fell in love with the other's home place,
and they solemnly pledged to make the journey together,
and to spend, together, six months in the one's Swedish
home and six months in the other's Norwegian home. And
for the rest of the voyage they could hardly be pried apart,
so infatuated did they become with discussing their plans.

Long John was not a home-body. But he was tired of
the forecastle. No boarding-house sharks in his. He, too,
would get a room in a quiet family, and he would go to
a navigation school and study to be a captain. And so it
went. Each man swore that for once he would be sensible
and not squander his money. No boarding-house sharks,
no sailor-town, no drink, was the slogan of our forecastle.

The men became stingy. Never was there such economy.
They refused to buy anything more from the slop-chest.
Old rags had to last, and they sewed patch upon patch,

turning out what are called 'homeward-bound patches' of
the most amazing dimensions. They saved on matches,
even, waiting till two or three were ready to light their
pipes from the same match.

As we sailed up the San Francisco water-front, the
moment the port doctors passed us the boarding-house
runners were alongside in whitehall boats. They swarmed
on board, each drumming for his own boarding-house, and
each with a bottle of free whisky inside his shirt. But we
waved them grandly and blasphemously away. We wanted
none of their boarding-houses and none of their whisky.
We were sober, thrifty sailormen, with better use for our
money.

Came the paying off before the Shipping Commissioner.
We emerged upon the sidewalk, each with a pocketful of
money. About us, like buzzards, clustered the sharks and
harpies. And we looked at each other. We had been seven
months together, and our paths were separating. One last
farewell rite of comradeship remained. (Oh, it was the
way, the custom.) 'Come on, boys,' said our sailing-master.
There stood the inevitable adjacent saloon. There were a
dozen saloons all around. And when we had followed the
sailing-master into the one of his choice, the sharks were
thick on the sidewalk outside. Some of them even ventured
inside, but we would have nothing to do with them.

There we stood at the long bar—the sailing-master, the
mates, the six hunters, the six boat-steerers, and the five
boat-pullers. There were only five of the last, for one of
our number had been dropped overboard, with a sack of
coal at his feet, between two snow squalls in a driving gale
off Cape Jerimo. There were nineteen of us, and it was to
be our last drink together. With seven months of men's
work in the world, blow high, blow low, behind us, we were
looking on each other for the last time. We knew it, for
sailors' ways go wide. And the nineteen of us drank the
sailing-master's treat. Then the mate looked at us with

eloquent eyes and called for another round. We liked the mate just as well as the sailing-master, and we liked them both. Could we drink with one, and not the other?

And Pete Holt, my own hunter (lost next year in the *Mary Thomas* with all hands), called a round. The time passed, the drinks continued to come on the bar, our voices rose, and the maggots began to crawl. There were six hunters, and each insisted, in the sacred name of comradeship, that all hands drink with him just once. There were six boat-steerers and five boat-pullers and the same logic held with them. There was money in all our pockets, and our money was as good as any man's, and our hearts were as free and generous.

Nineteen rounds of drinks. What more would John Barleycorn ask in order to have his will with men? They were ripe to forget their dearly cherished plans. They rolled out of the saloon and into the arms of the sharks and harpies. They didn't last long. From two days to a week saw the end of their money and saw them being carted by the boarding-house master on board outward-bound ships. Victor was a fine body of a man, and through a lucky friendship managed to get into the life-saving service. He never saw the dancing-school nor placed his advertisement for a room in a working-class family. Nor did Long John win to navigation-school. By the end of the week he was a transient lumper on a river steamboat. Red John and Axel did not send their pay-days home to the old country. Instead, and along with the rest, they were scattered on board sailing ships bound for the four quarters of the globe, where they had been placed by the boarding-house masters and where they were working out advance money which they had neither seen nor spent.

What saved me was that I had a home and people to go to.* I crossed the bay to Oakland, and, among other things, took a look at the death-road. Nelson was gone— shot to death while drunk and resisting the officers. His partner in that affair was lying in prison. Whisky Bob was gone. Old Cole, Old Smoudge and Bob Smith were gone. Another Smith, he of the belted guns and the *Annie*, was drowned. French Frank, they said, was lurking up river, afraid to come down because of something he had done. Others were wearing stripes in San Quentin or Folsom. Big Alec, the King of the Greeks, whom I had known well in the old Benicia days, and with whom I had drunk whole nights through, had killed two men and fled to foreign parts. Fitzsimmons, with whom I had sailed on the Fish Patrol, had been stabbed in the lung through the back and had died a lingering death from tuberculosis. And so it went, a very lively and well patronized road, and, from what I knew of all of them, John Barleycorn was responsible, with the sole exception of Smith of the *Annie*.

CHAPTER XVIII

MY infatuation for the Oakland water-front was quite dead. I didn't like the looks of it nor the life. I didn't care for the drinking, nor the vagrancy of it, and I wandered back to the Oakland Free Library and read the books with greater understanding. Then, too, my mother said I had sown my wild oats and it was time I settled down to a regular job. Also, the family needed the money. So I got a job at the jute mills—a ten-hour day at ten cents an hour. Despite my increase in strength and general efficiency, I was receiving no more than when I worked in the cannery several years before.* But, then, there was a promise of a raise to a dollar and a quarter a day after a few months.

And here, so far as John Barleycorn is concerned, began a period of innocence. I did not know what it was to take a drink from month end to month end. Not yet eighteen years old, healthy and with labor-hardened but unhurt muscles, like any young animal I needed diversion, excitement, something beyond the books and the mechanical toil.

I strayed into Young Men's Christian Associations. The life there was healthful and athletic, but too juvenile. For me it was too late. I was not boy, nor youth, despite my paucity of years. I had bucked big with men. I knew mysterious and violent things. I was from the other side of life so far as concerned the young men I encountered in the Y.M.C.A. I spoke another language, possessed a sadder and more terrible wisdom. (When I come to think it over, I realize, now, that I have never had a boyhood.) At any rate, the Y.M.C.A. young men were too juvenile for me, too unsophisticated. This I would not have minded, could they have met me and helped me mentally. But I had got more out of the books than they. Their meager physical experiences, plus their meager intellectual experiences, made a negative sum so vast that it overbalanced their wholesome morality and healthful sports.

In short, I couldn't play with the pupils of a lower grade. All the clean splendid young life that was theirs was denied me—thanks to my earlier tutelage under John Barleycorn. I knew too much too young. And yet, in the good time coming, when alcohol is eliminated from the needs and the institutions of men, it will be the Y.M.C.A., and similar unthinkably better and wiser and more virile congregating places, that will receive the men who now go to saloons to find themselves and one another. In the meantime, we live to-day, here and now, and we discuss to-day, here and now.

I was working ten hours a day in the jute mills. It was humdrum machine toil. I wanted life. I wanted to realize myself in other ways than at a machine for ten cents an hour. And yet I had had my fill of saloons. I wanted something new. I was growing up. I was developing unguessed and troubling potencies and proclivities. And at this very stage, fortunately, I met Louis Shattuck and we became chums.

Louis Shattuck, without one vicious trait, was a real innocently devilish young fellow who was quite convinced that he was a sophisticated townboy. And I wasn't a town-boy at all. Louis was handsome, and graceful, and filled with love for the girls. With him it was an exciting and all-absorbing pursuit. I didn't know anything about girls. I had been too busy being a man. This was an entirely new phase of existence which had escaped me. And when I saw Louis say good-by to me, raise his hat to a girl of his acquaintance, and walk on by her side down the sidewalk, I was made excited and envious. I, too, wanted to play this game.

'Well—there's only one thing to do,' said Louis, 'and that is, you must get a girl.'

Which is more difficult than it sounds. Let me show you, at the expense of a slight going aside. Louis did not know girls in their home life. He had the entrée to no girl's home. And of course, I, a stranger in this new world, was similarly circumstanced. But further, Louis and I were unable to go to dancing-schools, or to public dances, which were very good places for getting acquainted. We didn't have the money. He was a blacksmith's apprentice, and was earning but slightly more than I. We both lived at home and paid our way. When we had done this, and bought our cigarettes, and the inevitable clothes and shoes, there remained to each of us, for personal spending, a sum that varied between seventy cents and a dollar for the week. We whacked this up, shared it, and sometimes loaned all of what was left of it when one of us needed it for some more gorgeous girl-adventure, such as carfare out to Blair's Park and back—twenty cents, bang, just like that; and ice-cream for two—thirty cents; or tamales, which came cheaper and which for two cost only twenty cents.

I did not mind this money meagerness. The disdain for money I had learned from the oyster pirates had never left me. I didn't care overweeningly for it for personal gratification; and in my philosophy I completed the circle, finding myself as equable with the lack of a ten-cent piece as I was with the squandering of scores of dollars in calling all men and hangers-on up to the bar to drink with me.

But how to get a girl? There was no girl's home to which Louis could take me and where I might be introduced to girls. I knew none. And Louis' several girls he wanted for himself; and anyway, in the very human nature of boys' and girls' ways, he couldn't turn any of them over to me. He did persuade them to bring girlfriends for me; but I found them weak sisters, pale and ineffectual alongside the choice specimens he had.

'You'll have to do like I did,' he said finally. 'I got these by getting them. You'll have to get one the same way.'

And he initiated me. It must be remembered that Louis and I were hard situated. We really had to struggle to pay our board and maintain a decent appearance. We met each other in the evening, after the day's work, on the street corner, or in a little candy store on a side street, our sole frequenting place. Here we bought our cigarettes, and occasionally, a nickel's worth of 'red-hots'. (Oh, yes; Louis and I unblushingly ate candy—all we could get. Neither of us drank. Neither of us ever went into a saloon.)

But the girl. In quite primitive fashion, as Louis advised me, I was to select her and make myself acquainted with her. We strolled the streets in the early evenings. The girls, like us, strolled in pairs. And strolling girls *will* look at strolling boys who look. (And to this day, in any town, city, or village, in which I, in my middle age, find myself, I look on with the eye trained of old experience, and watch the sweet game played by the strolling boys and girls who just *must* stroll when the spring and summer evenings call.)

The trouble was that in this Arcadian phase of my history, I, who had come through, case-hardened, from the other side of life, was timid and bashful. Again and again Louis nerved me up. But I didn't know girls. They were strange and wonderful to me after my precocious man's life. I failed of the bold front and the necessary forwardness when the crucial moment came.

Then Louis would show me how—a certain, eloquent glance of eye, a smile, a daring, lifted hat, a spoken word, hesitancies, giggles, coy nervousness, and, behold, Louis acquainted and nodding me up to be introduced. But, when we paired off to stroll along boy and girl together, I noted that Louis had invariably picked the goodlooker and left to me the little lame sister.

I improved, of course, after experiences too numerous

to enter upon, so that there were divers girls to whom I could lift my hat and who would walk beside me in the early evenings. But girl's love did not immediately come to me. I was excited, interested, and I pursued the quest. And the thought of drink never entered my mind. Some of Louis' and my adventures have since given me serious pause when casting sociological generalizations. But it was all good and innocently youthful, and I learned one generalization, biological rather than sociological, namely, that the 'Colonel's lady and Judy O'Grady are sisters under their skins.'*

And before long I learned girl's love, all the dear fond deliciousness of it, all the glory and the wonder. I shall call her Haydee. She was between fifteen and sixteen. Her little skirt reached her shoe-tops. We sat side by side in a Salvation Army meeting. She was not a convert, nor was her aunt, who sat on the other side of her and who, visiting from the country, where at that time the Salvation Army was not, had dropped in to the meeting for half an hour out of curiosity. And Louis sat beside me and observed—I do believe he did no more than observe, because Haydee was not his style of girl.

We did not speak, but in that great half-hour we glanced shyly at each other, and shyly avoided or as shyly returned and met each other's glances more than several times. She had a slender oval face. Her brown eyes were beautiful. Her nose was a dream, as was her sweet-lipped, petulant-hinting mouth. She wore a tam o'shanter, and I thought her brown hair the prettiest shade of brown I had ever seen. And from that single experience of half an hour I have ever since been convinced of the reality of love at first sight.

All too soon the aunt and Haydee departed. (This is permissible at any stage of a Salvation Army meeting.) I was no longer interested in the meeting, and after an appropriate interval of a couple of minutes or less, started to leave with Louis. As we passed out, at the back of the hall a woman recognized me with her eyes, arose, and followed me. I shall not describe her. She was of my own kind and friendship of the old time on the water-front. When Nelson was shot, he had died in her arms, and she knew me as his one comrade. And she must tell me how Nelson had died, and I did want to know; so I went with her across the width of life from dawning boy's love for a brown-haired girl in a tam o'shanter back to the old sad savagery I had known.

And when I had heard the tale, I hurried away to find Louis, fearing that I had lost my first love with the first glimpse of her. But Louis was dependable. Her name was—Haydee. He knew where she lived. Each day she passed the blacksmith-shop where he worked, going to or from the Lafayette school. Further, he had seen her on occasion with Ruth, another schoolgirl; and, still further, Nita, who sold us red-hots at the candy store, was a friend of Ruth. The thing to do was to go around to the candy store and see if we could get Nita to give a note to Ruth to give to Haydee. If that could be arranged, all I had to do was write the note.

And it so happened. And in stolen half-hours of meeting I came to know all the sweet madness of boy's love and girl's love. So far as it goes it is not the biggest love in the world, but I do dare to assert that it is the sweetest. Oh, as I look back on it! Never did girl have more innocent boy-lover than I who had been so wicked-wise and violent beyond my years. I didn't know the first thing about girls. I, who had been hailed Prince of the Oyster Pirates, who could go anywhere in the world as a man amongst men; who could sail boats, lay aloft in black and storm, or go into the toughest hang-outs in sailor town and play my part in any rough-house that started or call all hands to the bar—I didn't know the first thing I might say or do with this slender little chit of a girl-woman whose scant

skirt just reached her shoe-tops and who was as abysmally
ignorant of life, as I was, or thought I was, profoundly wise.

I remember we sat on a bench in the starlight. There
was fully a foot of space between us. We slightly faced
each other, our near elbows on the back of the bench;
and once or twice our elbows just touched. And all the
time, deliriously happy, talking in the gentlest and most
delicate terms that might not offend her sensitive ears, I
was cudgeling my brains in an effort to divine what I was
expected to do. What did girls expect of boys, sitting on a
bench and tentatively striving to find out what love was?
What did she expect me to do? Was I expected to kiss
her? Did she expect me to try? And if she did expect me,
and I didn't, what would she think of me?

Ah, she was wiser than I—I know it now—the little
innocent girl-woman in her shoe-top skirt. She had known
boys all her life. She encouraged me in the ways a girl
may. Her gloves were off and in one hand, and I remember,
lightly and daringly, in mock reproof for something I had
said, how she tapped my lips with a tiny flirt of those
gloves. I was like to swoon with delight. It was the most
wonderful thing that had ever happened to me. And I
remember yet the faint scent that clung to those gloves
and that I breathed in the moment they touched my lips.

Then came the agony of apprehension and doubt.
Should I imprison in my hand that little hand with the
dangling, scented gloves which had just tapped my lips?
Should I dare to kiss her there and then, or slip my arm
around her waist? Or dared I even sit closer?

Well, I didn't dare. I did nothing. I merely continued to
sit there and love with all my soul. And when we parted
that evening I had not kissed her. I do remember the
first time I kissed her, on another evening, at parting—
a mighty moment, when I took all my heart of courage
and dared. We never succeeded in managing more than
a dozen stolen meetings, and we kissed perhaps a dozen

times—as boys and girls kiss, briefly and innocently, and wonderingly. We never went anywhere—not even to a matinée. We once shared together five cents' worth of redhots. But I have always fondly believed that she loved me. I know I loved her; and I dreamed day dreams of her for a year and more, and the memory of her is very dear.

CHAPTER XIX

WHEN I was with folk who did not drink, I never thought of drinking. Louis did not drink. Neither he nor I could afford it; but, more significant than that, we had no desire to drink. We were healthy, normal, non-alcoholic. Had we been alcoholic, we would have drunk whether or not we could have afforded it.

Each night, after the day's work, washed up, clothes changed and supper eaten, we met on the street corner or in the little candy store. But the warm, fall weather passed, and on bitter nights of frost or damp nights of drizzle the street corner was not a comfortable meeting place. And the candy store was unheated. Nita, or whoever waited on the counter, between waitings lurked in a back living-room that was heated. We were not admitted to this room, and in the store it was as cold as out-of-doors.

Louis and I debated the situation. There was only one solution: the saloon, the congregating place of men, the place where men hobnobbed with John Barleycorn. Well do I remember the damp and draughty evening, shivering without overcoats because we could not afford them, that Louis and I started out to select our saloon. Saloons are always warm and comfortable. Now Louis and I did not go into this saloon because we wanted a drink. Yet we knew that saloons were not charitable institutions. A man could not make a lounging place of a saloon without occasionally buying something over the bar.

Our dimes and nickels were few. We could ill spare any of them when they were so potent in buying carfare for oneself and a girl. (We never paid carfare when by ourselves, being content to walk.) So, in this saloon, we desired to make the most of our expenditure. We called for a deck of cards and sat down at a table and played euchre for an hour, in which time Louis treated once, and

I treated once, to beer—the cheapest drink, ten cents for two. Prodigal! How we grudged it!

We studied the men who came into the place. They seemed all middle-aged and elderly workmen, most of them Germans, who flocked by themselves in old acquaintance groups, and with whom we could have only the slightest contacts. We voted against that saloon, and went out cast-down with the knowledge that we had lost an evening and wasted twenty cents for beer that we didn't want.

We made several more tries on succeeding nights, and at last found our way into the National, a saloon on Tenth and Franklin. Here was a more congenial crowd. Here Louis met a fellow or two he knew, and here I met fellows I had gone to school with when a little lad in knee pants. We talked of old days, and of what had become of this fellow, and what that fellow was doing now, and of course we talked it over drinks. They treated, and we drank. Then, according to the code of drinking, we had to treat. It hurt, for it meant forty to fifty cents a clatter.

We felt quite enlivened when the short evening was over; but at the same time we were bankrupt. Our week's spending-money was gone. We decided that that was the saloon for us, and we agreed to be more circumspect thereafter in our drink-buying. Also, we had to economize for the rest of the week. We didn't even have carfare. We were compelled to break an engagement with two girls from West Oakland with whom we were attempting to be in love. They were to meet us up town the next evening, and we hadn't the carfare necessary to take them home. Like many others financially embarrassed, we had to disappear for a time from the gay whirl—at least until Saturday night pay-day. So Louis and I rendezvoused in a livery stable, and with coats buttoned and chattering teeth played euchre and casino until the time of our exile was over.

Then we returned to the National Saloon and spent no more than we could decently avoid spending for the comfort and warmth. Sometimes we had mishaps, as when one got stuck twice in succession in a five-handed game of Sancho Pedro for the drinks. Such a disaster meant anywhere between twenty-five to eighty cents, just according to how many of the players ordered ten-cent drinks. But we could temporarily escape the evil effects of such disaster by virtue of an account we ran behind the bar. Of course, this only set back the day of reckoning and seduced us into spending more than we would have spent on a cash basis. (When I left Oakland suddenly for the adventure-path the following spring,* I well remember I owed that saloon keeper one dollar and seventy cents. Long after, when I returned, he was gone. I still owe him that dollar and seventy cents, and if he should chance to read these lines I want him to know that I'll pay on demand.)

The foregoing incident of the National Saloon I have given in order again to show the lure, or draw, or compulsion, toward John Barleycorn in society as at present organized with saloons on all the corners. Louis and I were two healthy youths. We didn't want to drink. We couldn't afford to drink. And yet we were driven by the circumstances of cold and rainy weather to seek refuge in a saloon, where we had to spend part of our pitiful dole for drink. It will be urged by some critics that we might have gone to the Y.M.C.A., to night school, and to the social circles and homes of young people. The only reply is that we didn't. That is the irrefragable fact. We didn't. And to-day, at this moment, there are hundreds of thousands of boys like Louis and me doing just what Louis and I did, with John Barleycorn, warm and comfortable, beckoning and welcoming, tucking their arms in his and beginning to teach them his mellow ways.

CHAPTER XX

THE jute mills failed of its agreement to increase my pay to a dollar and a quarter a day, and I, a free-born American boy whose direct ancestors had fought in all the wars from the old pre-Revolutionary Indian wars down, exercised my sovereign right of free contract by quiting the job.

I was still resolved to settle down, and I looked about me. One thing was clear. Unskilled labor didn't pay. I must learn a trade, and I decided on electricity. The need for electricians was constantly growing. But how to become an electrician? I hadn't the money to go to a technical school or university; besides, I didn't think much of schools. I was a practical man in a practical world. Also, I still believed in the old myths which were the heritage of the American boy when I was a boy.

A canal boy could become a president. Any boy, who took employment with any firm, could, by thrift, energy, and sobriety, learn the business and rise from position to position until he was taken in as a junior partner. After that the senior partnership was only a matter of time. Very often—so ran the myth—the boy, by reason of his steadiness and application, married his employer's daughter. By this time I had been encouraged to such faith in myself in the matter of girls that I was quite certain I would marry my employer's daughter. There wasn't a doubt of it. All the little boys in the myths did it as soon as they were old enough.

So I bade farewell forever to the adventure-path, and went out to the power-plant of one of our Oakland street-railways. I saw the superintendent himself, in a private office so fine that it almost stunned me. But I talked straight up. I told him I wanted to become a practical electrician, that I was unafraid of work, that I was used to hard work, and that all he had to do was look at me to see I was fit and strong. I told him that I wanted to begin right at the bottom and work up, that I wanted to devote my life to this one occupation and this one employment.

The superintendent beamed as he listened. He told me that I was the right stuff for success, and that he believed in encouraging American youth that wanted to rise. Why, employers were always on the lookout for young fellows like me, and alas, they found them all too rarely. My ambition was fine and worthy, and he would see to it that I got my chance. (And as I listened with swelling heart, I wondered if it was his daughter I was to marry.)

'Before you can go out on the road and learn the more complicated and higher details of the profession,' he said, 'you will, of course, have to work in the car house with the men who install and repair the motors.' (By this time I was sure that it was his daughter, and I was wondering how much stock he might own in the company.)

'But,' he said, 'as you yourself so plainly see, you couldn't expect to begin as a helper to the car house electricians. That will come when you have worked up to it. You will really begin at the bottom. In the car house your first employment will be sweeping up, washing the windows, keeping things clean. And after you have shown yourself satisfactory at that, then you may become a helper to the car house electricians.'

I didn't see how sweeping and scrubbing a building was any preparation for the trade of electrician; but I did know that in the books all the boys started with the most menial tasks and by making good ultimately won to the ownership of the whole concern.

'When shall I come to work?' I asked, eager to launch on this dazzling career.

'But,' said the superintendent, 'as you and I have already agreed, you must begin at the bottom. Not immediately can you in any capacity enter the car house.

Before that you must pass through the engine room as an oiler.'

My heart went down slightly and for the moment, as I saw the road lengthen between his daughter and me; then it rose again. I would be a better electrician with knowledge of steam engines. As an oiler in the great engine room I was confident that few things concerning steam would escape me. Heavens! My career shone more dazzling than ever.

'When shall I come to work?' I asked gratefully.

'But,' said the superintendent, 'you could not expect to enter immediately into the engine room. There must be preparation for that. And through the fire room, of course. Come, you see the matter clearly, I know. And you will see that even the mere handling of coal is a scientific matter and not to be sneezed at. Do you know that we weigh every pound of coal we burn? Thus, we learn the value of the coal we buy; we know to a tee the last penny of cost of every item of production, and we learn which firemen are the most wasteful, which firemen, out of stupidity or carelessness, get the least out of the coal they fire.' The superintendent beamed again. 'You see how very important the little matter of coal is, and by as much as you learn of this little matter you will become that much better a workman—more valuable to us, more valuable to yourself. Now, are you prepared to begin?'

'Any time,' I said valiantly. 'The sooner the better.'

'Very well,' he answered. 'You will come to-morrow morning at seven o'clock.'

I was taken out and shown my duties. Also, I was told the terms of my employment—a ten-hour day, every day in the month including Sundays and holidays, with one day off each month, with a salary of thirty dollars a month. It wasn't exciting. Years before, at the cannery, I had earned a dollar a day for a ten-hour day. I consoled myself with the thought that the reason my earning capacity had not increased with my years and strength was because I had remained an unskilled laborer. But it was different now. I was beginning to work for skill, for a trade, for career and fortune and the superintendent's daughter.

And I was beginning in the right way—right at the beginning. That was the thing. I was passing coal to the firemen, who shoveled it into the furnaces where its energy was transformed into steam, which, in the engine room, was transformed into the electricity with which the electricians worked. This passing of coal was surely the very beginning . . . unless the superintendent should take it into his head to send me to work in the mines from which the coal came in order to get a completer understanding of the genesis of electricity for street railways.

Work! I, who had worked with men, found that I didn't know the first thing about real work. A ten-hour day! I had to pass coal for the day and night shifts, and, despite working through the noon-hour, I never finished my task before eight at night. I was working a twelve- to thirteen-hour day, and I wasn't being paid overtime as in the cannery.

I might as well give the secret away right here. I was doing the work of two men. Before me, one mature able-bodied laborer had done the day shift and another equally mature able-bodied laborer had done the night shift. They had received forty dollars a month each. The superintendent, bent on an economical administration, had persuaded me to do the work of both men for thirty dollars a month. I thought he was making an electrician of me. In truth and fact, he was saving fifty dollars a month operating expenses to the company.

But I didn't know I was displacing two men. Nobody told me. On the contrary, the superintendent warned everybody not to tell me. How valiantly I went at it that first day. I worked at top speed, filling the iron wheelbarrow with coal, running it on the scales and weighing the load, then trundling it into the fire room and dumping it on the plates before the fires.

Work! I did more than the two men whom I had displaced. They had merely wheeled in the coal and dumped it on the plates. But while I did this for the day coal, the night coal I had to pile against the wall of the fire room. Now the fire room was small. It had been planned for a night coal-passer. So I had to pile the night coal higher and higher, buttressing up the heap with stout planks. Toward the top of the heap I had to handle the coal a second time, tossing it up with a shovel.

I dripped with sweat, but I never ceased from my stride, though I could feel exhaustion coming on. By ten o'clock in the morning, so much of my body's energy had I consumed, I felt hungry and snatched a thick double-slice of bread and butter from my dinner pail. This I devoured, standing, grimed with coal dust, my knees trembling under me. By eleven o'clock, in this fashion, I had consumed my whole lunch. But what of it? I realized that it would enable me to continue working through the noon hour. And I worked all afternoon. Darkness came on, and I worked under the electric lights. The day fireman went off and the night fireman came on. I plugged away.

At half-past eight, famished, tottering, I washed up, changed my clothes, and dragged my weary body to the car. It was three miles to where I lived, and I had received a pass with the stipulation that I could sit down as long as there were no paying passengers in need of a seat. As I sank into a corner outside seat I prayed that no passenger might require my seat. But the car filled up, and, half way in, a woman came on board, and there was no seat for her. I started to get up, and to my astonishment found that I could not. With the chill wind blowing on me, my spent body had stiffened into the seat. It took me the rest of the run in to unkink my complaining joints and muscles and get into a standing position on the lower step. And when the car stopped at my corner I nearly fell to the ground when I stepped off.

I hobbled two blocks to the house and limped into the kitchen. While my mother started to cook I plunged into bread and butter; but before my appetite was appeased, or the steak fried, I was sound asleep. In vain my mother strove to shake me awake enough to eat the meat. Failing in this, with the assistance of my father she managed to get me to my room, where I collapsed dead asleep on the bed. They undressed me and covered me up. In the morning came the agony of being awakened. I was terribly sore, and worst of all my wrists were swelling. But I made up for my lost supper, eating an enormous breakfast, and when I hobbled to catch my car I carried a lunch twice as big as the one the day before.

Work! Let any youth just turned eighteen try to out-shovel two man-grown coal-shovelers. Work! Long before midday I had eaten the last scrap of my huge lunch. But I was resolved to show them what a husky young fellow determined to rise could do. The worst of it was that my wrists were swelling and going back on me. There are few who do not know the pain of walking on a sprained ankle. Then imagine the pain of shoveling coal and trundling a loaded wheel-barrow with two sprained wrists.

Work! More than once I sank down on the coal where no one could see me, and cried with rage, and mortification, and exhaustion, and despair. That second day was my hardest, and all that enabled me to survive it and get in the last of the night coal at the end of thirteen hours was the day fireman, who bound both my wrists with broad leather straps. So tightly were they buckled that they were like slightly flexible plaster casts. They took the stresses and pressures which thitherto had been borne by my wrists, and they were so tight that there was no room for the inflammation to rise in the sprains.

And in this fashion I continued to learn to be an

electrician. Night after night I limped home, fell asleep before I could eat my supper, and was helped into bed and undressed. Morning after morning, always with huger lunches in my dinner pail, I limped out of the house on my way to work.

I no longer read my library books. I made no dates with the girls. I was a proper work-beast. I worked, and ate, and slept, while my mind slept all the time. The whole thing was a nightmare. I worked every day, including Sunday, and I looked far ahead to my one day off at the end of a month, resolved to lie abed all that day and just sleep and rest up.

The strangest part of this experience was that I never took a drink nor thought of taking a drink.* Yet I knew that men under hard pressure almost invariably drank. I had seen them do it, and in the past had often done it myself. But so sheerly non-alcoholic was I that it never entered my mind that a drink might be good for me. I instance this to show how entirely lacking from my make-up was any predisposition toward alcohol. And the point of this instance is that later on, after more years had passed, contact with John Barleycorn at last did induce in me the alcoholic desire.

I had often noticed the day fireman staring at me in a curious way. At last, one day, he spoke. He began by swearing me to secrecy. He had been warned by the superintendent not to tell me, and in telling me he was risking his job. He told me of the day coal-passer and the night coal-passer, and of the wages they had received. I was doing for thirty dollars a month what they had received eighty dollars for doing. He would have told me sooner, the fireman said, had he not been so certain that I would break down under the work and quit. As it was, I was killing myself, and all to no good purpose. I was merely cheapening the price of labor, he argued, and keeping two men out of a job.

Being an American boy, and a proud American boy, I did not immediately quit.* This was foolish of me, I know; but I resolved to continue the work long enough to prove to the superintendent that I could do it without breaking down. Then I would quit, and he would realize what a fine young fellow he had lost.

All of which I faithfully and foolishly did. I worked on until the time came when I got in the last of the night coal by six o'clock. Then I quit the job of learning electricity by doing more than two men's work for a boy's wages, went home, and proceeded to sleep the clock around.

Fortunately, I had not stayed by the job long enough to injure myself—though I was compelled to wear straps on my wrists for a year afterward. But the effect of this work orgy in which I had indulged was to sicken me with work. I just wouldn't work. The thought of work was repulsive. I didn't care if I never settled down. Learning a trade could go hang. It was a whole lot better to royster and frolic over the world in the way I had previously done. So I headed out on the adventure-path again, starting to tramp East by beating my way on the railroads.

CHAPTER XXI

BUT behold! As soon as I went out on the adventure-path I met John Barleycorn again. I moved through a world of strangers, and the act of drinking together made one acquainted with men and opened the way to adventures. It might be in a saloon with jingled townsmen, or with a genial railroad man well lighted up and armed with pocket flasks, or with a bunch of alki-stiffs in a hang-out. Yes; and it might be in a prohibition state, such as Iowa was in 1894, when I wandered up the main street of Des Moines and was variously invited by strangers into various blind pigs—I remember drinking in barber-shops, plumbing establishments, and furniture stores.

Always it was John Barleycorn. Even a tramp, in those halcyon days, could get most frequently drunk. I remember, inside the prison at Buffalo,* how some of us got magnificently jingled, and how, on the streets of Buffalo after our release, another jingle was financed with pennies begged on the main-drag.

I had no call for alcohol, but when I was with those who drank I drank with them. I insisted on traveling or loafing with the livest, keenest men, and it was just these live, keen ones that did most of the drinking. They were the more comradely men, the more venturous, the more individual. Perhaps it was too much temperament that made them turn from the commonplace and humdrum to find relief in the lying and fantastic sureties of John Barleycorn. Be that as it may, the men I liked best, desired most to be with, were invariably to be found in John Barleycorn's company.

In the course of my tramping over the United States I achieved a new concept. As a tramp, I was behind the scenes of society—ay, and down in the cellar. I could watch the machinery work. I saw the wheels of the social machine go around, and I learned that the dignity of manual labor wasn't what I had been told it was by the teachers, preachers, and politicians. The men without trades were helpless cattle. If one learned a trade, he was compelled to belong to a union in order to work at his trade. And his union was compelled to bully and slug the employers' unions in order to hold up wages or hold down hours. The employers' unions likewise bullied and slugged. I couldn't see any dignity at all. And when a workman got old, or had an accident, he was thrown into the scrap-heap like any worn-out machine. I saw too many of this sort who were making anything but dignified ends of life.

So my new concept was that manual labor was undignified, and that it didn't pay. No trade for me, was my decision, and no superintendent's daughter. And no criminality, I also decided. That would be almost as disastrous as to be a laborer. Brains paid, not brawn, and I resolved never again to offer my muscles for sale in the brawn market. Brain, and brain only, would I sell.

I returned to California with the firm intention of developing my brain.* This meant school education. I had gone through the grammar school long ago, so I entered the Oakland High School. To pay my way, I worked as a janitor. My sister helped me, too; and I was not above mowing anybody's lawn or taking up and beating carpets when I had half a day to spare. I was working to get away from work, and I buckled down to it with a grim realization of the paradox.

Boy and girl love was left behind, and along with it, Haydee and Louis Shattuck, and the early evening strolls. I hadn't the time. I joined the Henry Clay Debating Society. I was received into the homes of some of the members, where I met nice girls whose skirts reached the ground. I dallied with little home clubs wherein we discussed poetry and art and the nuances of grammar. I joined the socialist local, where we studied and orated political economy, philosophy, and politics. I kept half-a-dozen membership cards working in the free library and did an immense amount of collateral reading.

And for a year and a half on end I never took a drink nor thought of taking a drink. I hadn't the time, and I certainly did not have the inclination. Between my janitor-work, my studies, and innocent amusements such as chess, I hadn't a moment to spare. I was discovering a new world, and such was the passion of my exploration that the old world of John Barleycorn held no inducements for me.

Come to think of it, I did enter a saloon. I went to see Johnny Heinhold in the Last Chance, and I went to borrow money. And right here is another phase of John Barleycorn. Saloon-keepers are notoriously good fellows. On an average they perform vastly greater generosities than do business men. When I simply had to have ten dollars, desperate, with no place to turn, I went to Johnny Heinhold. Several years had passed since I had been in his place or spent a cent across his bar. And when I went to borrow the ten dollars I didn't buy a drink, either. And Johnny Heinhold let me have the ten dollars, without security or interest.

More than once, in the brief days of my struggle for an education, I went to Johnny Heinhold to borrow money.* When I entered the university, I borrowed forty dollars from him, without interest, without security, without buying a drink. And yet—and here is the point, the custom and the code—in the days of my prosperity, after the lapse of years, I have gone out of my way by many a long block to spend across Johnny Heinhold's bar deferred interest on the various loans. Not that Johnny Heinhold asked me to do it or expected me to do it. I did it, as I have said, in obedience to the code I had learned along with all the other things connected with John Barleycorn. In distress, when a man has no other place to turn, when he hasn't the slightest bit of security which a savage-hearted pawnbroker would consider, he can go to some saloon keeper he knows. Gratitude is inherently human. When the man so helped has money again, depend upon it that a portion will be spent across the bar of the saloon keeper who befriended him.

Why, I recollect the early days of my writing career,* when the small sums of money I earned from the magazines came with tragic irregularity, while at the same time I was staggering along with a growing family*—a wife, children, a mother, a nephew, and my Mammy Jennie and her old husband fallen on evil days. There were two places at which I could borrow money; a barber shop and a saloon. The barber charged me five per cent. per month in advance. That is to say, when I borrowed one hundred dollars, he handed me ninety-five. The other five dollars he retained as advance interest for the first month. And on the second month I paid him five dollars more, and continued so to do each month until I made a ten-strike* with the editors and lifted the loan.

The other place to which I came in trouble was the saloon. This saloon keeper I had known by sight for a couple of years. I had never spent my money in his saloon, and even when I borrowed from him I didn't spend any money. Yet never did he refuse me any sum I asked of him. Unfortunately, before I became prosperous, he moved away to another city. And to this day I regret that he is gone. It is the code I have learned. The right thing to do, and the thing I'd do right now did I know where he is, would be to drop in on occasion and spend a few dollars across his bar for old sake's sake and gratitude.

This is not to exalt saloon keepers. I have written it to exalt the power of John Barleycorn, and to illustrate one more of the myriad ways by which a man is brought in contact with John Barleycorn, until in the end he finds he cannot get along without him.

But to return to the run of my narrative. Away from the adventure-path, up to my ears in study, every moment occupied, I lived oblivious to John Barleycorn's existence. Nobody about me drank. If any had drunk, and had they offered it to me, I surely would have drunk. As it was, when I had spare moments I spent them playing chess, or going with nice girls who were themselves students, or in riding a bicycle whenever I was fortunate enough to have it out of the pawnbroker's possession.

What I am insisting upon all the time is this: in me was not the slightest trace of alcoholic desire, and this despite the long and severe apprenticeship I had served under John Barleycorn. I had come back from the other side of life to be delighted with this Arcadian simplicity of student youths and student maidens. Also, I had found my way into the realm of the mind, and I was intellectually intoxicated. Alas! as I was to learn at a later period, intellectual intoxication, too, has its katzenjammer.*

CHAPTER XXII

THREE years was the time required to go through high school.* I grew impatient. Also, my schooling was becoming financially impossible. At such rate I could not last out, and I did greatly want to go to the state university.* When I had done a year of high school, I decided to attempt a short cut. I borrowed the money and paid to enter the senior class of a 'cramming joint' or academy.* I was scheduled to graduate right into the university at the end of four months, thus saving two years.

And how I did cram! I had two years' new work to do in a third of a year. For five weeks I crammed, until simultaneous quadratic equations and chemical formulas fairly oozed from my ears. And then the master of the academy took me aside. He was very sorry, but he was compelled to give me back my tuition fee and to ask me to leave the school. It wasn't a matter of scholarship. I stood well in my classes, and did he graduate me into the university he was confident that in that institution I would continue to stand well. The trouble was that tongues were gossiping about my case. What! In four months accomplish two years' work! It would be a scandal, and the universities were becoming severer in their treatment of accredited prep schools. He couldn't afford such a scandal, therefore I must gracefully depart.

I did. And I paid back the borrowed money, and gritted my teeth, and started to cram by myself. There were three months yet before the university entrance-examinations. Without laboratories, without coaching, sitting in my bedroom, I proceeded to compress that two years' work into three months and to keep reviewed on the previous year's work.

Nineteen hours a day I studied. For three months I kept this pace, only breaking it on several occasions. My body grew weary, my mind grew weary, but I stayed with it. My eyes grew weary and began to twitch, but they did not break down. Perhaps, toward the last, I got a bit dotty. I know that at the time I was confident I had discovered the formula for squaring the circle; but I resolutely deferred the working of it out until after the examinations. Then I would show them.

Came the several days of the examinations, during which time I scarcely closed my eyes in sleep, devoting every moment to cramming and reviewing. And when I turned in my last examination paper I was in full possession of a splendid case of brain-fag. I didn't want to see a book. I didn't want to think nor to lay eyes on anybody who was liable to think.

There was but one prescription for such a condition, and I gave it to myself—the adventure-path. I didn't wait to learn the result of my examinations. I stowed a roll of blankets and some cold food into a borrowed whitehall boat* and set sail. Out of the Oakland Estuary I drifted on the last of an early morning ebb, caught the first of the flood up bay, and raced along with a spanking breeze. San Pablo Bay was smoking, and the Carquinez Straits off the Selby Smelter were smoking, as I picked up ahead and left astern the old landmarks I had first learned with Nelson in the unreefed *Reindeer*.

Benicia showed before me. I opened the bight of Turner's Shipyard, rounded the *Solano* wharf, and surged along abreast of the patch of tules and the clustering fishermen's-arks where in the old days I had lived and drunk deep.

And right here something happened to me, the gravity

of which I never dreamed for many a long year to come. I had no intention of stopping at Benicia. The tide favored, the wind was fair and howling—glorious sailing for a sailor. Bull Head and Army Points showed ahead, marking the entrance to Suisun Bay, which I know was smoking. And yet, when I laid eyes on those fishing-arks lying in the water-front tules, without debate, on the instant, I put down my tiller, came in on the sheet, and headed for the shore. On the instant, out of the profound of my brain-fag, I knew what I wanted. I wanted to drink. I wanted to get drunk.

The call was imperative. There was no uncertainty about it. More than anything else in the world, my frayed and frazzled mind wanted surcease from weariness in the way it knew surcease would come. And right here is the point. For the first time in my life I consciously, deliberately desired to get drunk. It was a new, a totally different manifestation of John Barleycorn's power. It was not a body need for alcohol. It was a mental desire. My overworked and jaded mind wanted to forget.

And here the point is drawn to its sharpest. Granted my prodigious brain-fag, nevertheless, had I never drunk in the past, the thought would never have entered my mind to get drunk now. Beginning with physical intolerance for alcohol, for years drinking only for the sake of comradeship and because alcohol was everywhere on the adventure-path, I had now reached the stage where my brain cried out, not merely for a drink, but for a drunk. And had I not been so long used to alcohol, my brain would not have so cried out. I should have sailed on past Bull Head, and in the smoking white of Suisun Bay, and in the wine of wind that filled my sail and poured through me, I should have forgotten my weary brain and rested and refreshed it.

So I sailed in to shore, made all fast, and hurried

up among the arks. Charley Le Grant fell on my neck.
His wife, Lizzie, folded me to her capacious breast. Billy
Murphy, and Joe Lloyd, and all the survivors of the old
guard, got around me and their arms around me. Charley
seized the can and started for Jorgensen's saloon across
the railroad tracks. That meant beer. I wanted whisky, so
I called after him to bring a flask.

Many times that flask journeyed across the railroad
tracks and back. More old friends of the old free and
easy times dropped in, fishermen, Greeks, and Russians,
and French. They took turns in treating, and treated all
around in turn again. They came and went, but I stayed
on and drank with all. I guzzled, I swilled. I ran the liquor
down and joyed as the maggots mounted in my brain.

And Clam came in, Nelson's partner before me, handsome as ever, but more reckless, half insane, burning
himself out with whisky. He had just had a quarrel with his
partner on the sloop *Gazelle*, and knives had been drawn,
and blows struck, and he was bent on maddening the fever
of the memory with more whisky. And while we downed it,
we remembered Nelson and that he had stretched out his
great shoulders for the last long sleep in this very town
of Benicia; and we wept over the memory of him, and
remembered only the good things of him, and sent out
the flask to be filled and drank again.

They wanted me to stay over, but through the open
door I could see the brave wind on the water, and my ears
were filled with the roar of it. And while I forgot that I
had plunged into the books nineteen hours a day for three
solid months, Charley Le Grant shifted my outfit into a
big Columbia River salmon boat. He added charcoal and
a fisherman's brazier, a coffee pot and frying-pan, and the
coffee and the meat, and a black bass fresh from the water
that day.

They had to help me down the rickety wharf and into

the salmon boat. Likewise they stretched my boom and sprit until the sail set like a board. Some feared to set the sprit; but I insisted, and Charley had no doubts. He knew me of old, and knew that I could sail as long as I could see. They cast off my painter. I put the tiller up, filled away before it, and with dizzy eyes checked and steadied the boat on her course and waved farewell.

The tide had turned, and the fierce ebb, running in the teeth of a fiercer wind, kicked up a stiff, upstanding sea. Suisun Bay was white with wrath and sea-lump. But a salmon boat can sail, and I knew how to sail a salmon boat. So I drove her into it, and through it, and across, and maundered aloud and chanted my disdain for all the books and schools. Cresting seas filled me a foot or so with water, but I laughed at it sloshing about my feet, and chanted my disdain for the wind and the water. I hailed myself a master of life, riding on the back of the unleashed elements, and John Barleycorn rode with me. Amid dissertations on mathematics and philosophy and spoutings and quotations, I sang all the old songs learned in the days when I went from the cannery to the oyster boats to be a pirate—such songs as: 'Black Lulu', 'Flying Cloud', 'Treat My Daughter Kind-i-ly', 'The Boston Burglar', 'Come All You Rambling Gambling Men', 'I Wisht I Was a Little Bird', 'Shenandoah', and 'Ranzo, Boys, Ranzo'.

Hours afterward, in the fires of sunset, where the Sacramento and the San Joaquin tumble their muddy floods together, I took the New York Cut-Off, skimmed across the smooth land-locked water past Black Diamond, on into the San Joaquin, and on the Antioch, where, somewhat sobered and magnificently hungry, I laid alongside a big potato sloop that had a familiar rig. Here were old friends aboard, who fried my black bass in olive oil. Then, too, there was a meaty fisherman's stew, delicious with garlic,

and crusty Italian bread without butter, and all washed
down with pint mugs of thick and heady claret.

My salmon boat was a-soak, but in the snug cabin of
the sloop dry blankets and a dry bunk were mine; and we
lay and smoked and yarned of old days, while overhead
the wind screamed through the rigging and taut halyards
drummed against the mast.

CHAPTER XXIII

MY cruise in the salmon boat lasted a week, and I returned ready to enter the university. During the week's cruise I did not drink again. To accomplish this I was compelled to avoid looking up old friends, for as ever the adventure-path was beset with John Barleycorn. I had wanted the drink that first day, and in the days that followed I did not want it. My tired brain had recuperated. I had no moral scruples in the matter. I was not ashamed nor sorry because of that first day's orgy at Benicia, and I thought no more about it, returning gladly to my books and studies.

Long years were to pass ere I looked back upon that day and realized its significance. At the time, and for a long time afterward, I was to think of it only as a frolic. But still later, in the slough of brain-fag and intellectual weariness, I was to remember and know the craving for the anodyne that resides in alcohol.

In the meantime, after this one relapse at Benicia, I went on with my abstemiousness, primarily because I didn't want to drink. And next, I was abstemious because my way led among books and students, where no drinking was. Had I been out on the adventure-path, I should as a matter of course have been drinking. For that is the pity of the adventure-path, which is one of John Barleycorn's favorite stamping-grounds.

I completed the first half of my freshman year, and in January of 1897 took up my course for the second half. But the pressure from lack of money, plus a conviction that the university was not giving me all that I wanted in the time I could spare for it, forced me to leave.* I was not very disappointed. For two years I had studied, and in those two years, what was far more valuable, I had done a prodigious amount of reading. Then, too, my grammar had improved. It is true, I had not yet learned that I must say 'It is I'; but I no longer was guilty of the double negative in writing, though still prone to that error in excited speech.

I decided immediately to embark on my career. I had four preferences: first, music; second, poetry; third, the writing of philosophic, economic, and political essays; and, fourth, and last, and least, fiction writing. I resolutely cut out music as impossible, settled down in my bedroom, and tackled my second, third and fourth choices simultaneously. Heavens, how I wrote!* Never was there a creative fever such as mine from which the patient escaped fatal results. The way I worked was enough to soften my brain and send me to a mad-house. I wrote, I wrote everything— ponderous essays, scientific and sociological, short stories, humorous verse, verse of all sorts from triolets and sonnets to blank verse tragedy and elephantine epics in Spenserian stanzas. On occasion I composed steadily, day after day, for fifteen hours a day. At times I forgot to eat, or refused to tear myself away from my passionate outpouring in order to eat.

And then there was the matter of typewriting. My brother-in-law owned a machine* which he used in the daytime. In the night I was free to use it. That machine was a wonder. I could weep now as I recollect my wrestlings with it. It must have been a first model in the year one of the typewriter era. Its alphabet was all capitals. It was informed with an evil spirit. It obeyed no known laws of physics, and overthrew the hoary axiom that like things performed to like things produce like results. I'll swear that machine never did the same thing in the same way twice. Again and again it demonstrated that unlike actions produce like results.

How my back used to ache with it! Prior to that experience, my back had been good for every violent strain put upon it in a none too gentle career. But that typewriter proved to me that I had a pipe-stem for a back. Also, it made me doubt my shoulders. They ached as with rheumatism after every bout. The keys of that machine had to be hit so hard that to one outside the house it sounded like distant thunder or some one breaking up the furniture. I had to hit the keys so hard that I strained my first fingers to the elbows, while the ends of my fingers were blisters burst and blistered again. Had it been my machine I'd have operated it with a carpenter's hammer.

The worst of it was that I was actually typing my manuscripts at the same time I was trying to master that machine. It was a feat of physical endurance and a brain storm combined to type a thousand words, and I was composing thousands of words every day which just had to be typed for the waiting editors.

Oh, between the writing and the typewriting I was well a-weary. I had brain- and nerve-fag, and body-fag as well, and yet the thought of drink never suggested itself. I was living too high to stand in need of any anodyne. All my waking hours, except those with that infernal typewriter, were spent in a creative heaven. And along with this I had no desire for drink, because I still believed in many things—in the love of all men and women in the matter of man and woman love; in fatherhood; in human justice; in art—in the whole host of fond illusions that keep the world turning around.

But the waiting editors elected to keep on waiting. My manuscripts made amazing round-trip records between the Pacific and the Atlantic. It might have been the weirdness of the typewriting that prevented the editors from accepting at least one little offering of mine. I don't know, and goodness knows the stuff I wrote was as weird as its typing. I sold my hard-bought school books for ridiculous sums to second-hand bookmen. I borrowed small sums of money wherever I could, and suffered my old father to feed me with the meager returns of his failing strength.

It didn't last long, only a few weeks, when I had to surrender and go to work. Yet I was unaware of any need for the drink-anodyne. I was not disappointed. My career was retarded, that was all. Perhaps I did need further preparation. I had learned enough from the books to realize that I had touched only the hem of knowledge's garment. I still lived on the heights. My waking hours, and most of the hours I should have used for sleep, were spent with the books.

CHAPTER XXIV

OUT in the country, at the Belmont Academy,* I went to work in a small, perfectly appointed steam laundry. Another fellow and myself did all the work from sorting and washing to ironing the white shirts, collars and cuffs, and the 'fancy starch' of the wives of the professors. We worked like tigers, especially as summer came on and the academy boys took to the wearing of duck trousers. It consumes a dreadful lot of time to iron one pair of duck trousers. And there were so many pairs of them. We sweated our way through long sizzling weeks at a task that was never done; and many a night, while the students snored in bed, my partner and I toiled on under the electric light at steam mangle or ironing board.

The hours were long, the work was arduous, despite the fact that we became past masters in the art of eliminating waste motion. And I was receiving thirty dollars a month and board—a slight increase over my coal-shoveling and cannery days, at least to the extent of board, which cost my employer little (we ate in the kitchen), but which was to me the equivalent of twenty dollars a month. My robuster strength of added years, my increased skill, and all I had learned from the books, were responsible for this increase of twenty dollars. Judging by my rate of development, I might hope before I died to be a night watchman for sixty dollars a month, or a policeman actually receiving a hundred dollars with pickings.

So relentlessly did my partner and I spring into our work throughout the week that by Saturday night we were frazzled wrecks. I found myself in the old familiar work-beast condition, toiling longer hours than the horses toiled, thinking scarcely more frequent thoughts than horses think. The books were closed to me. I had brought a trunkful to the laundry, but found myself unable to read them. I fell asleep the moment I tried to read; and if I did manage to keep my eyes open for several pages, I could not remember the contents of those pages. I gave over attempts on heavy study, such as jurisprudence, political economy, and biology, and tried lighter stuff, such as history. I fell asleep. I tried literature, and fell asleep. And finally, when I fell asleep over lively novels, I gave up. I never succeeded in reading one book in all the time I spent in the laundry.

And when Saturday night came, and the week's work was over until Monday morning, I knew only one desire besides the desire to sleep, and that was to get drunk. This was the second time in my life that I had heard the unmistakable call of John Barleycorn. The first time it had been because of brain-fag. But I had no overworked brain now. On the contrary, all I knew was the dull numbness of a brain that was not worked at all. That was the trouble. My brain had become so alert and eager, so quickened by the wonder of the new world the books had discovered to it, that it now suffered all the misery of stagnancy and inaction.

And I, the long-time intimate of John Barleycorn, knew just what he promised me—maggots of fancy, dreams of power, forgetfulness, anything and everything save whirling washers, revolving mangles, humming centrifugal wringers, and fancy starch and interminable processions of duck trousers moving in steam under my flying iron. And that's it. John Barleycorn makes his appeal to weakness and failure, to weariness and exhaustion. He is the easy way out. And he is lying all the time. He offers false strength to the body, false elevation to the spirit, making things seem what they are not and vastly fairer than what they are.

But it must not be forgotten that John Barleycorn is protean. As well as to weakness and exhaustion, does he appeal to too much strength, to superabundant vitality, to the ennui of idleness. He can tuck in his arm the arm of any man in any mood. He can throw the net of his lure over all men. He exchanges new lamps for old, the spangles of illusion for the drabs of reality, and in the end cheats all who traffic with him.

I didn't get drunk, however, for the simple reason that it was a mile and a half to the nearest saloon. And this, in turn, was because the call to get drunk was not very loud in my ears. Had it been loud, I would have traveled ten times the distance to win to the saloon. On the other hand, had the saloon been just around the corner, I should have got drunk. As it was, I would sprawl out in the shade on my one day of rest and dally with the Sunday papers. But I was too weary even for their froth. The comic supplement might bring a pallid smile to my face, and then I would fall asleep.

Although I did not yield to John Barleycorn while working in the laundry, a certain definite result was produced. I had heard the call, felt the gnaw of desire, yearned for the anodyne. I was being prepared for the stronger desire of later years.

And the point is that this development of desire was entirely in my brain. My body did not cry out for alcohol. As always, alcohol was repulsive to my body. When I was bodily weary from shoveling coal, the thought of taking a drink had never flickered into my consciousness. When I was brain-wearied after taking the entrance examinations to the university, I promptly got drunk. At the laundry, I was suffering physical exhaustion again, and physical exhaustion that was not nearly as profound as that of the coal-shoveling. But there was a difference. When I went coal-shoveling, my mind had not yet awakened. Between that time and the laundry my mind had found the kingdom of the mind. While shoveling coal, my mind was somnolent. While toiling in the laundry, my mind, informed and eager to do and be, was crucified.

And whether I yielded to drink, as at Benicia, or whether I refrained, as at the laundry, in my brain the seeds of desire for alcohol were germinating.

CHAPTER XXV

AFTER the laundry, my sister and her husband grubstaked me into the Klondike.* It was the first gold
rush into that region, the early fall rush of 1897. I was
twenty-one years old, and in splendid physical condition.
I remember, at the end of the twenty-eight-mile portage
across Chilkoot from Dyea Beach to Lake Linderman, I
was packing up with the Indians and outpacking many an
Indian.* The last pack into Linderman was three miles. I
back-tripped it four times a day, and on each forward trip
carried one hundred and fifty pounds. This means that
over the worst trails I daily traveled twenty-four miles,
twelve of which were under a burden of one hundred and
fifty pounds.

Yes, I had let career go hang, and was on the adventure-
path again in quest of fortune. And of course, on the
adventure-path, I met John Barleycorn. Here were the
chesty men again, rovers and adventurers, and while they
didn't mind a grub famine, whisky they could not do
without. Whisky went over the trail, while the flour lay
cached and untouched by the trail-side.

As good fortune would have it, the three men in my
party* were not drinkers. Therefore I didn't drink save on
rare occasions and disgracefully when with other men. In
my personal medicine chest was a quart of whisky. I never
drew the cork till six months afterward, in a lonely camp,
where, without anesthetics, a doctor was compelled to
operate on a man. The doctor and the patient emptied my
bottle between them and then proceeded to the operation.

Back in California a year later, recovering from scurvy,
I found that my father was dead and that I was the head
and the sole bread-winner of a household. When I state
that I had passed coal on a steamship from Behring Sea to

British Columbia, and traveled in the steerage from there to San Francisco, it will be understood that I brought nothing back from the Klondike but my scurvy.*

Times were hard. Work of any sort was difficult to get. And work of any sort was what I had to take, for I was still an unskilled laborer. I had no thought of career. That was over and done with. I had to find food for two mouths beside my own and keep a roof over our heads—yes, and buy a winter suit, my one suit being decidedly summery. I had to get some sort of work immediately. After that, when I had caught my breath, I might think about my future.

Unskilled labor is the first to feel the slackness of hard times, and I had no trades save those of sailor and laundryman. With my new responsibilities I didn't dare go to sea, and I failed to find a job at laundrying. I failed to find a job at anything. I had my name down in five employment bureaus. I advertised in three newspapers. I sought out the few friends I knew who might be able to get me work; but they were either uninterested or unable to find anything for me.

The situation was desperate. I pawned my watch, my bicycle, and a mackintosh of which my father had been very proud and which he had left to me. It was and is my sole legacy in this world. It had cost fifteen dollars, and the pawnbroker let me have two dollars on it. And—oh, yes—a water-front comrade of earlier years drifted along one day with a dress suit wrapped in newspapers. He could give no adequate explanation of how he had come to possess it, nor did I press for an explanation. I wanted the suit myself. No; not to wear. I traded him a lot of rubbish which, being unpawnable, was useless to me. He peddled the rubbish for several dollars, while I pledged the dress suit with my pawnbroker for five dollars. And for all I know, the pawnbroker still has the suit. I had never intended to redeem it.

But I couldn't get any work. Yet I was a bargain in the labor market. I was twenty-two years old, weighed one hundred and sixty-five pounds stripped, every pound of which was excellent for toil; and the last traces of my scurvy were vanishing before a treatment of potatoes chewed raw. I tackled every opening for employment. I tried to become a studio model, but there were too many fine-bodied young fellows out of jobs. I answered advertisements of elderly invalids in need of companions. And I almost became a sewing machine agent, on commission, without salary. But poor people don't buy sewing machines in hard times, so I was forced to forego that employment.

Of course, it must be remembered that along with such frivolous occupations, I was trying to get work as wop, lumper, and roustabout.* But winter was coming on, and the surplus labor army was pouring into the cities. Also, I, who had romped along carelessly through the countries of the world and the kingdom of the mind, was not a member of any union.

I sought odd jobs. I worked days, and half-days, at anything I could get. I mowed lawns, trimmed hedges, took up carpets, beat them, and laid them again. Further, I took the civil service examinations for mail carrier and passed first. But alas, there was no vacancy, and I must wait. And while I waited, and in between the odd jobs I managed to procure, I started to earn ten dollars by writing a newspaper account of a voyage I had made, in an open boat down the Yukon, of nineteen hundred miles in nineteen days. I didn't know the first thing about the newspaper game, but I was confident I'd get ten dollars for my article.

But I didn't. The first San Francisco newspaper* to which I mailed it never acknowledged receipt of the manuscript, but held on to it. The longer it held on to it, the more certain I was that the thing was accepted.

And here is the funny thing. Some are born to fortune, and some have fortune thrust upon them. But in my case I was clubbed into fortune, and bitter necessity wielded the club. I had long since abandoned all thought of writing as a career. My honest intention in writing that article was to earn ten dollars. And that was the limit of my intention. It would help to tide me along until I got steady employment. Had a vacancy occurred in the post office at that time, I should have jumped at it.

But the vacancy did not occur, nor did a steady job; and I employed the time between odd jobs and writing a twenty-one-thousand-word serial for the 'Youth's Companion'.* I turned it out and typed it in seven days. I fancy that was what was the matter with it, for it came back.

It took some time for it to go and come, and in the meantime I tried my hand at short stories. I sold one to the *Overland Monthly* for five dollars. The *Black Cat* gave me forty dollars for another.* The *Overland Monthly* offered me seven dollars and a half, pay on publication, for all the stories I should deliver. I got my bicycle, my watch, and my father's mackintosh out of pawn and rented a typewriter. Also, I paid up the bills I owed to the several groceries that allowed me a small credit. I recall the Portuguese groceryman who never permitted my bill to go beyond four dollars. Hopkins, another grocer, could not be budged beyond five dollars.

And just then came the call from the post office to go to work. It placed me in a most trying predicament. The sixty-five dollars I could earn regularly every month was a terrible temptation. I couldn't decide what to do. And I'll never be able to forgive the postmaster of Oakland. I answered the call, and I talked to him like a man. I frankly told him the situation. It looked as if I might win out at writing. The chance was good, but not certain. Now, if he would pass me by and select the next man on the eligible list, and give me a call at the next vacancy—

But he shut me off with: 'Then you don't want the position?'

'But I do,' I protested. 'Don't you see, if you will pass me over this time—'

'If you want it you will take it,' he said coldly.

Happily for me, the cursed brutality of the man made me angry.

'Very well,' I said. 'I won't take it.'

CHAPTER XXVI

HAVING burned my one ship,* I plunged into writing. I am afraid I always was an extremist. Early and late I was at it—writing, typing, studying grammar, studying writing and all the forms of writing, and studying the writers who succeeded in order to find out how they succeeded. I managed on five hours' sleep in the twenty-four, and came pretty close to working the nineteen waking hours left to me. My light burned till two and three in the morning, which led a good neighbor woman into a bit of sentimental Sherlock Holmes deduction. Never seeing me in the daytime, she concluded that I was a gambler, and that the light in my window was placed there by my mother to guide her erring son home.

The trouble with the beginner at the writing game is the long, dry spells, when there is never an editor's check and everything pawnable is pawned. I wore my summer suit pretty well through that winter, and the following summer experienced the longest, dryest spell of all, in the period when salaried men are gone on vacation and manuscripts lie in editorial offices until vacation is over.

My difficulty was that I had no one to advise me. I didn't know a soul who had written or who had ever tried to write. I didn't even know one reporter. Also, to succeed at the writing game, I found I had to unlearn about everything the teachers and professors of literature of the high school and university had taught me. I was very indignant about this at the time; though now I can understand it. They did not know the trick of successful writing in the years of 1895 and 1896. They knew all about 'Snow Bound' and 'Sartor Resartus';* but the American editors of 1899 did not want such truck. They wanted the 1899 truck, and offered to pay so well for it that the teachers and professors of literature would have quit their jobs could they have supplied it.

I struggled along, stood off the butcher and the grocer, pawned my watch and bicycle and my father's mackintosh, and I worked. I really did work, and went on short commons of sleep. Critics have complained about the swift education one of my characters, Martin Eden,* achieved. In three years, from a sailor with a common school education, I made a successful writer of him. The critics say this is impossible. Yet I was Martin Eden. At the end of three working years, two of which were spent in high school and the university and one spent at writing, and all three in studying immensely and intensely, I was publishing stories in magazines such as the *Atlantic Monthly*, was correcting proofs of my first book (issued by Houghton, Mifflin Co.), was selling sociological articles to *Cosmopolitan* and *McClure's*, had declined an associate editorship proffered me by telegraph from New York City, and was getting ready to marry.

Now the foregoing means work, especially the last year of it, when I was learning my trade as a writer. And in that year, running short on sleep and tasking my brain to its limit, I neither drank nor cared to drink. So far as I was concerned, alcohol did not exist. I did suffer from brain-fag on occasion, but alcohol never suggested itself as an ameliorative. Heavens! Editorial acceptances and checks were all the amelioratives I needed. A thin envelope from an editor in the morning's mail was more stimulating than half-a-dozen cocktails. And if a check of decent amount came out of the envelope, such incident in itself was a whole drunk.

Furthermore, at that time in my life I did not know what a cocktail was. I remember, when my first book was published, several Alaskans who were members of the Bohemian Club* entertained me one evening at the club in San Francisco. We sat in most wonderful leather chairs, and drinks were ordered. Never had I heard such an ordering of liqueurs and of highballs of particular brands of Scotch. I didn't know what a liqueur or a highball was, and I didn't know that 'Scotch' meant whisky. I knew only poor men's drinks, the drinks of the frontier and of sailor-town—cheap beer and cheaper whisky that was just called whisky and nothing else. I was embarrassed to make a choice, and the waiter nearly collapsed when I ordered claret as an after-dinner drink.

CHAPTER XXVII

AS I succeeded with my writing, my standard of living rose and my horizon broadened. I confined myself to writing and typing a thousand words a day, including Sundays and holidays; and I still studied hard, but not so hard as formerly. I allowed myself five and one-half hours of actual sleep. I added this half-hour because I was compelled. Financial success permitted me more time for exercise. I rode my wheel more, chiefly because it was permanently out of pawn; and I boxed and fenced, walked on my hands, jumped high and broad, put the shot and tossed the caber, and went swimming. And I learned that more sleep is required for physical exercise than for mental exercise. There were tired nights, bodily, when I slept six hours; and on occasion of very severe exercise I actually slept seven hours. But such sleep orgies were not frequent. There was so much to learn, so much to be done, that I felt wicked when I slept seven hours. And I blessed the man who invented the alarm clock.

And still no desire to drink. I possessed too many fine faiths, was living at too keen a pitch. I was a socialist, intent on saving the world, and alcohol could not give me the fervors that were mine from ideas and ideals. My voice, on account of my successful writing, had added weight, or so I thought. At any rate, my reputation as a writer drew me audiences that my reputation as a speaker never could have drawn. I was invited before clubs and organizations of all sorts to deliver my message. I fought the good fight, and went on studying and writing, and was very busy.

Up to this time I had had a very restricted circle of friends. But now I began to go about. I was invited out, especially to dinner; and I made many friends and acquaintances whose economic lives were easier than mine had been. And many of them drank. In their own houses they drank and offered me drink. They were not drunkards any of them. They just drank temperately, and I drank temperately with them as an act of comradeship and accepted hospitality. I did not care for it, neither wanted it nor did not want it, and so small was the impression made by it that I do not remember my first cocktail nor my first Scotch highball.

Well, I had a house.* When one is asked into other houses, he naturally asks others into his house. Behold the rising standard of living. Having been given drink in other houses, I could expect nothing else of myself than to give drink in my own house. So I laid in a supply of beer and whisky and table claret. Never since that has my house not been well supplied.

And still, through all this period, I did not care in the slightest for John Barleycorn. I drank when others drank, and with them, as a social act. And I had so little choice in the matter that I drank whatever they drank. If they elected whisky, then whisky it was for me. If they drank root beer or sarsaparilla, I drank root beer or sarsaparilla with them. And when there were no friends in the house, why, I didn't drink anything. Whisky decanters were always in the room where I wrote, and for months and years I never knew what it was, when by myself, to take a drink.

When out at dinner, I noticed the kindly, genial glow of the preliminary cocktail. It seemed a very fitting and gracious thing. Yet so little did I stand in need of it, with my own high intensity and vitality, that I never thought it worth while to have a cocktail before my own meal when I ate alone.

On the other hand, I well remember a very brilliant man,* somewhat older than I, who occasionally visited me. He liked whisky, and I recall sitting whole afternoons in my den, drinking steadily with him, drink for drink, until he was mildly lighted up and I was slightly aware that I had drunk some whisky. Now why did I do this? I don't know, save that the old schooling held, the training of the old days and nights, glass in hand, with men, the drinking ways of drink and drinkers.

Besides, I no longer feared John Barleycorn. Mine was that most dangerous stage when a man believes himself John Barleycorn's master. I had proved it to my satisfaction in the long years of work and study. I could drink when I wanted, refrain when I wanted, drink without getting drunk, and to cap everything I was thoroughly conscious that I had no liking for the stuff. During this period I drank precisely for the same reason I had drunk with Scotty and the harpooner and with the oyster pirates—because it was an act performed by men with whom I wanted to behave as a man. These brilliant ones, these adventurers of the mind, drank. Very well. There was no reason I should not drink with them,—I who knew so confidently that I had nothing to fear from John Barleycorn.

And the foregoing was my attitude of mind for years. Occasionally I got well jingled, but such occasions were rare. It interfered with my work, and I permitted nothing to interfere with my work. I remember, when spending several months in the East End of London,* during which time I wrote a book and adventured much amongst the worst of the slum classes, that I got drunk several times and was mightily wroth with myself because it interfered with my writing. Yet these very times were because I was out on the adventure-path, where John Barleycorn is always to be found.

Then, too, with the certitude of long training and unholy intimacy, there were occasions when I engaged

in drinking-bouts with men. Of course, this was on the
adventure-path in various parts of the world, and it was a
matter of pride. It is a queer man-pride that leads one to
drink with men in order to show as strong a head as they.
But this queer man-pride is no theory. It is a fact.

For instance, a wild band of young revolutionists invited
me as the guest of honor to a beer bust.* It is the only
technical beer bust I ever attended. I did not know the
true inwardness of the affair when I accepted. I imagined
that the talk would be wild and high, that some of them
might drink more than they ought, and that I would
drink discreetly. But it seemed these beer busts were
a diversion of these high-spirited young fellows whereby
they whiled away the tedium of existence by making fools
of their betters. As I learned afterward, they had got their
previous guest of honor, a brilliant young radical, unskilled
in drinking, quite pipped.

When I found myself with them, and the situation
dawned on me, up rose my queer man-pride. I'd show
them, the young rascals. I'd show them who was husky
and chesty, who had the vitality and the constitution,
the stomach and the head, who could make most of a
swine of himself and show it least. These unlicked cubs
who thought they could out-drink *me!*

You see, it was an endurance test, and no man likes
to give another best. Faugh! It was steam beer. I had
learned more expensive brews. Not for years had I drunk
steam beer; but when I had, I had drunk with men, and I
guessed I could show these youngsters some ability in beer-
guzzling. And the drinking began, and I had to drink with
the best of them. Some of them might lag, but the guest
of honor was not permitted to lag.

And all my austere nights of midnight oil, all the books I
had read, all the wisdom I had gathered, went glimmering
before the ape and tiger in me that crawled up from the

abysm of my heredity, atavistic, competitive and brutal, lustful with strength and desire to outswine the swine.

And when the session broke up I was still on my feet, and I walked erect, unswaying—which was more than can be said of some of my hosts. I recall one of them in indignant tears on the street corner, weeping as he pointed out my sober condition. Little he dreamed the iron clutch, born of old training, with which I held to my consciousness in my swimming brain, kept control of my muscles and my qualms, kept my voice unbroken and easy and my thoughts consecutive and logical. Yes, and mixed up with it all I was privily a-grin. They hadn't made a fool of me in that drinking bout. And I was proud of myself for the achievement. Darn it, I am still proud, so strangely is man compounded.

But I didn't write my thousand words next morning. I was sick, poisoned. It was a day of wretchedness. In the afternoon I had to give a public speech. I gave it, and I am confident it was as bad as I felt. Some of my hosts were there in the front rows to mark any signs on me of the night before. I don't know what signs they marked, but I marked signs on them and took consolation in the knowledge that they were just as sick as I.

Never again, I swore. And I have never been inveigled into another beer bust. For that matter, that was my last drinking bout of any sort. Oh, I have drunk ever since, but with more wisdom, more discretion, and never in a competitive spirit. It is thus the seasoned drinker grows seasoned.

To show that at this period in my life drinking was wholly a matter of companionship, I remember crossing the Atlantic in the old *Teutonic*. It chanced, at the start, that I chummed with an English cable operator and a younger member of a Spanish shipping firm. Now the only thing they drank was 'horse's neck'—a long, soft, cool

drink with an apple peel or an orange peel floating in
it. And for that whole voyage I drank horse's necks with
my two companions. On the other hand, had they drunk
whisky, I should have drunk whisky with them. From this
it must not be concluded that I was merely weak. I didn't
care. I had no morality in the matter. I was strong with
youth, and unafraid, and alcohol was an utterly negligible
question so far as I was concerned.

CHAPTER XXVIII

NOT yet was I ready to tuck my arm in John Barleycorn's. The older I got, the greater my success, the more money I earned, the wider was the command of the world that became mine and the more prominently did John Barleycorn bulk in my life. And still I maintained no more than a nodding acquaintance with him. I drank for the sake of sociability, and when alone I did not drink. Sometimes I got jingled, but I considered such jingles the mild price I paid for sociability.

To show how unripe I was for John Barleycorn, when, at this time, I descended into my slough of despond, I never dreamed of turning to John Barleycorn for a helping hand. I had life troubles and heart troubles which are neither here nor there in this narrative. But, combined with them, were intellectual troubles which are indeed germane.

Mine was no uncommon experience. I had read too much positive science* and lived too much positive life. In the eagerness of youth I had made the ancient mistake of pursuing Truth too relentlessly. I had torn her veils from her, and the sight was too terrible for me to stand. In brief, I lost my fine faiths in pretty well everything except humanity, and the humanity I retained faith in was a very stark humanity indeed.

This long sickness of pessimism is too well known to most of us to be detailed here. Let it suffice to state that I had it very bad. I meditated suicide coolly, as a Greek philosopher might. My regret was that there were too many dependent directly upon me for food and shelter for me to quit living. But that was sheer morality. What really saved me was the one remaining illusion—the PEOPLE.

The things I had fought for and burned my midnight oil

for, had failed me. Success—I despised it. Recognition—it was dead ashes. Society, men and women above the ruck and the muck of the water-front and the forecastle—I was appalled by their unlovely mental mediocrity. Love of woman—it was like all the rest. Money—I could sleep in only one bed at a time, and of what worth was an income of a hundred porterhouses a day when I could eat only one? Art, culture—in the face of the iron facts of biology such things were ridiculous, the exponents of such things only the more ridiculous.

From the foregoing it can be seen how very sick I was. I was a born fighter. The things I had fought for had proved not worth the fight. Remained the PEOPLE. My fight was finished, yet something was left still to fight for—the PEOPLE.

But while I was discovering this one last tie to bind me to life, in my extremity, in the depths of despond, walking in the valley of the shadow, my ears were deaf to John Barleycorn. Never the remotest whisper arose in my consciousness that John Barleycorn was the anodyne, that he could lie me along to live. One way only was uppermost in my thought—my revolver, the crashing eternal darkness of a bullet. There was plenty of whisky in the house—for my guests. I never touched it. I grew afraid of my revolver—afraid during the period in which the radiant, flashing vision of the PEOPLE was forming in my mind and will. So obsessed was I with the desire to die, that I feared I might commit the act in my sleep, and I was compelled to give my revolver away to others who were to lose it for me where my subconscious hand might not find it.

But the PEOPLE saved me. By the PEOPLE was I handcuffed to life. There was still one fight left in me, and here was the thing for which to fight. I threw all precaution to the winds, threw myself with fiercer zeal into the fight for socialism, laughed at the editors and publishers who warned me and who were the sources of my hundred porterhouses a day, and was brutally careless of whose feelings I hurt and of how savagely I hurt them. As the 'well-balanced radicals' charged at the time, my efforts were so strenuous, so unsafe and unsane, so ultra-revolutionary, that I retarded the socialist development in the United States by five years.* In passing, I wish to remark, at this late date, that it is my fond belief that I accelerated the socialist development in the United States by at least five minutes.

It was the PEOPLE, and no thanks to John Barleycorn, who pulled me through my long sickness. And when I was convalescent, came the love of woman to complete the cure and lull my pessimism asleep for many a long day, until John Barleycorn again awoke it. But, in the meantime, I pursued Truth less relentlessly, refraining from tearing her last veils aside even when I clutched them in my hand. I no longer cared to look upon Truth naked. I refused to permit myself to see a second time what I had once seen. And the memory of what I had that time seen I resolutely blotted from my mind.

And I was very happy. Life went well with me. I took delight in little things. The big things I declined to take too seriously. I still read the books, but not with the old eagerness. I still read the books to-day, but never again shall I read them with that old glory of youthful passion when I harked to the call from over and beyond that whispered me on to win to the mystery at the back of life and behind the stars.

The point of this chapter is that, in the long sickness that at some time comes to most of us, I came through without any appeal for aid to John Barleycorn. Love, socialism, the PEOPLE—healthful figments of man's mind—were the things that cured and saved me. If ever

a man was not a born alcoholic, I believe that I am
that man. And yet . . . well, let the succeeding chapters
tell their tale, for in them will be shown how I paid for
my previous quarter of a century of contact with ever-
accessible John Barleycorn.

CHAPTER XXIX

AFTER my long sickness my drinking continued to be convivial. I drank when others drank and I was with them. But, imperceptibly, my need for alcohol took form and began to grow. It was not a body need. I boxed, swam, sailed, rode horses, lived in the open an arrantly healthful life, and passed life insurance examinations* with flying colors. In its inception, now that I look back upon it, this need for alcohol was a mental need, a nerve need, a good-spirits need. How can I explain?

It was something like this. Physiologically, from the standpoint of palate and stomach, alcohol was, as it had always been, repulsive. It tasted no better than beer did when I was five, than bitter claret did when I was seven. When I was alone, writing or studying, I had no need for it. But—I was growing old, or wise, or both, or senile as an alternative. When I was in company I was less pleased, less excited, with the things said and done. Erstwhile worthwhile fun and stunts seemed no longer worth while; and it was a torment to listen to the insipidities and stupidities of women, to the pompous, arrogant sayings of the little half-baked men. It is the penalty one pays for reading the books too much, or for being oneself a fool. In my case it does not matter which was my trouble. The trouble itself was the fact. The condition of the fact was mine. For me the life, and light, and sparkle of human intercourse were dwindling.

I had climbed too high among the stars,* or, maybe, I had slept too hard. Yet I was not hysterical nor in any way overwrought. My pulse was normal. My heart was an amazement of excellence to the insurance doctors. My lungs threw the said doctors into ecstasies. I wrote a thousand words every day. I was punctiliously exact in dealing with all the affairs of life that fell to my lot. I exercised in joy and gladness. I slept at night like a babe. But—

Well, as soon as I got out in the company of others I was driven to melancholy and spiritual tears. I could neither laugh with nor at the solemn utterances of men I esteemed ponderous asses; nor could I laugh with nor at, nor engage in my old-time lightsome persiflage, with the silly superficial chatterings of women, who, underneath all their silliness and softness, were as primitive, direct, and deadly in their pursuit of biological destiny as the monkey women were before they shed their furry coats and replaced them with the furs of other animals.

And I was not pessimistic. I swear I was not pessimistic. I was merely bored. I had seen the same show too often, listened too often to the same songs and the same jokes. I knew too much about the box-office receipts. I knew the cogs of the machinery behind the scenes so well, that the posing on the stage, and the laughter and the song, could not drown the creaking of the wheels behind.

It doesn't pay to go behind the scenes and see the angel-voiced tenor beat his wife.* Well, I'd been behind, and I was paying for it. Or else I was a fool. It is immaterial which was my situation. The situation is what counts, and the situation was that social intercourse for me was getting painful and difficult. On the other hand, it must be stated that on rare occasions, on very rare occasions, I did meet rare souls, or fools like me, with whom I could spend magnificent hours among the stars, or in the paradise of fools. I was married to a rare soul, or a fool, who never bored me and who was always a source of new and unending surprise and delight. But I could not spend all my hours solely in her company. Nor would it have been fair, nor wise, to compel her to spend all her hours in my company. Besides, I had written a string of successful books, and society demands some portion of the recreative hours of a fellow that writes books. And any normal man, of himself and his needs, demands some hours of his fellow man.

And now we begin to come to it. How to face social intercourse with the glamour gone? John Barleycorn! The ever-patient one had waited a quarter of a century and more for me to reach my hand out in need of him. His thousand tricks had failed, thanks to my constitution and good luck, but he had more tricks in his bag. A cocktail or two, or several, I found, cheered me up for the foolishness of foolish people. A cocktail, or several, before dinner, enabled me to laugh whole-heartedly at things which had long since ceased being laughable. The cocktail was a prod, a spur, a kick, to my jaded mind and bored spirits. It recrudesced the laughter and the song, and put a lilt into my own imagination so that I could laugh and sing and say foolish things with the liveliest of them, or platitudes with verve and intensity to the satisfaction of the pompous mediocre ones who knew no other way to talk.

A poor companion without a cocktail, I became a very good companion with one. I achieved a false exhilaration, drugged myself to merriment. And the thing began so imperceptibly, that I, old intimate of John Barleycorn, never dreamed whither it was leading me. I was beginning to call for music and wine; soon I should be calling for madder music and more wine.

It was at this time I became aware of waiting with expectancy for the pre-dinner cocktail. I *wanted* it, and I was *conscious* that I wanted it. I remember, while war-corresponding in the Far East, of being irresistibly attracted to a certain home. Besides accepting all invitations to dinner, I made a point of dropping in almost every afternoon. Now, the hostess was a charming woman, but it was not for her sake that I was under her roof so frequently. It happened that she made by far the finest cocktail procurable in that large city where drink-mixing on the

part of the foreign population was indeed an art. Up at
the club, down at the hotels, and in other private houses,
no such cocktails were created. Her cocktails were subtle.
They were masterpieces. They were the least repulsive
to the palate and carried the most 'kick'. And yet, I
desired her cocktails only for sociability's sake, to key
myself to sociable moods. When I rode away from that
city, across hundreds of miles of rice-fields and mountains,
and through months of campaigning, and on with the
victorious Japanese into Manchuria,* I did not drink.
Several bottles of whisky were always to be found on the
backs of my pack-horses. Yet I never broached a bottle
for myself, never took a drink by myself, and never knew
a desire to take such a drink. Oh, if a white man came
into my camp, I opened a bottle and we drank together
according to the way of men, just as he would open a bottle
and drink with me if I came into his camp. I carried that
whisky for social purposes, and I so charged it up in my
expense account to the newspaper for which I worked.

Only in retrospect can I mark the almost imperceptible
growth of my desire. There were little hints then that I
did not take, little straws in the wind that I did not see,
little incidents the gravity of which I did not realize.

For instance, for some years it had been my practice
each winter to cruise for six or eight weeks on San
Francisco Bay. My stout sloop yacht, the *Spray*,* had a
comfortable cabin and a coal stove. A Korean boy* did
the cooking, and I usually took a friend or so along to
share the joys of the cruise. Also, I took my machine along
and did my thousand words a day. On the particular trip
I have in mind, Cloudesley* and Toddy came along. This
was Toddy's first trip. On previous trips Cloudesley had
elected to drink beer; so I had kept the yacht supplied
with beer and had drunk beer with him.

But on this cruise the situation was different. Toddy
was so nicknamed because of his diabolical cleverness

in concocting toddies. So I brought whisky along—a
couple of gallons. Alas! Many another gallon I bought,
for Cloudesley and I got into the habit of drinking
a certain hot toddy of huge dimensions that actually
tasted delicious going down and that carried the most
exhilarating kick imaginable.

I *liked* those toddies. I grew to look forward to the
making of them. We drank them regularly, one before
breakfast, one before dinner, one before supper, and a final
one when we went to bed. We never got drunk. But I will
say that four times a day we were very genial. And when,
in the middle of the cruise, Toddy was called back to San
Francisco on business, Cloudesley and I saw to it that the
Korean boy mixed toddies regularly for us according to
formula.

But that was only on the boat. Back on the land, in
my house, I took no before-breakfast eye-opener, no bed-
going nightcap. And I haven't drunk hot toddies since, and
that was many a year ago. But the point is, I *liked* those
toddies. The geniality of which they were provocative
was marvelous. They were eloquent proselyters for John
Barleycorn in their small insidious way. They were tickles
of the something destined to grow into daily and deadly
desire. And I didn't know, never dreamed—I, who had
lived with John Barleycorn for so many years and laughed
at all his unavailing attempts to win me.

CHAPTER XXX

PART of the process of recovering from my long sickness was to find delight in little things, in things unconnected with books and problems, in play, in games of tag in the swimming pool, in flying kites, in fooling with horses, in working out mechanical puzzles. As a result, I grew tired of the city. On the ranch,* in the Valley of the Moon, I found my paradise. I gave up living in cities. All the cities held for me were music, the theater, and Turkish baths.

And all went well with me. I worked hard, played hard, and was very happy. I read more fiction and less fact. I did not study a tithe as much as I had studied in the past. I still took an interest in the fundamental problems of existence, but it was a very cautious interest; for I had burned my fingers that time I clutched at the veils of Truth and rent them from her. There was a bit of lie in this attitude of mine, a bit of hypocrisy; but the lie and the hypocrisy were those of a man desiring to live. I deliberately blinded myself to what I took to be the savage interpretation of biological fact. After all, I was merely forswearing a bad habit, foregoing a bad frame of mind. And I repeat, I was very happy. And I add, that in all my days, measuring them with cold, considerative judgment, this was, far and away beyond all other periods, the happiest period of my life.

But the time was at hand, rimeless and reasonless so far as I can see, when I was to begin to pay for my score of years of dallying with John Barleycorn. Occasionally guests journeyed to the ranch and remained a few days. Some did not drink. But to those who did drink, the absence of all alcohol on the ranch was a hardship. I could not violate my sense of hospitality by compelling them to endure this hardship. I ordered in a stock . . . for my guests.

I was never interested enough in cocktails to know how they were made. So I got a barkeeper in Oakland to make them in bulk and ship them to me. When I had no guests I didn't drink. But I began to notice, when I finished my morning's work, that I was glad if there were a guest, for then I could drink a cocktail with him.

Now I was so clean of alcohol that even a single cocktail was provocative of pitch. A single cocktail would glow the mind and tickle a laugh for the few minutes prior to sitting down to table and starting the delightful process of eating. On the other hand, such was the strength of my stomach, of my alcoholic resistance, that the single cocktail was only the glimmer of a glow, the faintest tickle of a laugh. One day a friend frankly and shamelessly suggested a second cocktail. I drank the second one with him. The glow was appreciably longer and warmer, the laughter deeper and more resonant. One does not forget such experiences. Sometimes I almost think that it was because I was so very happy that I started on my real drinking.

I remember one day Charmian and I took a long ride over the mountains on our horses. The servants had been dismissed for the day, and we returned late at night to a jolly chafing-dish supper. Oh, it was good to be alive that night while the supper was preparing, the two of us alone in the kitchen. I, personally, was at the top of life. Such things as the books and ultimate truth did not exist. My body was gloriously healthy, and healthily tired from the long ride. It had been a splendid day. The night was splendid. I was with the woman who was my mate, picnicking in gleeful abandon. I had no troubles. The bills were all paid, and a surplus of money was rolling in on me. The future ever widened before me. And right there, in the kitchen, delicious things bubbled in the chafing dish, our laughter bubbled, and my stomach was keen with a most delicious edge of appetite.

I felt so good, that somehow, somewhere, in me arose an insatiable greed to feel better. I was so happy that I wanted to pitch my happiness even higher. And I knew the way. Ten thousand contacts with John Barleycorn had taught me. Several times I wandered out of the kitchen to the cocktail bottle, and each time I left it diminished by one man's cocktail. The result was splendid. I wasn't jingled, I wasn't lighted up; but I was warmed, I glowed, my happiness was pyramided. Munificent as life was to me, I added to that munificence. It was a great hour— one of my greatest. But I paid for it, long afterwards, as you shall see. One does not forget such experiences, and, in human stupidity, cannot be brought to realize that there is no immutable law which decrees that same things shall produce same results. For they don't, else would the thousandth pipe of opium be provocative of similar delights to the first, else would one cocktail, instead of several, produce an equivalent glow after a year of cocktails.

One day, just before I ate midday dinner, after my morning's writing was done, when I had no guest, I took a cocktail by myself. Thereafter, when there were no guests, I took this daily pre-dinner cocktail. And right there John Barleycorn had me. I was beginning to drink regularly. I was beginning to drink alone. And I was beginning to drink, not for hospitality's sake, not for the sake of the taste, but for the effect of the drink.

I *wanted* that daily pre-dinner cocktail. And it never crossed my mind that there was any reason I should not have it. I paid for it. I could pay for a thousand cocktails each day if I wanted. And what was a cocktail—one cocktail—to me who on so many occasions for so many years had drunk inordinate quantities of stiffer stuff and been unharmed?

The program of my ranch life was as follows: Each morning, at eight-thirty, having been reading or correcting proofs in bed since four or five, I went to my desk. Odds and ends of correspondence and notes occupied me till nine, and at nine sharp, invariably, I began my writing. By eleven, sometimes a few minutes earlier or later, my thousand words were finished. Another half hour at cleaning up my desk, and my day's work was done, so that at eleven-thirty I got into a hammock under the trees with my mail bag and the morning newspaper. At twelve-thirty I ate dinner and in the afternoon I swam and rode.

One morning, at eleven-thirty, before I got into the hammock, I took a cocktail. I repeated this on subsequent mornings, of course, taking another cocktail just before I ate at twelve-thirty. Soon I found myself, seated at my desk in the midst of my thousand words, looking forward to that eleven-thirty cocktail.

At last, now, I was thoroughly conscious that I desired alcohol. But what of it? I wasn't afraid of John Barleycorn. I had associated with him too long. I was wise in the matter of drink. I was discreet. Never again would I drink to excess. I knew the dangers and the pitfalls of John Barleycorn, the various ways by which he had tried to kill me in the past. But all that was past, long past. Never again would I drink myself to stupefaction. Never again would I get drunk. All I wanted, and all I would take, was just enough to glow and warm me, to kick geniality alive in me and put laughter in my throat and stir the maggots of imagination slightly in my brain. Oh, I was thoroughly master of myself, and of John Barleycorn.

CHAPTER XXXI

BUT the same stimulus to the human organism will not continue to produce the same response. By and by I discovered there was no kick at all in one cocktail. One cocktail left me dead. There was no glow, no laughter tickle. Two or three cocktails were required to produce the original effect of one. And I wanted that effect. I drank my first cocktail at eleven-thirty when I took the morning's mail into the hammock, and I drank my second cocktail an hour later just before I ate. I got into the habit of crawling out of the hammock ten minutes earlier so as to find time and decency for two more cocktails ere I ate. This became schedule—three cocktails in the hour that intervened between my desk and dinner. And these were two of the deadliest drinking habits: regular drinking and solitary drinking.

I was always willing to drink when any one was around. I drank by myself when no one was around. Then I made another step. When I had for guest a man of limited drinking caliber, I took two drinks to his one—one drink with him, the other drink without him and of which he did not know. I *stole* that other drink, and, worse than that, I began the habit of drinking alone when there was a guest, a man, a comrade, with whom I could have drunk. But John Barleycorn furnished the extenuation. It was a wrong thing to trip a guest up with excess of hospitality and get him drunk. If I persuaded him, with his limited caliber, into drinking up with me, I'd surely get him drunk. What could I do but steal that every second drink, or else deny myself the kick equivalent to what he had got out of half the number?

Please remember, as I recite this development of my drinking, that I am no fool, no weakling. As the world

measures such things, I am a success—I dare say a
success more conspicuous than the success of the average
successful man, and a success that required a pretty fair
amount of brains and will power. My body is a strong
body. It has survived where weaklings died like flies. And
yet these things which I am relating happened to my
body and to me. I am a fact. My drinking is a fact. My
drinking is a thing that has happened, and is no theory
nor speculation; and, as I see it, it but lays the emphasis
on the power of John Barleycorn—a savagery that we still
permit to exist, a deadly institution that lingers from the
mad old brutal days and that takes its heavy toll of youth
and strength and high spirit, and of very much of all of
the best we breed.

To return. After a boisterous afternoon in the swimming pool, followed by a glorious ride on horseback over
the mountains or up or down the Valley of the Moon, I
found myself so keyed and splendid that I desired to be
more highly keyed, to feel more splendid. I knew the way.
A cocktail before supper was not the way. Two or three,
at the very least, was what was needed. I took them. Why
not? It was living. I had always dearly loved to live. This
also became part of the daily schedule.

Then, too, I was perpetually finding excuses for extra
cocktails. It might be the assembling of a particularly jolly
crowd; a touch of anger against my architect or against a
thieving stone-mason working on my barn; the death of
my favorite horse in a barbed wire fence;* or news of good
fortune in the morning mail from my dealings with editors
and publishers. It was immaterial what the excuse might
be, once the desire had germinated in me. The thing was:
I *wanted* alcohol. At last, after a score and more of years
of dallying and of not wanting, now I wanted it. And my
strength was my weakness. I required two, three, or four
drinks to get an effect commensurate with the effect the
average man got out of one drink.

One rule I observed. I never took a drink until my day's work of writing a thousand words was done. And, when done, the cocktails reared a wall of inhibition in my brain between the day's work done and the rest of the day of fun to come. My work ceased from consciousness. No thought of it flickered in my brain till next morning at nine o'clock when I sat at my desk and began my next thousand words. This was a desirable condition of mind to achieve. I conserved my energy by means of this alcoholic inhibition. John Barleycorn was not so black as he was painted. He did a fellow many a good turn, and this was one of them.

And I turned out work that was healthful, and wholesome, and sincere. It was never pessimistic. The way to life I had learned in my long sickness. I knew the illusions were right, and I exalted the illusions. Oh, I still turn out the same sort of work, stuff that is clean, alive, optimistic, and that makes toward life. And I am always assured by the critics of my superabundant and abounding vitality, and of how thoroughly I am deluded by these very illusions I exploit.

And while on this digression, let me repeat the question I have repeated to myself ten thousand times. *Why did I drink?* What need was there for it? I was happy. Was it because I was too happy? I was strong. Was it because I was too strong? Did I possess too much vitality? I don't know why I drank. I cannot answer, though I can voice the suspicion that ever grows in me. I had been in too familiar contact with John Barleycorn through too many years. A left-handed man, by long practice, can become a right-handed man. Had I, a non-alcoholic, by long practice, become an alcoholic?

I was so happy! I had won through my long sickness to the satisfying love of woman. I earned more money with less endeavor. I glowed with health. I slept like a babe. I continued to write successful books, and in sociological

controversy I saw my opponents confuted with the facts
of the times that daily reared new buttresses to my
intellectual position. From day's end to day's end I never
knew sorrow, disappointment, nor regret. I was happy all
the time. Life was one unending song. I begrudged the
very hours of blessed sleep because by that much was
I robbed of the joy that would have been mine had I
remained awake. And yet I drank. And John Barleycorn,
all unguessed by me, was setting the stage for a sickness
all his own.

The more I drank the more I was required to drink
to get an equivalent effect. When I left the Valley of the
Moon, and went to the city and dined out, a cocktail
served at table was a wan and worthless thing. There
was no pre-dinner kick in it. On my way to dinner I was
compelled to accumulate the kick—two cocktails, three,
and, if I met some fellows, four or five, or six, it didn't
matter within several. Once, I was in a rush. I had no
time decently to accumulate the several drinks. A brilliant
idea came to me. I told the barkeeper to mix me a double
cocktail. Thereafter, whenever I was in a hurry, I ordered
double cocktails. It saved time.

One result of this regular heavy drinking was to jade
me. My mind grew so accustomed to spring and liven by
artificial means, that without artificial means it refused
to spring and liven. Alcohol became more and more
imperative in order to meet people, in order to become
sociably fit. I had to get the kick and the hit of the
stuff, the crawl of the maggots, the genial brain glow, the
laughter tickle, the touch of devilishness and sting, the
smile over the face of things, ere I could join my fellows
and make one with them.

Another result was that John Barleycorn was beginning
to trip me up. He was thrusting my long sickness back
upon me, inveigling me into again pursuing Truth and
snatching her veils away from her, tricking me into looking

reality stark in the face. But this came on gradually. My thoughts were growing harsh again, though they grew harsh slowly.

Sometimes warnings crossed my mind. Where was this steady drinking leading? But trust John Barleycorn to silence such questions. 'Come on and have a drink and I'll tell you all about it,' is his way. And it works. For instance, the following is a case in point, and one which John Barleycorn never wearied of reminding me:

I had suffered an accident which required a ticklish operation.* One morning, a week after I had come off the table, I lay on my hospital bed, weak and weary. The sunburn of my face, what little of it could be seen through a scraggly growth of beard, had faded to a sickly yellow. My doctor stood at my bedside on the verge of departure. He glared disapprovingly at the cigarette I was smoking.

'That's what you ought to quit,' he lectured. 'It will get you in the end. Look at me.'

I looked. He was about my own age, broad-shouldered, deep-chested, eyes sparkling, and ruddy-cheeked with health. A finer specimen of manhood one would not ask.

'I used to smoke,' he went on. 'Cigars. But I gave even them up. And look at me.'

The man was arrogant, and rightly arrogant, with conscious well-being. And within a month he was dead. It was no accident. Half-a-dozen different bugs of long scientific names had attacked and destroyed him. The complications were astonishing and painful, and for days before he died the screams of agony of that splendid manhood could be heard for a block around. He died screaming.

'You see,' said John Barleycorn. 'He took care of himself. He even stopped smoking cigars. And that's what he got for it. Pretty rotten, eh? But the bugs will jump. There's no forefending them. Your magnificent doctor took every precaution, yet they got him. When the bug

jumps you can't tell where it will land. It may be you. Look
what he missed. Will you miss all I can give you, only to
have a bug jump on you and drag you down? There is no
equity in life. It's all a lottery. But I put the lying smile on
the face of life and laugh at the facts. Smile with me and
laugh. You'll get yours in the end, but in the meantime
laugh. It's a pretty dark world. I illuminate it for you. It's
a rotten world, when things can happen such as happened
to your doctor. There's only one thing to do; take another
drink and forget it.'

And of course I took another drink for the inhibition
that accompanied it. I took another drink every time John
Barleycorn reminded me of what had happened. Yet I
drank rationally, intelligently. I saw to it that the quality
of the stuff was of the best. I sought the kick and the
inhibition, and avoided the penalties of poor quality and of
drunkenness. It is to be remarked, in passing, that when a
man begins to drink rationally and intelligently he betrays
a grave symptom of how far along the road he has traveled.

But I continued to observe my rule of never taking my
first drink of the day until the last word of my thousand
words was written. On occasion, however, I took a day's
vacation from my writing. At such times, since it was no
violation of my rule, I didn't mind how early in the day
I took that first drink. And persons who have never been
through the drinking game wonder how the drinking habit
grows!

CHAPTER XXXII

WHEN the *Snark** sailed on her long cruise from San Francisco there was nothing to drink on board. Or, rather, we were all of us unaware that there was anything to drink, nor did we discover it for many a month. This sailing with a 'dry' boat was malice aforethought on my part. I had played John Barleycorn a trick. And it showed that I was listening ever so slightly to the faint warnings that were beginning to arise in my consciousness.

Of course, I veiled the situation to myself and excused myself to John Barleycorn. And I was very scientific about it. I said that I would drink only while in ports. During the dry sea-stretches my system would be cleansed of the alcohol that soaked it, so that when I reached a port I should be in shape to enjoy John Barleycorn more thoroughly. His bite would be sharper, his kick keener and more delicious.

We were twenty-seven days on the traverse between San Francisco and Honolulu. After the first day out, the thought of a drink never troubled me. This I take to show how intrinsically I am not a alcoholic. Sometimes, during the traverse, looking ahead and anticipating the delightful *lanai* luncheons and dinners of Hawaii (I had been there a couple of times before), I thought, naturally, of the drinks that would precede those meals. I did not think of those drinks with any yearning, with any irk at the length of the voyage. I merely thought they would be nice and jolly, part of the atmosphere of a proper meal.

Thus, once again I proved to my complete satisfaction that I was John Barleycorn's master. I could drink when I wanted, refrain when I wanted. Therefore I would continue to drink when I wanted.

Some five months were spent in the various islands of

the Hawaiian group. Being ashore, I drank. I even drank a bit more than I had been accustomed to drink in California prior to the voyage. The people in Hawaii seemed to drink a bit more, on the average, than the people in more temperate latitudes. I do not intend the pun, and can awkwardly revise the statement to 'latitudes more distant from the equator.' Yet Hawaii is only sub-tropical. The deeper I got into the tropics the deeper I found men drank, the deeper I drank myself.

From Hawaii we sailed for the Marquesas. The traverse occupied sixty days. For sixty days we never raised land, a sail, nor a steamer smoke. But early in those sixty days, the cook, giving an overhauling to the galley, made a find. Down in the bottom of a deep locker he found a dozen bottles of angelica and muscatel. These had come down from the kitchen cellar of the ranch along with the home-preserved fruits and jellies. Six months in the galley-heat had effected some sort of a change in the thick sweet wine—brandied it, I imagine.

I took a taste. Delicious! And thereafter, once each day, at twelve o'clock, after our observations were worked up and the *Snark's* position charted, I drank half a tumbler of the stuff. It had a rare kick to it. It warmed the cockles of my geniality and put a fairer face on the truly fair face of the sea. Each morning, below, sweating out my thousand words, I found myself looking forward to that twelve o'clock event of the day.

The trouble was I had to share the stuff, and the length of the traverse was doubtful. I regretted that there were not more than a dozen bottles. And when they were gone I even regretted that I had shared any of it. I was thirsty for the alcohol, and eager to arrive in the Marquesas.

So it was that I reached the Marquesas the possessor of a real, man's size thirst. And in the Marquesas were several white men, a lot of sickly natives, much magnif-icent scenery, plenty of trade rum, an immense quantity of absinthe, but neither whisky nor gin. The trade rum scorched the skin of one's mouth. I know, because I tried it. But I had ever been plastic, and I accepted the absinthe. The trouble with the stuff was that I had to take such inordinate quantities in order to feel the slightest effect.

From the Marquesas I sailed with sufficient absinthe in ballast to last me to Tahiti, where I outfitted with Scotch and American whisky, and thereafter there were no dry stretches between ports. But please do not misunderstand. There was no drunkenness, as drunkenness is ordinarily understood—no staggering and rolling around, no befuddlement of the senses. The skilled and seasoned drinker, with a strong constitution, never descends to anything like that. He drinks to feel good, to get a pleasant jingle, and no more than that. The things he carefully avoids are the nausea of over-drinking, the after-effect of over-drinking, the helplessness and loss of pride of over-drinking.

What the skilled and seasoned drinker achieves is a discreet and canny semi-intoxication. And he does it by the twelve-month around without any apparent penalty. There are hundreds of thousands of men of this sort in the United States to-day, in clubs, hotels, and in their own homes—men who are never drunk, and who, though most of them will indignantly deny it, are rarely sober. And all of them fondly believe, as I fondly believed, that they are beating the game.

On the sea-stretches I was fairly abstemious; but ashore I drank more. I seemed to need more, anyway, in the tropics. This is a common experience, for the excessive consumption of alcohol in the tropics by white men is a notorious fact. The tropics is no place for white-skinned men. Their skin-pigment does not protect them against the excessive white light of the sun. The ultraviolet rays, and other high-velocity and invisible rays from the upper end of the spectrum, rip and tear through their tissues, just as the X-ray ripped and tore through the tissues of so many laboratory experimenters before they learned the danger.

White men in the tropics undergo radical changes of nature. They become savage, merciless. They commit monstrous acts of cruelty that they would never dream of committing in their original temperate climate. They become nervous, irritable, and less moral. And they drink as they never drank before. Drinking is one form of the many forms of degeneration that set in when white men are exposed too long to too much white light. The increase of alcoholic consumption is automatic. The tropics is no place for a long sojourn. They seem doomed to die anyway, and the heavy drinking expedites the process. They don't reason about it. They just do it.

The sun-sickness* got me, despite the fact that I had been in the tropics only a couple of years. I drank heavily during this time, but right here I wish to forestall misunderstanding. The drinking was not the cause of the sickness, nor of the abandonment of the voyage. I was strong as a bull, and for many months I fought the sun-sickness that was ripping and tearing my surface and nervous tissues to pieces. All through the New Hebrides and the Solomons and up among the atolls on the Line, during this period, under a tropic sun, rotten with malaria, and suffering from a few minor afflictions such as Biblical leprosy with the silvery skin, I did the work of five men.

To navigate a vessel through the reefs and shoals and passages and unlighted coasts of the coral seas is a man's work in itself. I was the only navigator on board. There was no one to check me up on the working out of my observations, nor any one with whom I could advise in the ticklish darkness among uncharted reefs and shoals. And I stood all watches. There was no seaman on board whom I could trust to stand a mate's watch. I was mate as well as captain. Twenty-four hours a day were the watches I stood at sea, catching cat-naps when I might. Third, I was doctor. And let me say right here that the doctor's job on the *Snark* at that time was a man's job. All on board suffered from malaria—the real, tropical malaria that can kill in three months. All on board suffered from perforating ulcers and from the maddening itch of *ngari ngari.* A Japanese cook went insane from his too numerous afflictions. One of my Polynesian sailors lay at death's door with blackwater fever. Oh, yes, it was a full man's job, and I dosed and doctored, and pulled teeth, and dragged my patients through mild little things like ptomaine poisoning.

Fourth, I was a writer. I sweated out my thousand words a day, every day, except when the shock of fever smote me, or a couple of nasty squalls smote the *Snark,* in the morning. Fifth, I was a traveler and a writer, eager to see things and to gather material into my note books. And, sixth, I was master and owner of the craft that was visiting strange places where visitors are rare and where visitors are made much of. So here I had to hold up the social end, entertain on board, be entertained ashore by planters, traders, governors, captains of war vessels, kinky-headed cannibal kings, and prime ministers sometimes fortunate enough to be clad in cotton under shirts.

Of course I drank. I drank with my guests and hosts. Also, I drank by myself. Doing the work of five men, I thought, entitled me to drink. Alcohol was good for a man who overworked. I noted its effect on my small crew, when, breaking their backs and hearts at heaving up anchor in forty fathoms, they knocked off gasping and trembling at the end of half an hour and had new life put into them by stiff jolts of rum. They caught their breaths, wiped their mouths, and went to it again with a will. And when we careened the *Snark* and had to work in the water to our necks between shocks of fever, I noted how raw trade-rum helped the work along.

And here again we come to another side of many-sided John Barleycorn. On the face of it, he gives something for nothing. Where no strength remains he finds new strength. The wearied one rises to greater effort. For the time being there is an actual accession of strength. I remember passing coal on an ocean steamer through eight days of hell, during which time we coal-passers were kept to the job by being fed whisky. We toiled half drunk all the time. And without the whisky we could not have passed the coal.

This strength John Barleycorn gives is not fictitious strength. It is real strength. But it is manufactured out of the sources of strength, and it must ultimately be paid for, and with interest. But what weary human will look so far ahead? He takes this apparently miraculous accession of strength at its face value. And many an overworked business and professional man, as well as a harried common laborer, has traveled John Barleycorn's death-road because of this mistake.

CHAPTER XXXIII

I WENT to Australia to go into hospital and get tinkered up,* after which I planned to go on with the voyage. And during the long weeks I lay in hospital, from the first day I never missed alcohol. I never thought about it. I knew I should have it again when I was on my feet. But when I regained my feet I was not cured of my major afflictions. Naaman's silvery skin* was still mine. The mysterious sun-sickness, which the experts of Australia could not fathom, still ripped and tore my tissues. Malaria still festered in me and put me on my back in shivering delirium at the most unexpected moments, among other things compelling me to cancel a double lecture tour which had been arranged.

So I abandoned the *Snark* voyage and sought a cooler climate. The day I came out of hospital I took up drinking again as a matter of course. I drank wine at meals. I drank cocktails before meals. I drank Scotch highballs when anybody I chanced to be with was drinking them. I was so thoroughly the master of John Barleycorn, I could take up with him or let go of him whenever I pleased, just as I had done all my life.

After a time, for cooler climate, I went down to southernmost Tasmania in forty-three South. And I found myself in a place where there was nothing to drink. It didn't mean anything. I didn't drink. It was no hardship. I soaked in the cool air, rode horseback, and did my thousand words a day save when the fever shock came in the morning.

And for fear that the idea may still lurk in some minds that my preceding years of drinking were the cause of my disabilities, I here point out that my Japanese cabin-boy, Nakata,* still with me, was rotten with fever, as was Charmian, who in addition was in the slough of a tropical neurasthenia that required several years of temperate climate to cure, and that neither she nor Nakata drank or ever had drunk.

When I returned to Hobart Town, where drink was obtainable, I drank as of old. The same when I arrived back in Australia. On the contrary, when I sailed from Australia on a tramp steamer commanded by an abstemious captain, I took no drink along, and had no drink for the forty-three days' passage. Arrived in Ecuador, squarely under the equatorial sun, where the humans were dying of yellow fever, smallpox, and the plague, I promptly drank again—every drink of every sort that had a kick in it. I caught none of these diseases. Neither did Charmian nor Nakata, who did not drink.

Enamored of the tropics, despite the damage done me, I stopped in various places, and was a long while getting back to the splendid, temperate climate of California. I did my thousand words a day, traveling or stopping over, suffered my last faint fever shock, saw my silvery skin vanish and my sun-torn tissues healthily knit again, and drank as a broad-shouldered, chesty man may drink.

CHAPTER XXXIV

BACK on the ranch,* in the Valley of the Moon, I resumed my steady drinking. My program was no drink in the morning; first drink-time came with the completion of my thousand words. Then, between that and the midday meal, were drinks numerous enough to develop a pleasant jingle. Again, in the hour preceding the evening meal, I developed another pleasant jingle. Nobody ever saw me drunk, for the simple reason that I never was drunk. But I did get a jingle twice each day; and the amount of alcohol I consumed every day, if loosed in the system of one unaccustomed to drink, would have put such a one on his back and out.

It was the old proposition. The more I drank, the more I was compelled to drink in order to get an effect. The time came when cocktails were inadequate. I had neither the time in which to drink them nor the space to accommodate them. Whisky had a more powerful jolt. It gave quicker action with less quantity. Bourbon or rye, or cunningly aged blends, constituted the pre-midday drinking. In the late afternoon it was Scotch and soda.

My sleep, always excellent, now became not quite so excellent. I had been accustomed to read myself back to sleep when I chanced to awake. But now this began to fail me. When I had read two or three of the small hours away and was as wide awake as ever, I found that a drink furnished the soporific effect. Sometimes two or three drinks were required.

So short a period of sleep then intervened before early morning rising, that my system did not have time to work off the alcohol. As a result I awoke with mouth parched and dry, with a slight heaviness of head, and with a mild nervous palpitation in the stomach. In fact I did not feel good. I was suffering from the morning sickness of the steady, heavy drinker. What I needed was a pick-me-up, a bracer. Trust John Barleycorn, once he has broken down a man's defenses! So it was a drink before breakfast to put me right for breakfast—the old poison of the snake that has bitten one! Another custom, begun at this time, was that of the pitcher of water by the bedside to furnish relief to my scorched and sizzling membranes.

I achieved a condition in which my body was never free from alcohol. Nor did I permit myself to be away from alcohol. If I traveled to out-of-the-way places, I declined to run the risk of finding them dry. I took a quart, or several quarts, along in my grip. In the past I had been amazed by other men guilty of this practice. Now I did it myself unblushingly. And when I got out with the fellows, I cast all rules by the board. I drank when they drank, what they drank, and in the same way they drank.

I was carrying a beautiful alcoholic conflagration around with me. The thing fed on its own heat and flamed the fiercer. There was no time, in all my waking time, that I didn't want a drink. I began to anticipate the completion of my daily thousand words by taking a drink when only five hundred words were written. It was not long until I prefaced the beginning of the thousand words with a drink.

The gravity of this I realized too well. I made new rules. Resolutely I would refrain from drinking until my work was done. But a new and most diabolical complication arose. The work refused to be done without drinking. It just couldn't be done. I had to drink in order to do it. I was beginning to fight now. I had the craving at last, and it was mastering me. I would sit at my desk and dally with pad and pen, but words refused to flow. My brain could not think the proper thoughts because continually it was obsessed with the one thought that across the room in the liquor cabinet stood John Barleycorn. When, in despair,

I took my drink, at once my brain loosened up and began to roll off the thousand words.

In my town house, in Oakland, I finished the stock of liquor and wilfully refused to purchase more. It was no use, because, unfortunately, there remained in the bottom of the liquor cabinet a case of beer. In vain I tried to write. Now beer is a poor substitute for strong waters; besides, I didn't like beer; yet all I could think of was that beer so singularly accessible in the bottom of the cabinet. Not until I had drunk a pint of it did the words begin to reel off, and the thousand were reeled off to the tune of numerous pints. The worst of it was that the beer caused me severe heart-burn; but despite the discomfort I soon finished the case.

The liquor cabinet was now bare. I did not replenish it. By truly heroic perseverance, I finally forced myself to write the daily thousand words without the spur of John Barleycorn. But all the time I wrote I was keenly aware of the craving for a drink. And as soon as the morning's work was done, I was out of the house and away down-town to get my first drink. Merciful goodness!—if John Barleycorn could get such sway over me, a non-alcoholic, what must be the sufferings of the true alcoholic, battling against the organic demands of his chemistry while those closest to him sympathize little, understand less, and despise and deride him!

CHAPTER XXXV

BUT the freight has to be paid. John Barleycorn began
to collect, and he collected not so much from the body
as from the mind. The old long sickness, which had
been purely an intellectual sickness, recrudesced. The
old ghosts, long laid, lifted their heads again. But they
were different and more deadly ghosts. The old ghosts,
intellectual in their inception, had been laid by a sane
and normal logic. But now they were raised by the
White Logic* of John Barleycorn, and John Barleycorn
never lays the ghosts of his raising. For this sickness of
pessimism, caused by drink, one must drink further in
quest of the anodyne that John Barleycorn promises but
never delivers.

How to describe this White Logic to those who never
experienced it? It is perhaps better first to state how
impossible such a description is. Take Hasheesh Land,*
for instance, the land of enormous extensions of time and
space. In past years I have made two memorable journeys
into that far land. My adventures there are seared in
sharpest detail on my brain. Yet I have tried vainly, with
endless words, to describe any tiny particular phase to
persons who have not traveled there.

I use all the hyperbole of metaphor, and tell what
centuries of time and profounds of unthinkable agony and
horror can obtain in each interval of all the intervals
between the notes of a quick jig played quickly on the
piano. I talk for an hour, elaborating that one phase of
Hasheesh Land, and at the end I have told them nothing.
And when I cannot tell them this one thing of all the
vastness of terrible and wonderful things, I know I have
failed to give them the slightest concept of Hasheesh Land.

But, let me talk with some other traveler in that weird

region, and at once am I understood. A phrase, a word,
conveys instantly to his mind what hours of words and
phrases could not convey to the mind of the non-traveler.
So it is with John Barleycorn's realm where the White
Logic reigns. To those untraveled there, the traveler's
account must always seem unintelligible and fantastic. At
the best, I may only beg of the untraveled ones to strive
to take on faith the narrative I shall relate.

For there are fatal intuitions of truth that reside in
alcohol. Philip sober vouches for Philip drunk* in this
matter. There seem to be various orders of truth in this
world. Some sorts of truth are truer than others. Some
sorts of truth are lies, and these sorts are the very ones
that have the greatest use-value to life that desires to
realize and live. At once, O untraveled reader, you see
how lunatic and blasphemous is the realm I am trying
to describe to you in the language of John Barleycorn's
tribe. It is not the language of your tribe, all of whose
members resolutely shun the roads that lead to death and
tread only the roads that lead to life. For there are roads
and roads, and of truth there are orders and orders. But
have patience. At least, through what seems no more than
verbal yammerings, you may, perchance, glimpse faint far
vistas of other lands and tribes.

Alcohol tells truth, but its truth is not normal. What
is normal is healthful. What is healthful tends toward life.
Normal truth is a different order, and a lesser order, of
truth. Take a dray horse. Through all the vicissitudes of
its life, from first to last, somehow, in unguessably dim
ways, it must believe that life is good; that the drudgery
in harness is good; that death, no matter how blind-
instinctively apprehended, is a dread giant; that life is
beneficent and worthwhile; that, in the end, with fading
life, it will not be knocked about and beaten and urged
beyond its sprained and spavined best; that old age, even,
is decent, dignified, and valuable, though old age means

a ribby scarecrow in a hawker's cart, stumbling a step to every blow, stumbling dizzily on through merciless servitude and slow disintegration to the end—the end, the apportionment of its parts (of its subtle flesh, its pink and springy bone, its juices and ferments, and all the sensateness that informed it), to the chicken farm, the hide-house, the glue-rendering works, and the bone-meal fertilizer factory. To the last stumble of its stumbling end this dray horse must abide by the mandates of the lesser truth that is the truth of life and that makes life possible to persist.

This dray horse, like all other horses, like all other animals including man, is life-blinded and sense-struck. It will live, no matter what the price. The game of life is good, though all of life may be hurt, and though all lives lose the game in the end. This is the order of truth that obtains, not for the universe, but for the live things in it if they for a little space will endure ere they pass. This order of truth, no matter how erroneous it may be, is the sane and normal order of truth, the rational order of truth that life must believe in order to live.

To man, alone among the animals, has been given the awful privilege of reason. Man, with his brain, can penetrate the intoxicating show of things and look upon a universe brazen with indifference toward him and his dreams. He can do this, but it is not well for him to do it. To live, and live abundantly, to sting with life, to be alive (which is to be what he is), it is good that man be life-blinded and sense-struck. What is good is true. And this is the order of truth, lesser though it be, that man must know and guide his actions by, with unswerving certitude that it is absolute truth and that in the universe no other order of truth can obtain. It is good that man should accept at face value the cheats of sense and snares of flesh, and through the fogs of sentiency pursue the lures and lies of passion. It is good that he shall see neither shadows nor futilities, nor be appalled by his lusts and rapacities.

And man does this. Countless men have glimpsed that other and truer order of truth and recoiled from it. Countless men have passed through the long sickness and lived to tell of it and deliberately to forget it to the end of their days. They lived. They realized life, for life is what they were. They did right.

And now comes John Barleycorn with the curse he lays upon the imaginative man who is lusty with life and desire to live. John Barleycorn sends his White Logic, the argent messenger of truth beyond truth, the antithesis of life, cruel and bleak as interstellar space, pulseless and frozen as absolute zero, dazzling with the frost of irrefragable logic and unforgettable fact. John Barleycorn will not let the dreamer dream, the liver live. He destroys birth and death, and dissipates to mist the paradox of being, until his victim cries out, as in 'The City of Dreadful Night':* 'Our life's a cheat, our death a black abyss.' And the feet of the victim of such dreadful intimacy take hold of the way of death.

CHAPTER XXXVI

BACK to personal experiences and the effects in the past of John Barleycorn's White Logic on me. On my lovely ranch in the Valley of the Moon, brain-soaked with many months of alcohol, I am oppressed by the cosmic sadness that has always been the heritage of man. In vain do I ask myself why I should be sad. My nights are warm. My roof does not leak. I have food galore for all the caprices of appetite. Every creature-comfort is mine. In my body are no aches nor pains. The good old flesh-machine is running smoothly on. Neither brain nor muscle is overworked. I have land, money, power, recognition from the world, a consciousness that I do my meed of good in serving others, a mate whom I love, children that are of my own fond flesh. I have done, and am doing, what a good citizen of the world should do. I have built houses, many houses, and tilled many a hundred acres. And as for trees, have I not planted a hundred thousand?* Everywhere, from any window of my house, I can gaze forth upon these trees of my planting, standing valiantly erect and aspiring toward the sun.

My life has indeed fallen in pleasant places. Not a hundred men in a million have been so lucky as I. Yet, with all this vast good fortune, am I sad. And I am sad because John Barleycorn is with me. And John Barleycorn is with me because I was born in what future ages will call the dark ages before the ages of rational civilization. John Barleycorn is with me because in all the unwitting days of my youth John Barleycorn was accessible, calling to me and inviting me on every corner and on every street between the corners. The pseudo-civilization into which I was born permitted everywhere licensed shops for the sale of soul-poison. The system of life was so organized that I (and millions like me) was lured and drawn and driven to the poison shops.

Wander with me through one mood of the myriad of moods of sadness into which one is plunged by John Barleycorn. I ride out over my beautiful ranch. Between my legs is a beautiful horse. The air is wine. The grapes on a score of rolling hills are red with autumn flame. Across Sonoma Mountain wisps of sea fog are stealing. The afternoon sun smoulders in the drowsy sky. I have everything to make me glad I am alive. I am filled with dreams and mysteries. I am all sun and air and sparkle. I am vitalized, organic. I move, I have the power of movement, I command movement of the live thing I bestride. I am possessed with the pomps of being, and know proud passions and inspirations. I have ten thousand august connotations. I am a king in the kingdom of sense, and trample the face of the uncomplaining dust.

And yet, with jaundiced eye I gaze upon all the beauty and wonder about me, and with jaundiced brain consider the pitiful figure I cut in this world that endured so long without me and that will again endure without me. I remember the men who broke their hearts and their backs over this stubborn soil that now belongs to me. As if anything imperishable could belong to the perishable! These men passed. I, too, shall pass. These men toiled, and cleared, and planted, gazed with aching eyes, while they rested their labor-stiffened bodies, on these same sunrises and sunsets, at the autumn glory of the grape, and at the fog-wisps stealing across the mountain. And they are gone. And I know that I, too, shall some day, and soon, be gone.

Gone? I am going now. In my jaw are cunning artifices of the dentists* which replace the parts of me already gone. Never again will I have the thumbs of my youth. Old fights and wrestlings have injured them irreparably. That punch on the head of a man whose very name is forgotten, settled this thumb finally and forever. A slip-grip at catch-as-catch-can did for the other. My lean runner's stomach has passed into the limbo of memory. The joints of the legs that bear me up are not so adequate as they once were, when, in wild nights and days of toil and frolic, I strained and snapped and ruptured them. Never again can I swing dizzily aloft and trust all the proud quick that is I to a single rope-clutch in the driving blackness of storm. Never again can I run with the sled-dogs along the endless miles of Arctic trail.

I am aware that within this disintegrating body which has been dying since I was born I carry a skeleton; that under the rind of flesh which is called my face is a bony, noseless death's head. All of which does not shudder me. To be afraid is to be healthy. Fear of death makes for life. But the curse of the White Logic is that it does not make one afraid. The world-sickness of the White Logic makes one grin jocosely into the face of the Noseless One and to sneer at all the phantasmagoria of living.

I look about me as I ride, and on every hand I see the merciless and infinite waste of natural selection. The White Logic insists upon opening the long-closed books, and by paragraph and chapter states the beauty and wonder I behold in terms of futility and dust. About me is murmur and hum, and I know it for the gnat-swarm of the living, piping for a little space its thin plaint of troubled air.

I return across the ranch. Twilight is on, and the hunting-animals are out. I watch the piteous tragic play of life feeding on life. Here is no morality. Only in man is morality, and man created it—a code of action that makes toward living and that is of the lesser order of truth. Yet all this I knew before, in the weary days of my long sickness. These were the greater truths that I so successfully schooled myself to forget; the truths that were so serious that I refused to take them seriously, and played with gently, O so gently, as sleeping dogs at the back of consciousness which I did not care to waken. I did but stir them, and let them lie. I was too wise, too wicked wise, to wake them. But now White Logic willy nilly wakes them for me, for White Logic, most valiant, is unafraid of all the monsters of the earthy dream.

'Let the doctors of all the schools condemn me,' White Logic whispers as I ride along. 'What of it? I am truth. You know it. You cannot combat me. They say I make for death. What of it? It is truth. Life lies in order to live. Life is a perpetual lie-telling process. Life is a mad dance in the domain of flux, wherein appearances in mighty tides ebb and flow, chained to the wheels of moons beyond our ken. Appearances are ghosts. Life is ghost land, where appearances change, transfuse, permeate each the other and all the others, that are, that are not, that always flicker, fade, and pass, only to come again as new appearances, as other appearances. You are such an appearance, composed of countless appearances out of the past. All an appearance can know is mirage. You know mirages of desire. These very mirages are the unthinkable and incalculable congeries of appearances that crowd in upon you and form you out of the past, and that sweep you on to dissemination into other unthinkable and incalculable congeries of appearances to people the ghost land of the future. Life is apparitional, and passes. You are an apparition. Through all the apparitions that preceded you and that compose the parts of you, you rose gibbering from the evolutionary mire, and gibbering you will pass on, interfusing, permeating the procession of apparitions that will succeed you.'

And of course it is all unanswerable, and as I ride along through the evening shadows I sneer at that Great Fetish which Compte called the world.* And I remember what another pessimist of sentiency has uttered: 'Transient are

all. They, being born, must die; and, being dead, are glad
to be at rest.'

But here through the dusk comes one who is not glad
to be at rest. He is a workman on the ranch, an old man,
an immigrant Italian.* He takes his hat off to me in all
servility, because, forsooth, I am to him a lord of life. I am
food to him, and shelter, and existence. He has toiled like
a beast all his days, and lived less comfortably than my
horses in their deep-strawed stalls. He is labor-crippled. He
shambles as he walks. One shoulder is twisted higher than
the other. His hands are gnarled claws, repulsive, horrible.
As an apparition he is a pretty miserable specimen. His
brain is as stupid as his body is ugly.

'His brain is so stupid that he does not know he is
an apparition,' the White Logic chuckles to me. 'He is
sense-drunk. He is the slave of the dream of life. His brain
is filled with superrational sanctions and obsessions. He
has listened to the vagaries of the prophets, who have
blown for him the sumptuous bubble of Paradise. He feels
inarticulate affinities with self-conjured non-realities. He
sees penumbral visions of himself titubating fantastically
through days and nights of space and stars. Beyond the
shadow of any doubt he is convinced that the universe was
made for him, and that it is his destiny to live forever in
the immaterial and supersensuous realms he and his kind
have builded of the stuff of semblance and deception.

'But you, who have opened the books and who share
my awful confidence—you know him for what he is,
brother to you and the dust, a cosmic joke, a sport
of chemistry, a garmented beast that arose out of the
ruck of screaming beastliness by virtue and accident of
two opposable great toes. He is brother as well to the
gorilla and the chimpanzee. He thumps his chest in anger,
and roars and quivers with cataleptic ferocity. He knows
monstrous, atavistic promptings, and he is composed of
all manner of shreds of abysmal and forgotten instincts.'

'Yet he dreams he is immortal,' I agree feebly. 'It is vastly wonderful for so stupid a clod to bestride the shoulders of time and ride the eternities.'

'Pah!' is the retort. 'Would you then shut the books and exchange places with this thing that is only an appetite and a desire, a marionette of the belly and the lions?'

'To be stupid is to be happy,' I contend.

'Then your ideal of happiness is a jelly-like organism floating in a tideless, tepid, twilight sea, eh?'

—Oh, the victim cannot combat John Barleycorn!

'One step removed from the annihilating bliss of Buddha's Nirvana,' the White Logic adds. 'Oh, well, here's the house. Cheer up and take a drink. We know, we illuminated, you and I, all the folly and the farce.'

And in my book-walled den, the mausoleum of the thoughts of men, I take my drink, and other drinks, and roust out the sleeping dogs from the recesses of my brain and halloo them on over the walls of prejudice and law and through all the cunning labyrinths of superstition and belief.

'Drink,' says the White Logic. 'The Greeks believed that the gods gave them wine so that they might forget the miserableness of existence. And remember what Heine said.'

Well do I remember that flaming Jew's 'With the last breath all is done: joy, love, sorrow, macaroni, the theater, lime-trees, raspberry drops, the power of human relations, gossip, the barking of dogs, champagne.'*

'Your clear white light is sickness,' I tell the White Logic. 'You lie.'

'By telling too strong a truth,' he quips back.

'Alas, yes, so topsyturvy is existence,' I acknowledge sadly.

'Ah, well, Liu Ling* was wiser than you,' the White Logic girds. 'You remember him?'

I nod my head—Liu Ling, a hard drinker, one of the

group of bibulous poets who called themselves the Seven
Sages of the Bamboo Grove and who lived in China many
an ancient century ago.

'It was Liu Ling,' prompts the White Logic, 'who
declared that to a drunken man the affairs of this world
appear but as so much duckweed on a river. Very well.
Have another Scotch, and let semblance and deception
become duckweed on a river.'

And while I pour and sip my Scotch, I remember
another Chinese philosopher, Chuang Tzu,* who, four
centuries before Christ, challenged this dreamland of the
world, saying: 'How then do I know but that the dead
repent of having previously clung to life? Those who
dream of the banquet, wake to lamentation and sorrow.
Those who dream of lamentation and sorrow, wake to join
the hunt. While they dream, they do not know that they
dream. Some will even interpret the very dream they are
dreaming; and only when they awake do they know it
was a dream. . . . Fools think they are awake now, and
flatter themselves they know if they are really princes or
peasants. Confucius and you are both dreams; and I who
say you are dreams—I am but a dream myself.

'Once upon a time, I, Chuang Tzu, dreamt I was a
butterfly, fluttering hither and thither, to all intents and
purposes a butterfly. I was conscious only of following
my fancies as a butterfly, and was unconscious of my
individuality as a man. Suddenly, I awaked, and there I
lay, myself again. Now I do not know whether I was then
a man dreaming I was a butterfly, or whether I am now a
butterfly dreaming I am a man.'

CHAPTER XXXVII

'COME,' says the White Logic, 'and forget these Asian dreamers of old time. Fill your glass and let us look at the parchments of the dreamers of yesterday who dreamed their dreams on your own warm hills.'

I pore over the abstract of title of the vineyard called Tokay* on the rancho called Petaluma. It is a sad long list of the names of men, beginning with Manuel Micheltoreno, one time Mexican 'Governor, Commander-in-Chief, and Inspector of the Department of the Californias,' who deeded ten square leagues of stolen Indian land to Colonel Don Mariano Guadalupe Vallejo for services rendered his country and for moneys paid by him for ten years to his soldiers.

Immediately this musty record of man's land-lust assumes the formidableness of a battle—the quick struggling with the dust. There are deeds of trust, mortgages, certificates of release, transfers, judgments, foreclosures, writs of attachment, orders of sale, tax liens, petitions for letters of administration, and decrees of distribution. It is like a monster ever unsubdued, this stubborn land that drowses in this Indian summer weather and that survives them all, the men who scratched its surface and passed.

Who was this James King of William, so curiously named?* The oldest surviving settler in the Valley of the Moon knows him not. Yet only sixty years ago he loaned Mariano G. Vallejo eighteen thousand dollars on security of certain lands including the vineyard yet to be and to be called Tokay. Whence came Peter O'Connor, and whither vanished, after writing his little name of a day on the woodland that was to become a vineyard? Appears Louis Csomortanyi, a name to conjure with. He lasts through several pages of this record of the enduring soil.

Comes old American stock, thirsting across the Great American Desert, mule-backing across the Isthmus, wind-jamming around the Horn, to write brief and forgotten names where ten thousand generations of wild Indians are equally forgotten—names like Halleck, Hastings, Swett, Tait, Denman, Tracy, Grimwood, Carlton, Temple. There are no names like those to-day in the Valley of the Moon.

The names begin to appear fast and furiously, flashing from legal page to legal page and in a flash vanishing. But ever the persistent soil remains for others to scrawl themselves across. Come the names of men of whom I have vaguely heard but whom I have never known. Kohler and Frohling—who built the great stone winery on the vineyard called Tokay, but who built upon a hill up which other vinyardists refused to haul their grapes. So Kohler and Frohling lost the land; the earthquake of 1906 threw down the winery; and I now live in its ruins.

La Motte—he broke the soil, planted vines and orchards, instituted commercial fish-culture, built a mansion renowned in its day, was defeated by the soil, and passed. And my name of a day appears. On the site of his orchards and vineyards, of his proud mansion, of his very fish ponds, I have scrawled myself with a hundred thousand eucalyptus trees.

Cooper and Greenlaw—on what is called the Hill Ranch they left two of their dead, 'Little Lillie' and 'Little David', who rest to-day inside a tiny square of hand-hewn palings. Also, Cooper and Greenlaw in their time cleared the virgin forest from three fields of forty acres. Today I have those three fields sown with Canada peas, and in the spring they shall be plowed under for green manure.

Haska—a dim legendary figure of a generation ago, who went back up the mountain and cleared six acres of brush in the tiny valley that took his name. He broke the soil, reared stone walls and a house, and planted apple trees. And already the site of the house is undiscoverable, the location of the stone walls may be deduced from the configuration of the landscape, and I am renewing the battle, putting in Angora goats to browse away the brush that has overrun Haska's clearing and choked Haska's apple trees to death. So I, too, scratch the land with my brief endeavor and flash my name across a page of legal script ere I pass and the page grows musty.

'Dreamers and ghosts,' the White Logic chuckles.

'But surely the striving was not altogether vain,' I contend.

'It was based on illusion and is a lie.'

'A vital lie,' I retort.

'And pray what is a vital lie but a lie?' the White Logic challenges. 'Come. Fill your glass and let us examine these vital liars who crowd your bookshelves. Let us dabble in William James* a bit.'

'A man of health,' I say. 'From him we may expect no philosopher's stone, but at least we shall find a few robust tonic things to which to tie.'

'Rationality gelded to sentiment,' the White Logic grins. 'At the end of all his thinking he still clung to the sentiment of immortality. Facts transmuted in the alembic of hope into terms of faith. The ripest fruit of reason the stultification of reason. From the topmost peak of reason James teaches to cease reasoning and to have faith that all is well and will be well—the old, oh, ancient old, acrobatic flip of the metaphysicians whereby they reasoned reason quite away in order to escape the pessimism consequent upon the grim and honest exercise of reason.

'Is this flesh of yours you? Or is it an extraneous something possessed by you? Your body—what is it? A machine for converting stimuli into reactions. Stimuli and reactions are remembered. They constitute experience. Then you are in your consciousness these experiences. You are at any moment what you are thinking at that moment. Your I is both subject and object; it predicates things of itself and is the things predicated. The thinker is the thought, the knower is what is known, the possessor is the things possessed.

'After all, as you know well, man is a flux of states of consciousness, a flow of passing thoughts, each thought of self another self, a myriad thoughts, a myriad selves, a continual becoming but never being, a will-of-the-wisp flitting of ghosts in ghostland. But this, man will not accept of himself. He refuses to accept his own passing. He will not pass. He will live again if he has to die to do it.

'He shuffles atoms and jets of light, remotest nebulae, drips of water, prick-points of sensation, slime-oozings and cosmic bulks, all mixed with pearls of faith, love of woman, imagined dignities, frightened surmises, and pompous arrogances, and of the stuff builds himself an immortality to startle the heavens and baffle the immensities. He squirms on his dunghill, and like a child lost in the dark among goblins, calls to the gods that he is their younger brother, a prisoner of the quick that is destined to be as free as they—monuments of egotism reared by the epiphenomena; dreams and the dust of dreams, that vanish when the dreamer vanishes and are no more when he is not.

'It is nothing new, these vital lies men tell themselves, muttering and mumbling them like charms and incantations against the powers of Night. The voodoos and medicine men and the devil-devil doctors were the fathers of metaphysics. Night and the Noseless One were ogres that beset the way of light and life. And the metaphysicians would win by if they had to tell lies to do it. They were vexed by the brazen law of the Ecclesiast that men die like the beasts of the field and their end is the same. Their creeds were their schemes, their religions their nostrums, their philosophies their devices, by which they half-believed they would outwit the Noseless One and the Night.

'Bog-lights, vapors of mysticism, psychic overtones, soul orgies, wailings among the shadows, weird gnosticisms, veils and tissues of words, gibbering subjectivisms, gropings and maunderings, ontological fantasies, pan-psychic hallucinations—this is the stuff, the phantasms of hope, that fills your book shelves. Look at them, all the sad wraiths of sad mad men and passionate rebels—your Schopenhauers, your Strindbergs, your Tolstois and Nietzsches.*

'Come. Your glass is empty. Fill and forget.'

I obey, for my brain is now well a-crawl with the maggots of alcohol, and as I drink to the sad thinkers on my shelves I quote Richard Hovey:*

> 'Abstain not! Life and Love, like night and day,
>   Offer themselves to us on their own terms,
>   Not ours. Accept their bounty while ye may,
>   Before we be accepted by the worms.'

'I will cap you,' cries the White Logic.

'No,' I answer, while the maggots madden me. 'I know you for what you are, and I am unafraid. Under your mask of hedonism you are yourself the Noseless One and your way leads to the Night. Hedonism has no meaning. It, too, is a lie, at best the coward's smug compromise—'

'Now will I cap you!' the White Logic breaks in.

> 'But if you would not this poor life fulfil,
>   Lo, you are free to end it when you will,
>   Without the fear of waking after death.'

And I laugh my defiance; for now, and for the moment, I know the White Logic to be the arch-impostor of them all, whispering his whispers of death. And he is guilty of his own unmasking, with his own genial chemistry turning the tables on himself, with his own maggots biting alive the old illusions, resurrecting and making to sound again the old voice from beyond of my youth, telling me again that still are mine the possibilities and powers which life and the books had taught me did not exist.

And the dinner-gong sounds to the reversed bottom of my glass. Jeering at the White Logic, I go out to join my guests at table, and with assumed seriousness to discuss the current magazines and the silly doings of the world's day, whipping every trick and ruse of controversy through all the paces of paradox and persiflage. And, when the whim changes, it is most easy and delightfully disconcerting to play with the respectable and cowardly bourgeois fetishes and to laugh and epigram at the flitting god-ghosts and the debaucheries and follies of wisdom.

The clown's the thing! The clown! If one must be a philosopher, let him be Aristophanes. And no one at the table thinks I am jingled. I am in fine fettle, that is all. I tire of the labor of thinking, and, when the table is finished, start practical jokes and set all playing at games, which we carry on with bucolic boisterousness.

And when the evening is over and good night said, I go back through my book-walled den to my sleeping porch and to myself and to the White Logic which, undefeated, has never left me. And as I fall to fuddled sleep I hear Youth crying, as Harry Kemp* heard it:

'I heard Youth calling in the night:
"Gone is my former world-delight;
For there is naught my feet may stay;
The morn suffuses into day,
It dare not stand a moment still
But must the world with light fulfil.
More evanescent than the rose
My sudden rainbow comes and goes
Plunging bright ends across the sky—
Yea, I am Youth because I die!"'

CHAPTER XXXVIII

THE foregoing is a sample roaming with the White Logic through the dusk of my soul. To the best of my power I have striven to give the reader a glimpse of a man's secret dwelling when it is shared with John Barleycorn. And the reader must remember that this mood, which he has read in a quarter of an hour, is but one mood of the myriad moods of John Barleycorn, and that the procession of such moods may well last the clock around through many a day and week and month.

My alcoholic reminiscences draw to a close. I can say, as any strong, chesty drinker can say, that all that leaves me alive to-day on the planet is my unmerited luck—the luck of chest, and shoulders, and constitution. I dare to say that a not large percentage of youths, in the formative stage of fifteen to seventeen, could have survived the stress of heavy drinking that I survived between my fifteenth and seventeenth years; that a not large percentage of men could have punished the alcohol I have punished in my manhood years and lived to tell the tale. I survived, through no personal virtue, but because I did not have the chemistry of a dipsomaniac and because I possessed an organism unusually resistant to the ravages of John Barleycorn. And, surviving, I have watched the others die, not so lucky, down all the long sad road.

It was my unmitigated and absolute good fortune, good luck, chance, call it what you will, that brought me through the fires of John Barleycorn. My life, my career, my joy in living, have not been destroyed. They have been scorched, it is true; but, like the survivors of forlorn hopes, they have by unthinkably miraculous ways come through the fight to marvel at the tally of the slain.

And like such a survivor of old red War who cries out,

'Let there be no more war!' so I cry out, 'Let there be no more poison-fighting by our youths!' The way to stop war is to stop it. The way to stop drinking is to stop it. The way China stopped the general use of opium was by stopping the cultivation and importation of opium.* The philosophers, priests, and doctors of China could have preached themselves breathless against opium for a thousand years, and the use of opium, so long as opium was ever-accessible and obtainable, would have continued unabated. We are so made, that is all. We have with great success made a practice of not leaving arsenic and strychnine, and typhoid and tuberculosis germs, lying around for our children to be destroyed by. Treat John Barleycorn the same way. Stop him. Don't let him lie around, licensed and legal, to pounce upon our youth. Not of alcoholics nor for alcoholics do I write, but for our youths, for those who possess no more than the adventure-stings and the genial predispositions, the social man-impulses, which are twisted all awry by our barbarian civilization which feeds them poison on all the corners. It is the healthy, normal boys, now born or being born, for whom I write.

It was for this reason, more than any other, and more ardently than any other, that I rode down into the Valley of the Moon, all a-jingle, and voted for equal suffrage. I voted that women might vote, because I knew that they, the wives and mothers of the race, would vote John Barleycorn out of existence and back into the historical limbo of our vanished customs of savagery. If I thus seem to cry out as one hurt, please remember that I have been sorely bruised and that I do dislike the thought that any son or daughter of mine or yours should be similarly bruised.

The women are the true conservators of the race. The men are the wastrels, the adventure-lovers and gamblers, and in the end it is by their women that they are saved.

About man's first experiment in chemistry was the making of alcohol, and down all the generations to this day man has continued to manufacture and drink it. And there has never been a day when the women have not resented man's use of alcohol, though they have never had the power to give weight to their resentment. The moment women get the vote in any community, the first thing they proceed to do, or try to do, is to close the saloons. In a thousand generations to come men of themselves will not close the saloons. As well expect the morphine victims to legislate the sale of morphine out of existence.

The women know. They have paid an incalculable price of sweat and tears for man's use of alcohol. Ever jealous for the race, they will legislate for the babes of boys yet to be born; and for the babes of girls, too, for they must be the mothers, wives, and sisters of these boys.

And it will be easy. The only ones that will be hurt will be the topers and seasoned drinkers of a single generation. I am one of these, and I make solemn assurance, based upon long traffic with John Barleycorn, that it won't hurt me very much to stop drinking when no one else drinks and when no drink is obtainable. On the other hand, the overwhelming proportion of young men are so normally non-alcoholic, that, never having had access to alcohol, they will never miss it. They will know of the saloon only in the pages of history, and they will think of the saloon as a quaint old custom similar to bull-baiting and the burning of witches.

CHAPTER XXXIX

OF course, no personal tale is complete without bringing the narrative of the person down to the last moment. But mine is no tale of a reformed drunkard. I was never a drunkard, and I have not reformed.

It chanced, some time ago, that I made a voyage of one hundred and forty-eight days in a windjammer around the Horn.* I took no private supply of alcohol along, and, though there was no day of those one hundred and forty-eight days that I could not have got a drink from the captain, I did not take a drink. I did not take a drink because I did not desire a drink. No one else drank on board. The atmosphere for drinking was not present, and in my system there was no organic need for alcohol. My chemistry did not demand alcohol.

So there arose before me a problem, a clear and simple problem: *This is so easy, why not keep it up when you get back on land?* I weighed this problem carefully. I weighed it for five months, in a state of absolute non-contact with alcohol. And out of the data of past experience, I reached certain conclusions.

In the first place, I am convinced that not one man in ten thousand, or in a hundred thousand, is a genuine, chemical dipsomaniac. Drinking, as I deem it, is practically entirely a habit of mind. It is unlike tobacco, or cocaine, or morphine, or all the rest of the long list of drugs. The desire for alcohol is quite peculiarly mental in its origin. It is a matter of mental training and growth, and it is cultivated in social soil. Not one drinker in a million began drinking alone. All drinkers begin socially, and this drinking is accompanied by a thousand social connotations such as I have described out of my own experience in the first part of this narrative. These social connotations are the stuff of which the drink habit is largely composed. The part that alcohol itself plays is inconsiderable, when compared with the part played by the social atmosphere in which it is drunk. The human is rarely born these days, who, without long training in the social relations of drinking, feels the irresistible chemical propulsion of his system toward alcohol. I do assume that such rare individuals are born, but I have never encountered one.

On this long, five-months' voyage, I found that among all my bodily needs not the slightest shred of a bodily need for alcohol existed. But this I did find: my need was mental and social. When I thought of alcohol, the connotation was fellowship. When I thought of fellowship, the connotation was alcohol. Fellowship and alcohol were Siamese twins. They always occurred linked together.

Thus, when reading in my deck-chair or when talking with others, practically any mention of any part of the world I knew instantly aroused the connotation of drinking and good fellows. Big nights and days and moments, all purple passages and freedoms, thronged my memory. 'Venice' stares at me from the printed page, and I remember the café tables on the sidewalks. 'The Battle of Santiago,'* some one says, and I answer, 'Yes, I've been over the ground.' But I do not see the ground, nor Kettle Hill, nor the Peace Tree. What I see is the Café Venus, on the plaza of Santiago, where one hot night I talked long and drank deep with a dying consumptive.

The East End of London,* I read, or some one says; and first of all, under my eyelids, leap the visions of the shining pubs, and in my ears echo the calls for 'two of bitter' and 'three of Scotch'. The Latin Quarter—at once I am in the student cabarets, bright faces and keen spirits around me, sipping cool, well-dripped absinthe while our voices mount and soar in Latin fashion as we settle God and art and democracy and the rest of the simple problems of existence.

In a pampero off the River Plate, we speculate, if we are disabled, of running in to Buenos Ayres, the 'Paris of America', and I have visions of bright congregating-places of men, of the jollity of raised glasses, and of song and cheer and the hum of genial voices. When we have picked up the Northeast Trades in the Pacific, we try to persuade our dying captain to run for Honolulu,* and while I persuade I see myself again drinking cocktails on the cool *lanais*, and fizzes out at Waikiki where the surf rolls in. Some one mentions the way wild ducks are cooked in the restaurants of San Francisco, and at once I am transported to the light and clatter of many tables, where I gaze at old friends across the golden brims of long-stemmed Rhine-wine glasses.

And so I pondered my problem. I should not care to revisit all these fair places of the world except in the fashion I visited them before. *Glass in hand!* There is a magic in the phrase. It means more than all the words in the dictionary can be made to mean. It is a habit of mind to which I have been trained all my life. It is now part of the stuff that composes me. I like the bubbling play of wit, the chesty laughs, the resonant voices of men, when, glass in hand, they shut the gray world outside and prod their brains with the fun and folly of an accelerated pulse.

No, I decided; I shall take my drink on occasion.* With all the books on my shelves, with all the thoughts of the thinkers shaded by my particular temperament, I decided coolly and deliberately that I should continue to do what I had been trained to want to do. I would drink—but, oh, more skilfully, more discreetly, than ever before. Never again would I be a peripatetic conflagration. Never again would I invoke the White Logic. I had learned how not to invoke him.

The White Logic now lies decently buried alongside the Long Sickness. Neither will afflict me again. It is many a year since I laid the Long Sickness away; his sleep is sound.

And just as sound is the sleep of the White Logic. And yet, in conclusion, I can well say that I wish my forefathers had banished John Barleycorn before my time. I regret that John Barleycorn flourished everywhere in the system of society in which I was born, else I should not have made his acquaintance, and I was long trained in his acquaintance.*

THE END

EXPLANATORY NOTES

In these 'Alcoholic Memoirs' London concentrates on moments in his past which peculiarly mark and chart his drinking career. Consequently, the actual narrative of the author's life in *John Barleycorn* is patchy. These notes aim principally to fill in the biographical blanks. I have used four main sources: *The Letters of Jack London* (1988), edited by Earle Labor, Robert C. Leitz III, and I. Milo Shepard; Andrew Sinclair's *Jack* (1977); Richard O'Connor's *Jack London* (1964); Robert Barltrop's *Jack London, the Man, the Writer, the Rebel* (1976). For London's Yukon escapade in 1897 Franklin Walker's extraordinarily detailed *Jack London and the Klondike* (1966) is invaluable as in its different way is David Mike Hamilton's study of the annotated books in London's Library, *The Tools of my Trade* (1987).

1 *JOHN BARLEYCORN*: a traditional personification of malt liquor (whisky being Jack London's favourite tipple). The phrase was popularized by the heavy-drinking poet, Robert Burns, in *Tam O'Shanter*, 'Inspiring bold John Barleycorn—What dangers thou canst make us scorn'.

the Valley of the Moon: the Sonoma Valley, i.e. the area in the foothills of northern California in the environs of Glen Ellen ('the little village') in which London lived and worked during the last years of his life. Santa Rosa is the nearest large town. In 1960 the Jack London State Historical Park was established on the site of the author's Beauty Ranch. London himself is buried on a knoll looking down on the Valley of the Moon. The area grows some of the best wine grapes in the United States. In 1912–13, London was at pains to project an idyllic public picture of his life on his ranch. Thus a profile of him in the *Writer's Magazine* Aug. 1913, by Sue McNamara concluded: 'In this "Valley of the Moon" as the name Sonoma signifies, the great writer seems to have found his real happiness. His life is one of comradeship with nature and humanity, in his keen blue eyes is the light of perfect content. No matter how far he may roam, Jack London is always glad to come back to this peaceful valley where the cow bells tinkle and the giant redwoods whisper softly to the mountain.'

the Constitution of the State of California: the date is 10 Oct. 1911. The Progressive wing of the Republican Party (principally the Lincoln–Roosevelt League) succeeded in getting passed a wide-ranging set of twenty-two amendments to the state constitution, including one which enabled women to vote. It was the sixth state to do so. Like most thinking Californians, London saw October 1911 as the dawn of a new era of enlightenment in the State.

Charmian: i.e. Charmian London, *née* Kittredge. On the divorce from his first wife, Bessie (*née* Maddern) becoming final in November 1905, London married Charmian and a little later moved with her to Glen Ellen where he intended to live an idealized agrarian existence.

my ardent democracy: London was, as he often proclaimed, a Socialist (see chapter 28 for the psychological roots of London's political idealism). He resigned from the Party in March 1916, ostensibly 'because of its lack of fire and fight and its loss of emphasis on the class struggle'. For London's highly idiosyncratic theory of socialism—as hybridized with his Darwinistic 'individualism' and his unbridled personal capitalism— see his essay *Revolution* (1908). In it he presents the 'caveman' as the highest type of socialist.

3 *Canoe houses from which she had been barred in the*

South Pacific: from April 1907 to November 1908, the Londons had voyaged the South Seas in their 45-foot yacht, the *Snark*. This episode evidently occurred in the Solomon Islands in June 1908.

4 *vital lies*: the phrase comes from Vernon Lee's (i.e. Violet Paget's), book of that name, published in 1912 (see notes to chapter 37.) The book was in London's personal library and he evidently took it with him on the *Dirigo* cruise during which *John Barleycorn* was planned. In the Huntington archive there is a page of notes for an unwritten novel, to be called *The Vital Liars*.

6 *dipsomaniac*: an obsolete nineteenth-century medical term for a condition defined as 'a morbid and insatiable craving, often paroxysmal, for alcohol'.

7 *soul-sickness*: the phrase comes from William James's *The Varieties of Religious Experience* (1902), Lectures VI and VII, 'The Sick Soul'. London read James's book while meditating the composition of *John Barleycorn*, on board the *Dirigo*, March–July 1912.

8 *a pessimistic German philosopher*: i.e. Arthur Schopenhauer (1788–1860), one of London's favourite philosophers.

9 *my father*: in fact, London's adoptive father, John London. Modern biographers agree that Jack was the son of 'Professor' William H. Chaney, 'a footloose astrologer', and of Chaney's common-law wife, Flora Wellman. The couple lived together in 1874–75, separating before Jack was born. Shortly before Jack's birth, Flora (who was highly strung) had reportedly attempted suicide twice. According to Russ Kingman, Chaney and Wellman went through a form of marriage in June 1874. Jack London did not definitely learn the rumour that he was Chaney's 'bastard' (as it was cruelly put) until much later, when he was a student at Berkeley in

1896. He wrote to Chaney asking confirmation, but the now 75-year-old astrologer disingenuously denied Jack's paternity, claiming that he had been impotent in 1875, when 'married' to Flora and that she had been a promiscuous sexual partner. On 7 Sept. 1876 (Jack was born on 12 Jan. 1876), Flora married John London, a widower older than her with two daughters. London assumed the role of the baby Jack's father. On his part, the son was clearly grateful for the respectability which his mother's husband gave him. Thus in writing a profile for his first publisher Houghton Mifflin in 1900, he began: 'My father was Pennsylvania-born, a soldier, scout, backwoodsman, trapper and wanderer.' In fact, John London was a less exciting man than this. A veteran of the Civil War, he drifted unsuccessfully through a number of trades and occupations. He was first a sewing-machine salesman, then in 1879 the co-owner of a grocer's store in West Oakland (Oakland is the town across the bay from San Francisco, then connected by ferry). In 1881, when Jack was 5, the store failed and John London leased a 20-acre 'ranch' in Alameda where London went to the West End School. This ranch provides the setting here for London's first encounter with Barleycorn.

12 *south of San Francisco*: in 1882 the Londons had moved again, down the peninsula to a 75-acre ranch somewhere between Pedro Point and Moss Beach on whose flat land John London could grow vegetables.

14 *my mother was a blond*: despite the tense, London's mother outlived him.

19 *who was never allowed to talk back*: in a number of places, London recollects the severity of his mother. Andrew Sinclair imaginatively pictures their loveless relationship in the first chapter of *Jack*: 'one of the reasons he often felt afraid was that his mother Flora

hardly ever touched him. She was always busy . . . She often complained of heart trouble; she pretended she was dying when she was thwarted. Usually angry and melancholy and preoccupied at the same time, she ruled the home through her hysteria' (p. 2).

21 *the saloon at Colma*: London went to school there for two years. His early education was disturbed by the family's frequent moves, and he claimed to have taught himself to read and write by the age of 5: 'I always could read and write, and have no recollection antedating such a condition' (see *Letters*, I:148).

Horace Fletcher had nothing on me when it came to soda crackers: Horace Fletcher (1849–1919), American nutritionist. Fletcher was an enthusiast for slow and deliberate mastication, chewing every mouthful 'until it swallowed itself'. To 'fletcherize' was a current verb.

23 *By the time I was ten years old . . . the city*: there seems to have been yet another family move in 1884 to a ranch back across the bay and inland, near Livermore. Here John London built some ambitious facilities for chickens, on whose success the family laid great store. In late 1885 or 1886 the chickens died in an epidemic, the bank foreclosed, and the family was again bankrupt. They returned to an eight-room home in Seventeenth Street, Oakland, which Flora seems to have run as a boarding house. For a while, she also ran two cottages, as accommodation for female California Cotton Mill workers brought over from Scotland. The enterprise failed when Flora could not keep up the mortgage payments. John (whose health was failing) returned to the grocery trade, and ended up as a night watchman on Davies wharf with an occasional daytime job swabbing decks for members of the yacht club. The family thereafter lived in a number of meaner houses, constantly persecuted by demanding landlords.

23 *we needed the money*: see O'Connor: 'He carried morning and evening newspaper routes before and after school, getting up while it was still dark to deliver the morning papers. Saturdays he worked as an iceman's apprentice, and Sundays he set up pins in a bowling alley' (p. 41). All these endeavours brought in about $20 a month which he turned over to Flora to supplement John London's meagre Civil War pension. As he recalled, London was frequently hungry at this time of his life (particularly for meat, which he tells us he craved). In a letter ten years later to his first sweetheart Mabel Applegarth, London recalled: 'Duty!—at ten years I was on the street selling newspapers . . . Duty—from then on I had no childhood' (*Letters* I:24).

the free public library: London testified in a letter of 11 Dec. 1914 how important this institution had been to his early intellectual development: 'The second wonderful thing happened to me when, nine or ten years of age, my people were compelled to leave their mortgaged ranch and come to the City of Oakland to live. There I found access to the great world by means of the free public library of the City of Oakland. At that time Ina Coolbrith was the librarian of the Oakland Free Library. It was this world of books, now accessible, that practically gave me the basis of my education' (*Letters* III:1392). Ina Coolbrith was a remarkably cultivated woman, a literary editor and poet, who influenced London strongly at this formative stage of his life. The earliest surviving acquisition in London's personal library is Barrett Wendell's *English Composition*, a book which he evidently forgot to return to the library, around 1893.

the life of Garfield: Horatio Alger's *From Canal Boy to President, Or The Boyhood of James A. Garfield* (1881), written in the author's familiar 'from log cabin

to White House' style. The Alger genre of American
success biography had a clear influence on London's
mythmaking about his own past.

Paul du Chaillu's African travels: Paul Belloni du
Chaillu's *Explorations and Adventures in Equatorial
Africa* (1861). London had other volumes by the author
in his personal library.

a novel by Ouida with the last forty pages missing: *Signa*
(1875). Later, London recalled: 'I never knew the finish
until I grew up, for the closing chapters were missing
from my copy, so I kept on dreaming with the hero,
and like him, unable to see Nemesis at the end.' London
credited this novel, which he first read aged 8, as having
been a major literary influence on him (see *Letters*
I:148, III:1392). It is the story of an illegitimate son
of an Italian peasant girl and an artist who eventually
becomes a great composer. The romantic similarity to
London's own childhood situation may be significant.
Jack began reading *Signa* aloud to Charmian, on board
the *Dirigo* on 18 Mar. 1912, some two weeks after
leaving port.

Irving's 'Alhambra': the book of Spanish (more particularly Granada) sketches published by Washington
Irving in 1832, and enlarged in 1852. Andrew Sinclair
adds some details: 'Jack built in the dust of the ranch
a miniature Moorish palace from fallen chimney bricks
and plaster and beads, and he wept all the way home
from school when he returned his copy of Alhambra and
was not given another book to replace it' (p. 6).

the Adventures of Peregrine Pickle: published by Tobias
Smollett in 1751. Smollett's robust fiction was routinely
bowdlerised in the nineteenth century. Presumably the
author's nautical *Roderick Random* (1748) would have
been more to the juvenile London taste.

25 *steam beer*: cheap, effervescent beer. The phrase is

evidently peculiar to the West Coast of America. The beverage had its origins in gold-rush era San Francisco. Made without ice the beer was noted for its great 'head'.

27 *When I was fourteen . . . a small centerboard skiff*: see O'Connor for the intervening family history: 'At thirteen he graduated from grade school [i.e. Cole Grammar School] and his parents decided that instead of attending high school he would have to find work to supplement John London's inadequate income. He swept out the saloons at two of the local parks after busy Sundays, sold papers, hustled around after odd jobs of all kinds . . . No landlord would trust the Londons, and young Jack couldn't bring in enough money for both rent and food. So they lived for months in a shack near the estuary [i.e. on Pine Street. Franklin Walker more accurately calls it 'a neat little cottage near the railroad shops on the Point', p. 18]' (p. 42). The 14-foot, decked-over skiff which he mentions here was his second boat, his first being a battered old rowing boat ('just big enough for himself and Rollo his dog') which he bought for $2 when he was twelve or thirteen. This second vessel cost him $6.

29 *running the Easting down*: sailors' jargon for heading in an easterly direction.

36 *I was barely turned fifteen and working long hours in a cannery*: by 1891, John London was crippled and unable to provide for his family. Jack had to give up his sailing to become the family breadwinner, working in Hickmott's cannery near the estuary for 10 cents an hour. Some months, by working incredible amounts of overtime, Jack contrived to earn as much as $50. After a summer and autumn (some accounts say 'a year') of this toil, London had had enough of servitude. The final straw seems to have been his mother coming to his workplace to demand the $5 he had saved for

a new skiff. 'I could have killed myself that night', London later wrote. Instead he threw the cannery job in. London's emotional conflict is recalled in his fine short story, 'The Apostate' (1906).

37 *my Mammy Jennie*: Mrs Virginia Prentiss, his former wet nurse. Andrew Sinclair sees her as having played a crucial part in Jack's very early emotional development ('She had brought him up through his babyhood when his mother had neglected him'.) On this occasion Mrs Prentiss loaned Jack $300 in twenty-dollar goldpieces (some commentators have doubted the truth of this large amount). Prentiss was a former slave and the wife of a white man.

39 *A sugar bark towed from the 'boneyard' to sea*: on the Carquinez Straits there was (and is) a huge sugar refinery which provided the main occupation for the 2,000-strong community of Crockett. The refinery handled sugar cane imported from Hawaii, then trans-shipped across the United States. The 'boneyard' is the dump for discarded vessels.

40 *an oyster pirate*: Barltrop comments: 'Oyster piracy had been established for some time in San Francisco Bay. Californian oysters were despised until, after the building of the transcontinental railroad, seed and yearlings of the prized Atlantic varieties were transplanted to the mud flats of the Bay. The railroads [principally the hated Southern Pacific—the 'Octopus'] themselves took over the beds and sold them at high prices; by 1890, one or two companies controlled the industry. Piracy was a natural outcome' (p. 23). The beds were protected by board fences. The poachers moved in at night in shallow-bottomed boats, waited until low tide, scooped the oysters into sacks, and sailed away on the rising tide. Fog was particularly helpful to them. Oyster pirates could earn up to $50 a night and given the

universal detestation of the railroad companies there was some sympathy for their activities; but the risks were high, both from treacherous comrades and from the authorities. If caught, poaching from the company's beds was a felony, punishable by a spell in State Prison.

41 *Johnny Heinhold's 'Last Chance'*: Barltrop includes two photographs of 'Heinolds [sic] First and Last Chance' saloon, which has over it a signboard reading 'Jack London's Rendezvous'. The saloon which was built around 1880 is at 50 Webster Street, where it survives partly as a Jack London shrine. In March 1913 Heinold evidently sent Jack a postcard reading, 'Keep up the good work!' (see *Letters* III:1238).

47 *stringer-piece*: according to *Webster's* dictionary, 'a fore-and-aft member of a vessel designed to give longitudinal strength, in a wooden vessel in the form of heavy planking'.

48 *the pinch of poverty had been chronic*: O'Connor notes with reference to this passage: 'actually [in the 1880s] the Londons were no poorer than most of their neighbours and better off than many.'

cigarette albums: the first cigarette cards were issued in the US with the innovation of the slide box, in 1869. But the cigarette card craze took hold in the 1880s. American cards were typically less imaginative than the British, and usually featured either busty ladies of the stage or sporting heroes.

53 *the St Louis House*: on 27 May 1916 'Spider' Healey, an old drinking buddy (and uncle of Mamie, 'Queen of the oyster pirates'), having read *John Barleycorn*, wrote to Jack: 'there is not a day passes that tourists from the far east and all parts of the United States do not stand and gaze with astonishment at the old relics of the St Louis House'. It was, presumably, destroyed in the 1906 earthquake.

56 *burned my mainsail*: this is a very confused episode in London's career, in which no biographer has managed successfully to disentangle the truth from scanty details and the author's heroic exaggerations. When Jack and Charmian met Scotty in Melbourne in 1909, he insisted that it was Jack who burned the mainsail. Many other details (such as when Jack actually parted from his 'Queen', Mamie) are also vague or missing.

58 *rushed the growler*: in American slang of this period, sent for measured pails ('growlers') of draft beer from the saloon to be consumed off the premises.

67 *Benicia . . . my headquarters*: the abandoned *Razzle Dazzle* had meanwhile been raided, dismantled, and set adrift by a rival oyster gang, or—as Barltrop conjectures—by former comrades running Jack off their territory. When he recovered the wrecked sloop, Jack got $20 for its scrap. He seems, at this stage, temporarily to have severed ties with his home and family. (Flora recalled much later in a newspaper interview that at this period 'Jack became awful bossy in the house. We couldn't stand him sometimes'.) Benicia is inland in the San Francisco Bay system, through the Carquinez Straits at the head of the San Pablo Bay, about twenty miles north of Oakland.

deputy fish patrolman: Oddly, London here underplays the fact that having established himself in 1891 as the 'Prince of the Oyster Pirates' he turned coat in 1892 and joined the Fish Patrol of San Francisco Bay. As he says, the partnership with young Nelson broke up; he returned to Oakland and was shot in the head two years later. The Patrol had been set up in 1883, principally to protect shrimp and salmon from illegal netting, mainly by Chinese immigrants. Since the Patrol also protected the companies' oyster beds, Jack was now pitted against his former mates, with whom—although he does not

mention it in *John Barleycorn*—he had evidently fallen
out. (See London's *Tales of the Fish Patrol*, 1905.)

69 *the 'Bight of Turner's Shipyard'*: a bight is a bay.
Matthew Turner's shipyard was located at Benicia,
just beyond the Carquinez Straits. It was the largest
manufacturer of its kind in the country, launching 228
vessels between 1883 and 1903.

70 *the* Solano *runs all night*: the *Solano* was 'one of the
wonders of the age'. A paddle steamer, it was built
by the Central Pacific railroad in 1879 to carry trains
across the straits from Benicia to Port Costa. It could
carry two complete passenger trains on its deck. The
Solano remained in service until the 1920s. London
has drifted through the one-mile-wide Carquinez Straits
(connected since 1927 by a bridge), the rapidly running
water connecting the San Pablo and Suisun bays. To the
north of him is Vallejo, Mare Island, and Napa County;
to the south San Francisco Bay.

the Selby smelter on the Contra Costa shore: the
Selby smelter, operated by the American Smelting and
Refining Company, was built in 1885, principally to
process lead ore. Its stack on the shore of San Pablo
Bay was 600 feet high.

Mare Island: the Mare Island is the spit of land (to the
north of London as he drifts) formed on one side by the
outlet of the Napa River, on the other side by the San
Pablo Bay. This episode was later drawn on by London
for the hero's (successful) suicide at the end of *Martin
Eden* (1909).

72 *So I left Benicia . . . and ranged wider afield*: another
vague interlude in the early biography. Andrew Sinclair
gives a convincing reconstruction: 'He teamed up with
the Road Kids [of West Oakland] the gangs of homeless
boys who lived like young wolves. They hunted in a
pack and dragged down their victims in a rush. Jack

learned from them how to beg, how to steal and roll
workingmen for their money, clothes and boots. He
called himself 'Frisco Kid and jumped the freight trains,
riding the rods up to the Sierras, and living free and
wild and perilous' (p. 13). His experiences are vividly
recalled in two chapters in *The Road* (1907), 'Road
Kids and Gay Cats' and 'Confession'. At this largely
unchronicled stage of his life, the 16-year-old London
seems to have been still alienated from his family.

no later than last year: from June to September 1911,
Jack and Charmian took a four-horse driving trip
through Northern California and Oregon.

79 *'The Rail-Splitter'*: i.e. Horatio Alger's *Abraham Lincoln, the Backwoods Boy; or how a young Rail-Splitter
became President* (1883).

80 *Haywards . . . San Leandro . . . Niles*: all in the Bay
Area, on what is now Interstate Highway 580, about 15
miles south of Oakland. Haywards is now Hayward.

86 *boat-puller*: the seals were hunted in herds, on the open
sea, intercepted during their annual migration to their
breeding grounds. Schooners would put out about six
small sealing boats, each manned by a steerer, one or
more boat pullers (or oarsmen) and a hunter with a
shotgun. On the trip to and from the northern waters
where the hunting took place, London doubled as an
able seaman—for which work he should legally have
been 19-years-old. Pelagic, or open-sea hunting of this
kind virtually exterminated the seal species and was
finally banned by international agreement in 1911.

87 Sophie Sutherland . . . *sealing schooner*: more properly
called the *Sophia Sutherland*. O'Connor describes the
vessel as: 'a three-topmast schooner of eighty tons
[156.8 tons, according to Walker], Captain Sutherland
commanding'. She was the original of Wolf Larson's
'hell ship', the *Ghost* in *The Sea-Wolf* (1904). But

unlike the fearsome Wolf Larsen, Captain Sutherland was a doddering 80-year-old. The *Sophia Sutherland* carried a crew of twenty-three, with twelve men quartered in her tiny forecastle, ten of whom were Scandinavians. London wrote many fictional recollections of this episode in his life, but his story 'The Human Drift' (1911) recalls his life in the *Sophia Sutherland* forecastle in some detail. In conversation with Joseph Noel (who is not entirely reliable) in 1912, London allegedly recalled the 'foc'stle lovers he had encountered . . . It was frank, brutal, disgusting'. Jack, Noel adds, 'despised homosexuals' (see Joseph Noel, *Footloose in Arcadia* (1940), p. 224).

88 *the Bonin Islands*: now called Ogassawarajima.

90 *Old lines*: this sentence down to the end of the paragraph was added in pencil to the manuscript by London, clearly at a somewhat later date than the pen and ink composition of the rest of the chapter. In his library, London had a book by Herbert A. Giles on the Vikings, a subject which evidently interested him.

96 *wild and heavy work off the Siberian coast*: it is surmised that the *Sophia Sutherland* did not actually sail this far north. For London's somewhat appalled reaction to the 'wanton slaughter' of pelagic seal-hunting, see chapter 17 of *The Sea-Wolf*.

98 *thirty-seven days of brave sailing*: Andrew Sinclair notes that Jack almost died of an attack of shingles during these five weeks, 'It was the first time his splendid body had let him down'(p. 17).

the Barbary Coast: two notorious blocks in San Francisco, off Pacific Avenue; an unofficial red light district.

99 *Red John*: the bully of the forecastle. Early in his voyage on the *Sophia Sutherland*, Jack was obliged to fight Red John and practically gouge his eyes out.

101 *a home and people to go to*: London was also still ill from his shingles, and probably not up to a proper drinking bout. It may have saved his life. Pete Holt had invited him to sign on with him as boat-puller on the ill-fated *Mary Thomas*, which similarly Jack was not up to. The vessel was lost at sea with all hands in circumstances that were never ascertained. What had transpired to reconcile Jack to his family at this time is not clear.

103 *in the cannery several years before*: it is the summer of 1893, and the country was in the grips of a savage depression. Jack's stepfather was meanwhile trying to keep the family going with a weekly few dollars earned as a part-time constable. London, who seems to have been at this time on good terms with his mother (who began to take an interest in his early writing efforts), undertook to support the household first with the remains of his seaman's wages, then by his labour in the jute factory. The employers had cartelised to establish a standard 10 cents an hour rate for all manual work. Jack's experiences as a wage slave over the next few months inspired his early socialist tendencies, as his slaughterous seal hunting a few months before confirmed his Darwinist convictions.

107 *sisters under their skins*: The refrain from Rudyard Kipling's poem *The Ladies* (1895).

113 *When I left Oakland suddenly for the adventure-path the following spring*: in 1894 London threw in his attempts to succeed by honest toil (the trade depression had not subsided, and would not for four years more). He became a tramp in 'Coxey's army', which intended to march on Washington to persuade the government to reverse the recession by injecting $500 million into roadbuilding and other public works schemes. London and a friend, Frank Davis, joined one of the battalions

of Jacob Coxey's 1,500-strong unemployed, organized under so-called 'generals', i.e. labour activists like the Oakland printer Charles T. Kelly. (See chapter 21 of *John Barleycorn* and *The Road*, 1907. For London's later thinking about Coxey's economic nostrum see *The Iron Heel*, 1908.)

120 *nor thought of taking a drink*: this is contradicted by London's disciple, the excessively sober Upton Sinclair, in his tract *The Cup of Fury* (1956). Based on conversations with Jack in 1905 and gossip from George Sterling, Sinclair asserts that at this period he took up the destructive habit of 'industrial' (i.e. heavy weekend) drinking. Sinclair is not to be trusted on this matter.

121 *I did not immediately quit*: elsewhere London gave a slightly different reason than pride for his quitting. He learned that one of the two men he replaced had killed himself in despair at not being able to support his wife and three children (see O'Connor, p. 58).

122 *inside the prison at Buffalo*: in spring 1894, London and Frank Davis tagged along with Kelly's army from Sacramento, over the Sierras, across the Great Plains (at which point a dispirited Davis turned back), to Nebraska, Omaha (where Kelly was arrested) and Iowa, where—as he recalls—Jack was warmed by the hospitality of the townspeople of Des Moines. In Illinois, Kelly's brigade began to break up, and only a few stragglers actually reached Washington (where their leader Jacob Coxey had been imprisoned, for walking on the White House grass). London deserted in Hannibal, Missouri, and from May 1894 he hopped freights and rode the rods and blind baggages to the eastern seaboard. After spending an uncomfortable few weeks in New York, Jack then hoboed up to Niagara where in late June he was arrested by a fee-hunting constable for vagrancy on his way to the Falls. He was

sentenced to thirty days' hard labour in the Erie County Penitentiary. The brutality which he witnessed there affected him powerfully. In later life, London would playfully refer to himself as an ex-con. (See the chapters 'Pinched' and 'The Pen' in *The Road*, 1907.)

123 *I returned to California . . . my brain*: London rode freight trains via Canada back to Vancouver, then worked his way to San Francisco as a deckhand and coal stoker. He arrived back at the end of 1894, after the most eventful and politically formative year of his life. He went back to live with his mother, stepfather (now working as a railroad depot guard) and stepsister Eliza. Jack himself picked up what work he could and for a time had the position of assistant janitor, sweeping the floor and cleaning the lavatories at Oakland High School. In the autumn of 1895, he enrolled in the school's sophomore class with a view eventually (in three years) to enter the University of California at Berkeley. He was, of course, at nineteen some three to four years older than his classmates. The high school paper, the *Aegis*, published some of London's early writing, including an early version of *John Barleycorn*'s Bonin Islands episode.

124 *I went to Johnny Heinhold to borrow money*: London may have been sentimentalizing. See O'Connor: 'Jack claimed in *John Barleycorn* that Johnny Heinhold, proprietor of the Last Chance, loaned him $50 to continue his education, an episode that aroused much sardonic laughter along the Oakland waterfront, where Heinhold was regarded as notably tight-fisted' (p. 331). In a letter of 28 Sept. 1913, London wrote to an admirer of *John Barleycorn*: 'Johnny Heinold [correct spelling] still runs the Last Chance on Webster Street, down near the old City Wharf. I was in to see him just the other day. When *John Barleycorn* was appearing serially in

The Saturday Evening Post, Johnny Heinold wrote to
me about it' (*Letters* III:1238).

125 *the early days of my writing career*: London returned
from his unlucky goldmining expedition to the Yukon in
summer 1898. While looking for any kind of work in the
autumn of that year, he wrote and submitted fiction to
various magazines. He actually published his first paid-
for piece of writing in Jan. 1899 when the *Overland
Monthly* gave him $5 for his story, 'To the Man on
Trail'. The magazine (called the *Transcontinental* in
chapter 25 of *Martin Eden*, 1909) was prestigious and
one of its founder editors was Ina Coolbrith, London's
patron from the Oakland Free Library (see *John Barleycorn*, chapter 5). Despite the niggardliness of the
$5 payment (which infuriated him), Jack immediately
devoted himself to authorship. The succeeding months
were extremely difficult and are recalled in chapters
20–43 of *Martin Eden*. At times, he and his mother
came near starving. On one occasion, he was obliged to
go to the office of the *Overland Monthly* and threaten
physical violence to get payment. Success actually came
rather faster than the fictional account suggests, however. The prestigious *Atlantic Monthly* accepted Jack's
'An Odyssey of the North' in July 1899 (for $120). In
December of that year, Houghton Mifflin offered him a
contract for a collection of his stories, entitled *The Son
of the Wolf* (1900). Thereafter, London was a popular
and well-paid professional author.

a growing family: London had married Bessie Maddern
in April 1900. They separated three years later (she taking their two daughters) and their divorce was finalised
in 1905. While London was away in the Klondike (1897–
98) his stepfather died. On his return in the summer of
1898, Jack took on the responsibility of looking after

his mother and his stepsister Ida's son Johnny Miller (whom he here calls his nephew).

I made a ten-strike: the term is from bowling, in which all the pins are knocked down with one ball.

126 *its katzenjammer*: literally 'cat's wailing', figuratively 'hangover'.

127 *through high school*: London has gone back in time to 1895–96.

want to go to the state university: although he does not mention it here, one of the main spurs for his sudden ambition to go to college was his love for Mabel Applegarth. As O'Connor puts it, 'She was three years older than Jack, was taking special courses in English at the University of California, and openly worshipped art, music and literature. Her fragility, her cultivated voice and delicate manner made her seem like a goddess to Jack' (p. 74). London commemorates the love affair in *Martin Eden*, in the proletarian hero's passion for the bourgeois beauty, Ruth Morse.

or academy: the cramming school, which Jack attended in early 1896, was Anderson's University Academy at Alameda. He remained there about five weeks, before being asked to leave for over-eagerness, as he describes in this chapter. The episode is pooh-poohed in Joseph Noel's *Footloose in Arcadia* (p. 278) where Jim Whitaker is reported as saying: 'Did you ever hear of anything so childish? I happen to know Jack's mental range. It was good, but not that good'. London was also helped at this time by his future wife, Bessie Maddern. The university entrance exams for which he was preparing were held on 10 Aug. 1896. He did well enough to pass on a probationary basis, as a 'social science special of the class of '00'.

128 *a borrowed whitehall boat*: a rowing boat, originally a New York term.

133 *forced me to leave*: some of Jack's biographers speculate that a motive contributing to his leaving college prematurely was the discovery, for the first time with any certainty, that he was the son of William H. Chaney. London actually quit the Berkeley campus on 4 Feb. 1897. His grades in his first term were As and Bs and academic competence was not an issue.

134 *Heavens how I wrote!*: Barltrop disputes this: 'One has to conclude that the *John Barleycorn* narrative pulls a curtain over his life at [this] time. The period of writing and submitting innumerable manuscripts belongs to a little later, after his return from the Yukon' (p. 58).

a machine: identified elsewhere as a Blickensdorfer. This frustrating typewriter, which only hammered out capital letters, plays a prominent part in the demonology of London's early writing career as portrayed in *Martin Eden*.

137 *the Belmont Academy*: a military academy. London worked there for a few months in early 1897, after leaving the University of California. A vivid recollection of this interlude in the steam laundry is given in *Martin Eden*, chapters 16–18.

141 *grubstaked me into the Klondike*: the great gold rush to the Yukon reached fever proportions in mid-1897. Jack persuaded his stepsister Eliza Shepard (nine years older than him) to give him her savings of $500 from the bank and take out a $1,000 mortgage on her home to finance his, and her husband's expedition to make their fortune in the Yukon. It was a somewhat reckless decision. James Shepard was in his fifties and had a weak heart. Jack was young and strong, but knew nothing about goldmining. They sailed in the steamship *Umatilla* on 25 July and disembarked at the Dyea Inlet, near the tent towns of Dyea and Skagway, at the head of the Chilkoot Pass leading to the Yukon Valley. After

an eventful year, much used in his subsequent fiction (e.g. *The Call of the Wild*, 1903), Jack returned broke and with scurvy to San Francisco in the summer of 1898. London's experiences are exhaustively detailed in Franklin Walker's *Jack London and the Klondike*.

outpacking many an Indian: as Walker notes, 'it was practically impossible to use horses or other pack animals to get over the [3,600 foot] Chilkoot saddle' so as to get inland to the Yukon valley. London's party had some 3,000 pounds of gear and provisions. It was normal to use Siwash Indians as human bearers. But at this stage of the rush, their rates had gone up from 8 cents to 22 cents a pound carried.

the three men in my party: Walker identifies these as I. M. Sloper, Jim Goodman, and F. C. Thompson. Thompson's diary survives, and is the basis for much that is known of this episode in London's life. Shepard, the fourth member of the group whom London does not mention, was invalided back to Oakland in Aug. 1897.

142 *but my scurvy*: Walker notes, 'on August 6 [1898] he sold to Treager's Loan Office in Oakland gold dust from the Klondike for the sum of $4.50' (p. 191).

143 *wop, lumper and roustabout*: a wop is an unskilled labourer (not necessarily Italian); a lumper is a labourer hired to load a vessel; a roustabout is a wharf labourer or dockhand.

San Francisco newspaper: London wrote to the *San Francisco Bulletin* on 17 Sept. 1898, offering them this 4,000 word essay (later published as 'From Dawson to the Sea', in the *Illustrated Buffalo Express*, June 1899). The editor declined it with the explanation 'Interest in Alaska has subsided [to] an amazing degree' (*Letters* I:18).

144 *for the 'Youth's Companion'*: i.e. *Where Boys are*

Men, never published under that title. The magazine returned the story (see *Letters* I:30).

forty dollars for another: 'A Thousand Deaths' (see *Letters* I:36–37.

146 *my one ship*: this phrase marks one of the very few places where London seems to have had trouble in composing *John Barleycorn*. In the manuscript he originally wrote 'Having burned my bridges', which he changed to 'Having burned my ship'. This did not sound right, however, and London changed it in the proofs to 'one ship'. Such corrections and improvements are rare in the manuscript.

'Snow Bound' and 'Sartor Resartus': the first (1866) is a winter idyll in verse, by John Greenleaf Whittier. The second (1836) is Thomas Carlyle's idiosyncratic essay in the philosophy of clothes.

147 *one of my characters, Martin Eden*: see London's *Martin Eden* (1909) which he called 'my artistic memoirs'.

my first book . . . the Bohemian Club: London's first book, *The Son of the Wolf*, was published by Houghton Mifflin in April 1900. The Bohemian Club is at the corner of Post and Taylor streets in San Francisco. Founded in 1872, it catered largely for newspapermen and writers. Its only woman member was Jack's old patron, Ina Coolbrith, who was also the club librarian. Jack later became a member of the club, despite resistance from some members on the paradoxical grounds of his being too bohemian by half.

150 *I had a house*: London married Bessie Maddern on 7 Apr. 1900. They settled down in a fairly large house at 1130 East Fifteenth Street, Oakland. Among the household initially were Jack's mother, Flora, and his 'nephew' Johnny Miller.

a very brilliant man: Jack London may mean George

Wharton James (1858–1923) the English-born expert
on southern California, several of whose books he had
in his library. The two men met in 1903, became friends,
and were on visiting terms from 1905 (see *Letters*
II:604).

151 *the East End of London*: Jack went to London in Aug.
1902, and from his six weeks experience in the slums
wrote his exposé book, *The People of the Abyss*.

152 *a beer bust*: O'Connor dates this beer bust (bout) with
students from the University of California as having
taken place in 1907, while the building of London's
yacht the *Snark* was being completed. It seems as
likely to have been in January 1905, when Jack was
lecturing on 'Socialism' at the University of California
(see *Letters* I:491).

155 *too much positive science*: i.e. 'Positivism', as popular-
ised by Herbert Spencer.

157 *I retarded the socialist development in the United States
by five years*: for socialist criticisms of London's highly
idiosyncratic 'individualistic' socialism, see Andrew
Sinclair, pp. 129–30 and London's essay, 'Revolution'
(1908). In the winter of 1911 London's 'comrades' in
New York had attacked him as a 'syndicalist and a
direct activist', which he may be thinking of here.

159 *life insurance examinations*: Russ Kingman notes: 'Jack
was examined by Dr Crepin on 24 October 1911 and
issued with a £2,500 [insurance] policy.'

I had climbed too high among the stars: Hamilton
(p. 220) notes that London was particularly struck by
Richard Le Gallienne's translation of one of the verses
from the *Rubaiyat of Omar Khayyam* which London
began reading shortly after the *Dirigo* left Baltimore
in March 1912: 'Up, up where Parrius' hoofs stamp
heaven's floor/My soul went knocking at each starry
door.'

160 *see the angel-voiced tenor beat his wife*: this seems to recall Thackeray's prefatory 'Before the Curtain' in *Vanity Fair* (1848).

162 *the victorious Japanese into Manchuria*: from Jan. to June 1904, London was in Korea as a war correspondent for the Hearst newspapers in the Russo-Japanese War.

the Spray: London bought this 'sloop yacht' in 1903, with part of his $2,000 earnings from *The Call of the Wild*.

a Korean boy: Manyoungi, whom Jack London brought back with him as his valet in 1904. He turned surly, and Jack dismissed him in 1907, just before going on the extended *Snark* cruise.

Cloudesley: Cloudesley Johns (1874–1948), whom London met in 1899. Johns was a post office worker, an aspiring writer, a southern Californian and a fellow-socialist. He became one of Jack's main correspondents (see *Letters* I:45).

164 *on the ranch*: London began living in his Sonoma Valley home in 1905; the same year he married his second wife, Charmian Kittredge. Eventually his landholding enlarged to become the 'Beauty Ranch'.

169 *the death of my favorite horse in a barbed wire fence*: see London's letter to George Sterling, 31 May 1906: 'Remember Ban, my saddle horse? Got in the barb wire, sawed a leg half off—had to shoot him yesterday' (*Letters* II:578).

172 *ticklish operation*: London had an operation in mid-March 1905 for the removal of a tumour which proved benign. But from the reference to his sunburn, it is possible that he refers here to the rectal operation he underwent in Sydney after the *Snark* cruise (see notes to p. 181).

174 *the* Snark: London's 45-foot yacht, built to his own
design in 1906. From Apr. 1907 to 1909 Jack and
Charmian (intending a seven-years' cruise) sailed the
Snark through the South Seas to Australia, from where
London returned, sick and exhausted in July 1909. See
The Cruise of the Snark (1911).

177 *the sun sickness*: the most mysterious of the ailments
which afflicted London on the *Snark* voyage. He developed a condition in which his exposed skin turned silver,
apparently in reaction to tropical sunlight. As Andrew
Sinclair notes, it 'appeared to be leprosy of the hands.
The disease may have been pellagra . . . but more likely
he was suffering from psoriasis.'

180 *tinkered up*: possibly an understatement. According to
Andrew Sinclair: 'during the voyage to Sydney, [Jack]
remained a very sick man. The doctors there put him
into hospital, then kept him as an outpatient for five
months. His rectal disease turned out to be a double
fistula, which an operation corrected. His malaria re-
sponded to quinine. His silver skin and psoriasis baffled
the physicians' (p. 153).

Naaman's silvery skin: in 2 Kings 5:27, Naaman is
afflicted with leprosy that turns his skin white.

Nakata: Yoshimatsu Nakata, a Hawaian-born Japanese
houseboy, who joined the Londons in Oct. 1907 and
remained with them for years after.

182 *back on the ranch*: London arrived back in late July
1909.

185 *the White Logic*: London's vivid term seems to owe
something to the Yukon wastes described in his early
story 'The White Silence' (1899):

Nature has many tricks wherewith she convinces man of
his finity – the ceaseless flow of the tides, the fury of the
storm, the shock of the earthquake, the long roll of heaven's
artillery—but the most tremendous, the most stupefying of

all, is the passive phase of the White Silence. All movement ceases, the sky clears, the heavens are as brass; the slightest whisper seems sacrilege, and man becomes timid, affrighted at the sound of his own voice. Sole speck of life journeying across the ghostly wastes of a dead world, he trembles at his audacity, realizes that his is a maggot's life, nothing more.

Hasheesh Land: according to Dr Herbert Stolz ('Bert' on the *Snark*), London used marijuana for the first time while cruising among the South Sea Islands, in 1907. If London is to believed here, he experimented with the drug on one other occasion.

186 *Philip drunk*: proverbial. 'To appeal from Philip drunk to Philip sober' is to assume that the drunken man is no reliable guide to what the same man will think or say when sober.

188 *'The City of Dreadful Night'*: the drunkard James Thomson's poem, published in 1880.

189 *have I not planted a hundred thousand?*: no exaggeration. London was infected with the eucalyptus-planting mania which swept California in 1909 in the (false) belief that the eastern US was running out of timber and that 'Circassian walnut' (as eucalyptus wood was called) would be commercially valuable. The following year, London tore up 700 acres of vines and planted 16,000 seedlings on his ranch. He informed his publisher that it was his intention to plant 25,000 more the next year. Before the mania subsided some years later London had planted around a quarter of a million trees, and spent some $50,000. It was an unprofitable speculation.

190 *cunning artifices of the dentists*: see Andrew Sinclair: 'He spent much of 1913 visiting the dentist, finally having all his upper teeth pulled out in mid-November' (p. 192).

192 *Great Fetish . . . Compte*: Auguste Comte, inventor of

'sociology', divided the intellectual progression of the world into three stages, of which the first and most primitive was Fetishistic, or Animistic (the succeeding two were Metaphysical and Positivistic.) Comte's ideas were known to London via his great disciple Herbert Spencer.

193 *an immigrant Italian*: see London in a letter to Herbert Forder, 3 Feb. 1911: 'with the exception of my German-Swiss ranch-foreman, I employ nothing but floating labor, and this is practically entirely Italian . . . it is all cheap, unskilled labor. I pay these Italians $1.75 a day . . . They get paid when they work and don't get paid when they don't work' (*Letters* II:978).

194 *dogs, champagne*: in London's library are the two volumes of Heinrich Heine's *Memoirs* (1910), which he annotated (see Hamilton, p. 151). Jack and Charmian read these volumes on board the *Dirigo* in mid-June 1912.

194 *Liu Ling*: Chinese poet of the third century. In her *Book of Jack London* (1921), Charmian recalls that while sailing on the *Dirigo*, Jack 'delved into Chinese legend'.

195 *Chuang Tzu*: according to the *Encyclopaedia Britannica*, 'the most significant of China's early interpreters of Taoism', who flourished in the fourth century BC. In illustration of Chuang Tzu's relativism, the *Britannica* quotes the same 'butterfly' passage as does London lower on this page. London had evidently been pondering Herbert A. Giles's *A History of Chinese Literature* (1909), a volume in his personal library.

196 *the vineyard called Tokay*: as London goes on to make clear, he is musing over the title deeds to the 700 acre Kohler-Frohling-Tokay ranch, which he bought in June 1910. José Manuel Micheltorena (1802–53) was a Mexican soldier, and Governor of Alta California from 1842 to 1845. The Petaluma Ranch was founded

in the early nineteenth century by Vallejo (1808–90), whom London mentions below. A great *cacique*, Vallejo encouraged Americans on to his territory and was a powerful agent in securing the submission of California to the United States. He had a house at Sonoma, where he entertained sumptuously. As Hamilton notes (p. 293), London made notes for this section of *John Barleycorn* in his copy of Josiah Flynt [Willard's] *My Life* (1908): 'White logic on ranch—I pore over deeds from days of old Spanish grants, the men who toiled, and cleared, and planted, and gazed with labor-stiffened bodies on these same sunsets and sunrises, the autumn red of the grape, the fogs across Sonoma mountain. These men are gone.' Josiah Flynt was the dedicatee of London's *The Road* and his *My Life* is probably a model for *John Barleycorn*.

James King of William so curiously named?: London's friend George Sterling, writing on 19 March 1913 (having seen the proofs of *John Barleycorn*) expressed surprise that London did not know King (1822–56), the San Francisco banker, 'why, the vigilante committee was started because Cora murdered him!'

198 *William James*: London read William James's *The Varieties of Religious Experience* on the *Dirigo* and scrawled some early notes for *John Barleycorn* in his copy. He also has in mind here James's *Principles of Psychology* (1909). The term 'vital liars' is taken from Violet Paget's *Vital Lies: Studies of Some Varieties of Recent Obscurantism* (1912) which Jack also evidently read on board the *Dirigo*.

200 *your Schopenhauers, your Strindbergs, your Tolstois and Nietzsches*: a group of London's favourite pessimists and melancholics. All are prominently represented in his library and Tolstoy's *Confession* (1882) was evidently a model for *John Barleycorn*. It is also

quoted extensively by William James in *The Varieties of Religious Experience*.

Richard Hovey: the quotation is from Hovey's (1864–1900) *Last Songs of Vagabondia* (1901), one of the author's many anthems to the open road and tramping.

201 *Harry Kemp*: quotation from the author's *The Cry of Youth* (1914). Kemp (1883–1960) was called 'the Tramp Poet'.

203 *China . . . importation of opium*: stopped in 1839.

205 *a windjammer round the Horn*: London refers to the five month voyage which he and Charmian took on the *Dirigo* from Baltimore to Seattle, March to July 1912.

206 *the Battle of Santiago*: the victory of Santiago in Cuba, during the Spanish–American war of 1898 in which the Spanish fleet was destroyed.

the East End of London: which London visited for six weeks in 1902 for his book of social reportage, *The People of the Abyss*.

207 *our dying captain to run for Honolulu*: during the *Dirigo* voyage, the captain, Omar E. Chapman, developed a terminal case of stomach cancer, as Charmian realized on 2 July 1912.

I shall take my drink on occasion: crossed out in the manuscript, there follows: 'when I am back on land again'.

208 *trained in his acquaintance*: there follows crossed out in the manuscript: 'These are unanswerable[?] facts. And the old dog likes the old tricks and does not care to learn new tricks. The young dogs will learn the new tricks'.

The Oxford World's Classics Website

www.worldsclassics.co.uk

- Browse the full range of Oxford World's Classics online

- Sign up for our monthly e-alert to receive information on new titles

- Read extracts from the Introductions

- Listen to our editors and translators talk about the world's greatest literature with our Oxford World's Classics audio guides

- Join the conversation, follow us on Twitter at OWC_Oxford

- Teachers and lecturers can order inspection copies quickly and simply via our website

www.worldsclassics.co.uk

American Literature

British and Irish Literature

Children's Literature

Classics and Ancient Literature

Colonial Literature

Eastern Literature

European Literature

Gothic Literature

History

Medieval Literature

Oxford English Drama

Poetry

Philosophy

Politics

Religion

The Oxford Shakespeare

A complete list of Oxford World's Classics, including Authors in Context, Oxford English Drama, and the Oxford Shakespeare, is available in the UK from the Marketing Services Department, Oxford University Press, Great Clarendon Street, Oxford OX2 6DP, or visit the website at www.oup.com/uk/worldsclassics.

In the USA, visit www.oup.com/us/owc for a complete title list.

Oxford World's Classics are available from all good bookshops. In case of difficulty, customers in the UK should contact Oxford University Press Bookshop, 116 High Street, Oxford OX1 4BR.